WHERE TO FIND WHAT:

A Handbook to Reference Service

by

JAMES M. HILLARD

The Scarecrow Press, Inc.

Metuchen, N. J.   1975

Library of Congress Cataloging in Publication Data

Hillard, James M   1920-
    Where to find what : a handbook to reference service.

    1. Reference books--Bibliography. I. Title.
Z1035.1.H54   011'.02   75-6723
ISBN 0-8108-0813-7

TABLE OF CONTENTS

INTRODUCTION

Seven years of teaching reference courses to in-service librarians of the Charleston area has convinced me that there is definite need for a new approach. Traditionally, reference has been taught as a book-oriented subject; that is, students were taught about types of reference books and then, within each type, about specific useful publications. As a result, new reference personnel had to spend the first months or even years on the job orienting the type of questions asked to the books with which they were familiar. This often resulted in a lack of self-confidence if the new librarian could not immediately think of a logical source to answer the needed inquiry.

Since the reference function is possibly the most important facet of any but a purely recreational library, our reputation is often dependent upon how well we can provide needed answers quickly. This book, then, is designed to help the harried reference person find needed items quickly. Its approach is the direct opposite of the textbook approach; in this book one finds a series of typical reference subjects and then a suggested reference source in which answers to these questions can be located. It will not, and of course, could not solve all the problems of the neophyte or the partially trained librarian but it will help enhance the reputation of the reference services offered by providing an immediate source for the questioner to consult while the librarian considers other solutions to the problem. The speed with which the user receives the initial information will do much to build confidence in the library's ability, and it is in the provision of that initial information that this book will be most valuable.

One of the most important facts that I learned while in Library School was that reference questions need not and often cannot be answered by that collection of books that we normally call the Reference Collection. Miss Rose Lefevre of the Illinois Library School always emphasized that the reference collection was only the beginning of the search and that a good reference person used every available source wherever it might be located. That has been the approach in this book. I have not limited the sources to any predetermined list but in each case have tried to give the most logical and, in my opinion, the best source of information on the subject. This means that many books cited may not currently be in your collection, but generally I have chosen those titles which could be recommended for purchase by any but the smallest libraries. However, certain essential reference books are included which will be too expensive for any but very large libraries but which are necessary for any thorough reference service in certain subject fields.

For example, such works as the abstracting services, Biological Abstracts and Chemical Abstracts, or the beautiful six-volume set of Wild Flowers of the United States are too expensive for the smaller library but would be readily available in nearby large libraries to which the patron could be referred. These and similar works are included for that reason.

Although this book is not intended as a buying guide, the full order information, including ISBN where available, is included except for price which changes too rapidly to be of much value in a very short time.

In most cases, individual books are annotated only in those cases where they might not be widely recognized. For example, there is no need to annotate well known dictionaries and encyclopedias since those have already been studied in the traditional reference text or can be easily understood. However, for lesser known works a full notation is given.

Two previous books have dealt with reference service in much the same way that this one is attempting. It is hoped that this one will supplement rather than duplicate those earlier efforts. The first and more desirable of these two previous books was A Subject Guide to Reference Books, by Herbert S. Hirschberg, published by the American Library Association in 1942. This excellent book was of invaluable service to a whole generation of librarians. Unfortunately, it is currently out-of-print and would be terribly out-of-date even if available. Its approach varied from this book's in that it was what it claimed to be: a subject guide to "reference books." My book will not only up-date the information found in Hirshberg's but will also broaden the scope by including many items which might not normally be referred to as "reference" material.

The second book, much newer, is How and Where to Look It Up, by Robert W. Murphey, published in 1958. This, too, was an excellent book but its approach differed from that of the present volume in that it was aimed at the non-librarian rather than the librarian and his clientele. It is a much larger book than mine because my standards of selection have been much more stringent than Mr. Murphey's. I have not included out-of-print items, nor many works which I could not recommend for purchase by a medium-sized library.

This book, in a sense, might be considered as a marriage of the previous two, but up-dated to list more recent sources.

ACKNOWLEDGMENTS

Although the final decisions concerning which subjects should be covered and which books should be cited have been mine, I have consulted with several outstanding persons in all areas of library work--public, college, school and special librarians--and have incorporated many of their suggestions into the final version of the book. The following persons graciously consented to review and comment upon my selection of subjects for the book: Nellie M. Baird, Larry E. Bone, Lucille Bostdorf, Frances Neel Cheney, Kathleen Dunn, Evan I. Farber, Katherine Foster, Mary Gaver, Martha Landis, Rachael S. Martin, Bernice B. Middleton, Michael H. Ridgeway, Edna H. Savoya, Charles A. Stevenson and William Urban.

I must also acknowledge the great help given me by the high school and public librarians of Charleston County, many of whom struggled through my course on Basic Reference Sources. They taught me not only humility but also brought to my attention the need for such a volume as this one.

I should also like to acknowledge how grateful I am to my wife, E. Louise Hillard, who as librarian of the best academic high school in the Charleston area was able to advise me on books needed for the small reference collection as well as giving suggestions of subjects to be covered.

I would be remiss if I did not acknowledge the most important person in the preparation of this book. Mrs. Catharine B. North typed, proofread and corrected all portions of the book and encouraged me during those periods in which I doubted if it would ever be completed. Without her help in all fields, this book would have taken several years longer to compile.

No one writing the subject of reference books would be honest unless he admitted his debt to those two great giants, Constance M. Winchell and Frances Neel Cheney, without whose writings one would be crippled. Finally, I must offer a belated thank you to Miss Rose Lefevre who first introduced me to the fascinating field of reference work so many years ago.

JAMES M. HILLARD
Librarian
The Citadel
Charleston, S. C. 29409

September 1, 1974

SUBJECT HEADINGS USED

ABBREVIATIONS
ABSTRACTS
ACADEMIC DEGREES
  see ACADEMIC REGALIA
ACADEMIC REGALIA
ACCOUNTING
ACTORS AND ACTRESSES
ADDRESS, FORMS OF
ADOPTION
ADVERBS
  see ENGLISH LANGUAGE
ADVERTISING
AERONAUTICS
  see AIRCRAFT
AGED
AGRICULTURE
AIR CONDITIONING
AIR FORCE
  see ARMED FORCES
AIRCRAFT
AIRLINES
ALCOHOL
ALLERGIES
ALMANACS
ALPHABET
ALTITUDES
AMERICAN GUIDE SERIES
AMISH
  see MENNONITES
AMPHIBIANS and REPTILES
ANECDOTES
ANNIVERSARIES
  see HOLIDAYS; WEDDINGS
ANTHEMS, NATIONAL
ANTHROPOLOGY
ANTIQUES
ANTONYMS
  see SYNONYMS AND ANTO-
  NYMS
AQUARIUMS
ARCHITECTURE
ARMAMENT

ARMED FORCES
ARMORED VEHICLES
ARMS AND ARMOR
ARMY
  see ARMED FORCES
ART AND ARTISTS
ASSOCIATIONS
ASTROLOGY
ASTRONOMY
ATHLETICS
  see SPORTS
ATLASES
ATMOSPHERE
ATOMIC POWER
AUDIO-VISUAL MATERIALS
AUDITING
  see ACCOUNTING
AUTHORS
AUTOGRAPHS
AUTOMOBILE LAWS
AUTOMOBILES
AVIATION
  see AIRCRAFT; AIRLINES
AWARDS
  see LITERARY AWARDS

BALLADS
  see FOLK SONGS
BALLET
BANKS AND BANKING
BASEBALL
BASKETBALL
BATTLES
BEAUTY
BEAUTY PAGEANTS
BEST BOOKS
BEST SELLERS
BIBLE
BIOGRAPHIES
BIOLOGY
BIRDS
BLACKS

DOGS
DRAMA
DRESS
  see COSTUME

ECOLOGY
  see also BIOLOGY; BOTANY;
  PLANTS, etc.
ECONOMICS
EDUCATION
ELECTIONS
ELECTRICITY
ENCYCLOPEDIAS
ENGINES
ENGLISH LANGUAGE
ENGRAVING AND ENGRAVERS
ENTOMOLOGY
  see INSECTS
EPIGRAMS
  see QUOTATIONS; ANEC-
  DOTES
ETHNOLOGY
ETIQUETTE
ETYMOLOGY
EVOLUTION
EXAMINATIONS AND TESTS

FACTS
FAIRY TALES
FELLOWSHIPS AND GRANTS
FESTIVALS
  see also HOLIDAYS
FILMS
  see MOTION PICTURES
FIREARMS
  see also ARMAMENT
FIRST AID
FISH
FISHING
FLAGS
FLOWERS
FOLK MUSIC
FOLKLORE
  see also FAIRY TALES
FOODS
FOOTBALL
FOREIGN AFFAIRS
FOREIGN WORDS AND PHRASES
FORESTRY
FORMULAS, CHEMICAL
FORMULAS, MATHEMATICAL
FOSSILS
FOUNDATIONS

  see FELLOWSHIPS AND
  GRANTS
FRATERNITIES AND SORORITIES
FREE MATERIALS
FROGS
  see also AMPHIBIANS AND
  REPTILES
FURNITURE
  see also ANTIQUES

GAMES
GARDENING
GEMS
GENEALOGY
  see also HERALDRY
GENETICS
GEOGRAPHY
GEOLOGY
GOLF
GOVERNMENT
  see also CONGRESS; CON-
  STITUTIONS; ELECTIONS
GOVERNMENT PUBLICATIONS
GRANTS IN AID
  see FELLOWSHIPS; COL-
  LEGES AND UNIVERSITIES;
  FOUNDATIONS
GRASSES
GUIDED MISSILES
GUNS
  see ARMAMENTS; FIRE-
  ARMS

HALL OF FAME
HALLMARKS
HANDICRAFTS
HARBORS AND PORTS
HEATING
HELICOPTERS
HERALDRY
HEREDITY
  see also GENETICS
HISTORIANS
HISTORY
HOCKEY
HOLIDAYS
  see also FESTIVALS
HONORARY SOCIETIES
  see FRATERNITIES AND
  SORORITIES; ASSOCIATIONS
HORSE RACING
  see RACING
HORSES

HOSPITALS
HOTELS AND MOTELS
HUNTING
see also FIREARMS
HYMNS

IDIOMS
INCOME TAX
INDIANS
INSECTS
INSURANCE AND INSURANCE
COMPANIES
INTERNAL REVENUE
see INCOME TAX
INTERNATIONAL RELATIONS
INVENTIONS
INVESTMENTS
IRON
IRRIGATION
ISLAM

JAZZ
JEWELRY
JEWISH PEOPLE
JOKES
see QUOTATIONS
JOURNALISM
JUDO AND JUJITSU

KARATE
see JUDO AND JUJITSU
KINGS AND RULERS
KNOTS AND SPLICES
KORAN
see also ISLAM

LABOR AND LABOR UNIONS
LAW
LEAVES
see TREES
LIBRARIES AND LIBRARIANS
LINGUISTICS
LITERARY AGENTS
LITERARY PRIZES AND
AWARDS
LITERATURE
LOCOMOTIVES
see ENGINES - RAILROAD

MAGAZINES
MAGIC
MAMMALS
MANNERS AND CUSTOMS

see also ETHNOLOGY
MANUFACTURERS
MAPS
MARINE CORPS
see ARMED FORCES
MARKETING
MARRIAGE
MATHEMATICS
see also FORMULAS,
MATHEMATICAL
MEDALS
see DECORATIONS AND
MEDALS
MEDICINE
METALS
METEORITES
METEOROLOGY
see also CLIMATE
METRIC SYSTEM
MICROFORMS
MILEAGES
see DISTANCES
MILITARY FORCES
see ARMED FORCES
MINERALOGY
MINING
see MINERALOGY; METALS
MISCELLANY
MOHAMMEDANISM
see ISLAM
MONASTIC ORDERS
MONEY
MOTELS
see HOTELS AND MOTELS
MOTION PICTURE DIRECTORS
see ACTORS AND ACTRESS-
ES
MOTTOES
MUSEUMS
MUSIC AND MUSICIANS
see also BALLADS; BALLET;
CONDUCTORS; COMPOSERS;
DANCES; OPERA; SONGS
MYTHOLOGY

NAMES
NATIONAL PARKS AND MONU-
MENTS
NATURAL RESOURCES
see also OBSERVATION
NATURALIZATION
NATURE STUDY
NAVIGATION

NAVY
  see ARMED FORCES
NEGROES
  see BLACKS
NEUROLOGY
NEWSPAPERS
NICKNAMES
NOBEL PRIZES
NOBILITY
  see HERALDRY
NUMBERS
NUMISMATICS
  see COINS; MONEY
NURSERY RHYMES
NUTRITION
  see also FOODS

OBITUARIES
OCCUPATIONS
  see CAREERS
OPERA
  see also MUSIC
ORGANIZATIONS
  see ASSOCIATIONS
OSCAR WINNERS
  see also MOTION PICTURES

PAINTERS
  see also ARTS AND ARTISTS -
  Biography
PALEONTOLOGY
  see FOSSILS; GEOLOGY
PARLIAMENTARY PROCEDURES
PASSPORTS
PATENTS
PENOLOGY
PERSONAL FINANCE
PERSONAL NAMES
  see NAMES
PETROLEUM
PETS
PHILATELY
  see STAMPS
PHILOLOGY
  see LINGUISTICS
PHILOSOPHY AND PHILOSO-
  PHERS
PHOTOGRAPHY
PLACE NAMES
  see GEOGRAPHY
PLANTS
PLASTICS
PLAYS - PLOTS

POETRY
POLICE
  see also CRIME AND CRIM-
  INALS
POLITICAL LEADERS
POLITICAL PARTIES
POPES
POPULATION
PORTRAITS
PORTS
  see HARBORS AND PORTS
PRECIOUS STONES
  see GEMS
PREPARATORY SCHOOLS
  see PRIVATE SCHOOLS
PRESIDENTS - U. S.
PRICES
PRISONS AND PRISONERS
  see PENOLOGY
PRIVATE SCHOOLS
PRIZES
  see LITERARY AWARDS;
  NOBEL PRIZES; OSCAR WIN-
  NERS
PRONUNCIATION
PROOFREADING
PROVERBS
PSEUDONYMS
  see NICKNAMES
PSYCHIATRY
PSYCHOLOGY
PUBLIC ADMINISTRATION
  see GOVERNMENT
PUBLIC HEALTH
PUNCTUATION
PUNS

QUOTATIONS

RACES
  see ANTHROPOLOGY
RACING
RADIO
RAILROADS
  see also ENGINES - RAIL-
  ROAD
RECORDS
  see SUPERLATIVES
REFERENCE BOOKS
  see also ATLASES; DICTION-
  ARIES; ENCYCLOPEDIAS
REPTILES
  see AMPHIBIANS AND REP-
  TILES

RETIREMENT
RHYMES
ROADS AND HIGHWAYS
ROCKETS
  see GUIDED MISSILES
ROCKS
  see also GEOLOGY; MINER-
  ALOGY
RODEOS
ROYALTY
  see KINGS AND RULERS

SAINTS
SAYINGS
  see QUOTATIONS
SCHOLARSHIPS
  see COLLEGE COSTS; FEL-
  LOWSHIPS AND GRANTS
SCULPTURE
SEX
SHAKESPEARE
SHELLS
SHIPS
SHORT STORIES
SIGNALS
SIGNS AND SYMBOLS
SKIN DIVING
SLANG
SNAKES
  see also AMPHIBIANS AND
  REPTILES
SOCIAL SCIENCES
SOCIAL SECURITY
SOCIOLOGY
  see SOCIAL SCIENCES
SOLAR ENERGY
SOLITAIRE
  see also CARD GAMES;
  GAMES
SONGS
  see also FOLK MUSIC
SPEECHES
SPELLING
SPIRITUALS
  see also FOLK MUSIC;
  SONGS
SPORTS
  see also names of individual
  sports
STAMP COLLECTING
STATE GOVERNMENT
  see GOVERNMENT - STATES
STATISTICS

STEEL
STOCKS AND BONDS
  see INVESTMENTS
SUPERLATIVES
SUPERSTITIONS
SUPREME COURT
SWIMMING
SYMBOLS
  see SIGNS AND SYMBOLS
SYNONYMS AND ANTONYMS

TAXES
  see also INCOME TAXES
TELEVISION
TENNIS
THEATER
  see also DRAMA
TIDES
  see also NAVIGATION
TIME
  see also NAVIGATION
TOYS
TRACK AND FIELD
TRADEMARKS AND TRADE
  NAMES
TRAVEL
TREATIES
TREES
TROPICAL FISH
TYPOGRAPHY

UNIFORMS
  see also ARMED FORCES;
  DECORATIONS AND MEDALS
UNITED NATIONS
UNITED STATES
UNIVERSITIES
  see COLLEGES AND UNIVER-
  SITIES

VALENTINES
VEGETABLES
  see GARDENING
VENEREAL DISEASES
VITAMINS
  see NUTRITION
VOCATIONS
  see CAREERS
VOTING QUALIFICATIONS

WEATHER
  see METEOROLOGY
WEDDINGS

see ETIQUETTE; MARRIAGE;
    CUSTOMS
WEIGHTS AND MEASURES
WILD FLOWERS
    see also FLOWERS
WILLS
WOMEN
WRESTLING
WRITING

ZOOS

WHERE TO FIND WHAT

ABBREVIATIONS

The use of abbreviations is continually on the increase and it is a common reference question in any type of library to be asked to identify certain combinations of letters. Many abbreviations which are identical or similar in nature may have widely variant meanings; you must, therefore, know the way the abbreviation is used in order to be sure that the meaning you find is the one you want. For example, PM normally means Post Meridian, i.e., afternoon, but it could as easily mean Postmaster or Provost Marshal.

One can easily find abbreviations in a variety of places such as almanacs, dictionaries, encyclopedias, etc., but the best first place to look is in a good dictionary of abbreviations.

Complete Dictionary of Abbreviations, by Robert J. Schwartz. Enl. ed. Crowell, 1959. (ISBN 0-690-20620-8)
This is the most complete of the various dictionaries since it does not specialize but lists in one alphabet the many abbreviations used in business, industry, history, geography, etc.

Cassell's Dictionary of Abbreviations, ed. by J. W. Gurnett, 2nd ed. International Publications Service. 1972.
While not quite as comprehensive as the Schwartz book, this book is newer and therefore often better for recent usage.

World Guide to Abbreviations of Associations and Institutions, by Paul Spillner. 2nd ed. Bowker, 1970-73. 3 Vols.

If you do not find the desired abbreviation in one of these, and it is possible that you will not since the field is so broad, try the following:

Funk and Wagnalls New Standard Dictionary
You will find two listings here; one under the word "abbreviations" and one under the proper alphabetical location of the abbreviation.

Webster's Third New International

Random House   Located alphabetically in its proper place.

1

Colliers Encyclopedia

Encyclopedia Americana

Encyclopaedia Britannica
	Excellent lists of abbreviations in use today arranged under "Abbreviations" in volume I.

ABSTRACTS

	Closely related to indexes and bibliographies, abstracts are both more or less than the other two forms. (Abstracts are, as their names would indicate, brief summaries of articles or books and are used as a handy way for social scientists, scientists and others to keep abreast of current literary output in their fields.) The abstract will often give the casual user enough information in itself; for the serious student it is one way of finding pertinent publications. Abstracting services are usually published periodically and therefore act not only as indexes but also as bibliographies for publications in the field during that period. The major abstracting services and their fields are as follows:

Biology

	Biological Abstracts. Philadelphia, Pa.: Biological Abstracts, 1926-
	Pollution Abstracts. LaJolla, California: Pollution Abstracts, 1970-

Chemistry

	Chemical Abstracts. Easton, Pennsylvania: American Chemical Society, 1907-

Congressional Publications and Public Laws

	CIS Annual. Washington, D.C.: Congressional Information Service, 1970-

Doctoral Dissertations

	Dissertation Abstracts International. Ann Arbor, Michigan: University Microfilms, 1938- (Also available on microfilm)

Education

	ERIC. Research in Education. Washington, D.C.: Educational Research Resources Information Center, 1965-
	Exceptional Child Education Abstracts. Arlington, Virginia: Council for Exceptional Children, 1969-

Mental Retardation Abstracts. Washington, D.C.: Dept. of
HEW, Public Health Service, 1964-

History

America: History and Life. Santa Barbara, California: American Bibliographical Center, 1964-
Historical Abstracts. Santa Barbara, California: American Bibliographical Center, 1955-

Mathematics

Mathematical Reviews. Providence, Rhode Island: American
Mathematical Society, 1946-

Psychology

Psychological Abstracts. Washington, D.C.: American Psychological Association, 1927-

Science

Computer and Control Abstracts. New York City, New York:
Institute of Electrical Engineers. (Series B of Science Ab-
stracts)
Electrical and Electronics Abstracts. New York City, New York:
Institute of Electrical Engineers. (Series A of Science Ab-
stracts)
Physics Abstracts. New York City, New York: Institute of
Electrical Engineers. (Series A of Science Abstracts)
Science Abstracts, one of the oldest abstracting services,
was begun in 1898. It was originally issued in two sections. A:
Physics, and B: Electrical, but a third section, C: Computer and
Control Abstracts, was added in 1966. Although all three are pub-
lished by the INSPEC (Information Service in Physics, Electrotech-
nical and Control) they may be purchased separately if desired.
There are three related publications entitled Current Papers in Physics, etc., which are listings of titles of current research papers in
each field. These are published monthly.

ACADEMIC DEGREES
see
ACADEMIC REGALIA

ACADEMIC REGALIA

Often a question arises as to the proper gown, cape, hood or
color to be worn in an academic or formal procession. The very

best work for this type of question is:

Academic Dress and Insignia of the World, by Hugh Smith.   Cape
Town, South Africa: Balkenia, 1970. 3 vols.
The first two volumes are devoted to a discussion of academic regalia by country and volume three is an appendix volume in
which are given the definitions of standard academic terms, identification tables and a complete listing of academic degrees giving
their correct abbreviations.

A less comprehensive but still worthwhile publication for the
United States is:

Academic Degrees, Earned and Honorary Degrees Conferred by Institutions of Higher Education in the U.S. Washington, D.C.:
U.S. Office of Education, 1961.

ACCOUNTING

Accountant's Handbook, ed. by Rufus Wixon. 5th ed. Ronald, 1970.
This is the basic handbook in the field which provides authoritative information on all forms of accounting. It is intended to provide in an easily located and applied manner those points of information needed by both the professional and the occasional accountant or
student.

Accountant's Encyclopedia, Prentice Hall, 1962. 4 vols. (ISBN
0-13-001073-1)
This set is the combined effort of over 50 well known authors
in the field, each writing on a specific aspect of accounting. This
set is excellent for forms and reports which can be used as examples.

A Dictionary for Accountants, by Eric L. Kohler. 4th ed. Prentice Hall, 1970. (ISBN 0-13-209809-1)
Over 2500 accounting terms are identified and explained.

ACTORS AND ACTRESSES

Questions concerning actors and actresses of stage, screen,
television and radio are so varied that only the more comprehensive
can be listed in a book of this size. If detailed information is
wanted concerning any personality the first and best place to look
for a full biography would be the card catalog under the name of
the individual. The sources listed below are for ready reference
information.

For periodical information consult:

Biography Index. H. W. Wilson

For simple dates and place of birth and death consult:

Information Please Almanac. Dan Golenpaul Associates.
Listed annually under heading, "Celebrated Persons."
World Almanac. Newspaper Enterprise Associates.
Listed annually under heading, "Noted Personalities."

For original names consult:

Information Please Almanac.
Under "Celebrated Persons."

For general information consult:

Celebrity Register, ed. by Earl Blackwell. Simon & Schuster, 1973.
Current Biography. H. W. Wilson Co.
Whatever Became Of... Crown Publishers.
Who's Who in the Theatre, ed. by Robert Finlay and Ian Herbert.
15th rev.ed. Pitman, 1974. (ISBN 0-273-07036-3)
Who's Who on the Screen, by C. D. Fox and Milton R. Silver.
Gordon Press, [1973].

ADDRESS, FORMS OF

Emily Post's Etiquette, ed. by Elizabeth L. Post. 12th ed. Funk
and Wagnall, 1968. (ISBN 0-308-10037-9)
See index under "forms of address" for proper usage with
all ranks.

Amy Vanderbilt's Etiquette, ed. by Amy Vanderbilt. Rev. ed.
Doubleday, 1972. (ISBN 0-385-03915-8)
See Chapter 47, "Correct forms of address."

Practical Protocol: A Guide to International Courtesies, by James
E. Lott. Gulf Publishing, 1973. (ISBN 0-87201-746-X)
This is the very best work on the protocol of dealing with
governmental and diplomatic figures. It gives a more complete listing of official forms of address than any other source, giving full
instructions for not only spoken address but also the outside address
on correspondence, the salutation and the close. It also gives proper forms for place cards.

ADOPTION

There are many books dealing with the psychological and

sociological aspects of adoption and a quick search of your card catalog under the heading will reveal these to you. However, there are two titles which can be highly recommended for any library.

Adoption and Family Life, by Margaret Kornitzer. Fernhill, 1968.
Adopted Children: How They Grow Up, by Alexina M. McWhinnie.
        Humanities, 1967.

More often though, questions concerning adoption have to do with the legal and technical aspects of the process. For the laws of a specific state there is no better place than the "Code of Laws of the State..." Check in the index volume under "Adoption" for the pertinent legal citations. However, many persons will be satisfied with the more general treatment of the subject found in the following books.

Adoption - Is It For You? by Colette T. Dywasuk. Harper & Row,
      1973. (ISBN 0-06-011147-X)
How To Adopt a Child, by Robert Farmer. Arco Press, 1968.
      (ISBN 0-688-01473-3)
Marriage, Divorce and Adoption Laws of the United States, by Editors of Gould Press. Gould Press, 1973. (ISBN 0-87526-045-4)

ADVERBS
see,
ENGLISH LANGUAGE AND GRAMMAR

ADVERTISING

Questions concerning advertising will generally fall in one of two categories: information concerning the business and techniques of advertising, or information on rates and sources for advertising.

Handbooks and Dictionaires

Handbook of Advertising Management, ed. by Roger Barton. McGraw Hill, 1970. (ISBN 0-07-003966-6)
      This is a very comprehensive reference book which, although aimed at the advertising manager, is excellent for the general public. There are nine sections dealing with every aspect of the field of advertising, written by 37 experts.

Encyclopedia of Advertising, by Irving Graham. 2nd ed. Fairchild, 1972. (ISBN 0-87005-014-1)
      An alphabetical encyclopedia to all facets of the business with more than a thousand entries relating to advertising, marketing, publishing, public relations and related fields. It is a useful working manual for everyday use.

A. A. A. A. Handbook for the Advertising Agency Account Executive,
    Addison-Wesley, 1969. (ISBN 0-201-00030-X)
    Rather specialized in approach, it is still an excellent source
for the how and why of advertising placement.

Directories

N. W. Ayer's and Sons Directory of Newspapers, Magazines, and
    Trade Publications, Ayer Press, annual since 1869.
    A comprehensive directory of all newspapers and periodic
publications in North America. It is arranged alphabetically by state
and then by city and lists the periodical publications for each city.
For each publication, it gives the political affiliation of the publications, the circulation and frequency as well as names of the editor
and publisher. There is also a classified list of publications by
subject field. For each city listed are given such pertinent data as
manufacturers, transportation etc.

Editor and Publisher's Market Guide. New York: Editor and Pub-
    lisher Company, annual since 1924.
    Excellent source material concerning every city which pub-
lishes newspapers in the United States. It is arranged alphabetically
by state and then by city and contains 1, 500 U. S. and Canadian market surveys. Each one gives, in a standard form, information
concerning transportation facilities, population, housing, banking,
automobiles, principal industries, number of wage earners and average salaries. Also of interest to the advertiser, it gives principal
pay days, shopping days and list of major commercial outlets and
shopping centers. For each newspaper it gives the official circulation and the name and address of the advertising manager.

Sales Management Survey of Buying Power. New York: Sales Man-
    agement Magazine, annual since 1929.
    This is a regular issue of Sales Management; the Marketing
Magazine, usually published in late May or early June, but it can be
purchased separately. It lists estimates of population and number
of households as well as the "Index of Effective Buying Power, "
cash income, retail sales and percentage of income by cash income
groups. There are also detailed lists of dollar values purchased by
each metropolitan area of different commodities, such as furniture,
appliances, drugstores, etc.

Standard Rate and Data Service. Skokie, Ill. : Standard Rate and
    Data Services, annual since 1919.
    The title will vary slightly from year to year and, while
scheduled annually, the date of publication also varies from year to
year. Probably the best source for information concerning the costs
of advertising in all media. It has a separate section for each type
including newspapers, radio, television, films, etc. It gives not
only American but also Mexican and Canadian rates.

Standard Advertising Register. New York: National Register Publi-
    cations, annual since 1915.

The title varies slightly from year to year. This is published in various parts throughout the year. It gives information on 16, 000 advertisers, products and type of media used. Some of the parts are: a geographic index, a product register, and an agency list which is published annually but updated weekly.

AERONAUTICS
see
AIRCRAFT

AGED

Questions concerning the aged most often deal with plans for retirement, social security benefits, hobbies, crafts, travel, etc. For information concerning those aspects of aging, look under the specific heading in this book. This section will deal with sources on gerontological problems.

A Classified Bibliography of Gerontology and Geriatrics, by Nathan W. Shocks. Standard Univ. Press, 1951. (op) Supplements 1 & 2, 1963. (ISBN 0-8047-0412-0)
Lists all pertinent monographs and journal articles dealing with problems of aging. It lists publications in all languages and covers not only the physical but also the sociological aspects of the problems. The bibliography is kept up to date by occasional supplements in the Journal of Gerontology.

The Nation and Its Older People, A Report of the White House Conference on Aging, January 9-12, 1961. Dept. of Health, Education & Welfare, 1961. (FS 1. 2:01 1/3)
This official report of the findings of the Conference gives an excellent overview of the problems in the United States. The U. S. Government is continually publishing new items in this field; for the most recent, check the G. P. O. price list 51, Health and Medical Services, or the monthly catalog of U. S. Government Publications.

AGRICULTURE

Although the subject of agriculture is a widely varied one covering many aspects, crops and procedures, it is generally possible to find the necessary answers quickly. The most prolific publisher in the field is the U. S. Department of Agriculture which publishes material on almost every aspect. The following price lists of the Superintendent of Documents are particularly helpful in finding materials in the field:

#38   Animal Industry
#41   Insects
#44   Plants
#46   Soils and Fertilizers
#68   Farm Management

In addition, the Department of Agriculture also prints a Year-book of Agriculture which deals each year with a specific aspect of agriculture. The following yearbooks are still available from the Superintendent of Documents.

1948. Grass. Cat. # A 1. 10:948.   S/N 0100-1542.
1949. Trees. Cat. # A 1. 10:949.   S/N 0100-0097.
1950-51. Crops in Peace and War. Cat. # A 1. 10:950-51. S/N 0100-0098.
1952. Insects. Cat. # A 1. 10:952.   S/N 0100-0099.
1953. Plant Diseases. Cat. # A 1. 10:953.   S/N 0100-0100.
1954. Marketing. Cat. # A 1. 10:954.   S/N 0100-0101.
1955. Water. Cat. # A 1. 10:955.   S/N 0100-0102.
1956. Animal Diseases. Cat. # A 1. 10:956.   S/N 0100-0103.
1957. Soil. Cat. # A 1. 10:957.   S/N 0100-0104.
1958. Land. Cat. # A 1. 10:958.   S/N 0100-0105.
1959. Food & Nutrition. Cat. # A 1. 10:959.   S/N 0100-0106.
1960. Power to Produce. Cat. # A 1. 10:960.   S/N 0100-0107.
1961. Seeds. Cat. # A 1. 10:961.   S/N 0100-0108.
1962. After a Hundred Years. Cat. # A 1. 10:962.   S/N 0100-0109.
1963. A Place to Live. Cat. # A 1. 10:963.   S/N 0100-0110.
1964. Farmer's World. Cat. # A 1. 10:964.   S/N 0100-0111.
1965. Consumers All. Cat. # A 1. 10:965.   S/N 0100-0112.
1966. Protecting Our Food. Cat. # A. 1. 10:966.   S/N 0100-0113.
1967. Outdoors USA. Cat. # A 1. 10:967.   S/N 0100-0114.
1968. Science for Better Living. Cat. # A 1. 10:968.   S/N 0100-0115.
1969. Food for Us All. Cat. # A 1. 10:969.   S/N 0100-0116.
1970. Contours of Change. Cat. # A 1. 10:970.   S/N 0100-1053.
1971. A Good Life for More People. Cat. # A 1. 10:971 S/N 0100-1459.
1972. Landscape for Living. Cat. # A 1. 10:972.   S/N 0100-2441.
1973. Handbook for the Home. Cat. # A 1. 10:973.   S/N 0100-02960.

The Yearbook of Agriculture has been published since 1894 with exception of the years 1943-44-45 and up until 1935 represented a summary of agricultural facts and statistics as well as latest developments. Beginning in 1936, each yearbook is devoted to a specific theme.

Agricultural Statistics. Department of Agriculture, annual since 1936.
Contains statistics and general information regarding crops and other products as well as brief summaries of economic conditions prior to 1936. The latter are derived from the Yearbook of Agriculture.

Agriculture Index. H. W. Wilson, 1919-
An excellent index of periodicals dealing with various aspects of agriculture arranged by subject. In addition, outstanding books, pamphlets and government documents are often listed. This is the most complete bibliography of current materials dealing with agriculture.

A check of the card catalog will reveal many more worthwhile titles but the following are useful for general information.

American Agriculture, by Edward C. Higbee. Wiley, 1958 (ISBN 0-471-38742-8)
Agricultural Regions of the United States, by Ladd Haystead. Oklahoma Univ. Press, 1963. (ISBN 0-8061-0323-X)

AIR CONDITIONING

Audel's Air Conditioning. Bobbs Merrill. (ISBN 0-672-23159-X)
The very best handbook for repair and maintenance of the home air conditioner.

Handbook of Air Conditioning, Heating and Ventilation, by Clifford Strock. 2nd ed. Industrial Press, 1965. (ISBN 0-8311-3015-6)
Excellent for technical references on all types of air conditioning problems.

Trouble Shooter's Bible for Refrigeration and Air Conditioning, by James H. Doolin. Wehman Bros., 1962.

Sincere's Air Conditioning Service, by William Ewers. Sincere Press, 2 vols. (Vol. I, Home. ISBN 0-912534-07-09; Vol. II, Auto. ISBN 0-912534-08-7)
This work devotes one volume to home air conditioning and one to air conditioning of the automobile. The latter is almost the only reliable source for the automobile information.

AIR FORCE
see
ARMED FORCES

AIRCRAFT

There are many sources of information on types of aircraft
and aircraft engines but the first two listed below are the most important and most comprehensive.

Jane's All the World's Aircraft, ed. by John J. W. Taylor. Franklin
    Watts, annual since 1909.
    This is the most comprehensive guide to both civil and mili-
tary aircraft of the world.   Each country of the world which has an
air potential is considered.   Photographs and line drawings of each
plane are given, plus detailed specifications as to size, performance
and capacities, and special features dealing with engines and construction.   This annual publication continually adds new planes and
engines as well as deleting obsolete models.   The annual index lists
any plane recorded within the past ten years, giving volume and
page.   An absolute must for any library having this type of question.

Aircraft, Engines and Airmen, by August Hanniball.   Scarecrow
    Press, 1972.   (ISBN 0-8108-0430-1)
    This is a selective review of the periodical literature, 1930-
1969, covering many periodicals dealing with aviation.   It is divided
into four parts: articles dealing with aircraft; with aircraft engines;
with biographies of fighter pilots; and with Air Forces.   In addition,
there are indexes by aircraft names, manufacturers, aircraft symbols and engine names and symbols.   This is sometimes the only
source of some information which is not even to be found in the Air
University Index.

Air University Library Index to Military Periodicals, Maxwell Air
    Force Base, Ala.:   Air University, published since 1949-
    This quarterly index to the more important military periodi-
cals from all over the world is often the only source of indexing for
those journals.   It is an excellent source of information on recent
and experimental planes.

    Other worthwhile books discussing various types of aircraft
are:

Famous Fighters of World War II, ed. by William Green.   Double-
    day, 1957.   10 vol.
    The definitive works on fighting planes of the Second World
War.   Its small size--it fits too well into a pocket--is something of
a hazard for library collections.

Aircraft Annual, ed. by J. W. Taylor.   Arco Publishing.

This book is published annually but the title varies from year to year. It is an excellent source of information on all phases of aeronautical development and design.

One of the most common questions concerns identification of aircraft. There are several excellent publications for this purpose:

Aircraft in Profile, ed. by Charles W. Cain. Doubleday. 10 vol.
    1968-1975.
    Well illustrated with silhouettes of all major planes of the world, concentrating on military aircraft. Excellent as a basic source for teaching the recognition of type.

Observer's Book of Aircraft, by William Green, Warne, 1973.
    (ISBN 0-7232-1514-6)
    Another excellent book by Green with the same pocketsized format as Famous Fighters... (above).

AIRLINES

There are two probable types of questions dealing with airlines: one concerning the history and background of various airlines or the air transport industry, the other seeking information on fares and schedules.

Although the user should be cautioned that the ticket agent or a good travel agency can be relied upon to give adequate information, many persons like the feeling of independence it gives them to plan and schedule their own flights. The very best source of information concerning tickets and schedules is:

Official Airlines Guide, Washington, D. C.: American Aviation Publ.,
    monthly since 1958.
    This monthly publication gives the latest fares and schedules for all airlines, both national and international, that serve the continental United States.

For information concerning the history and background of the various airlines:

Airlines of the United States Since 1914, by R. E. Davies. Rowman,
    1972.
History of the World's Airlines, by R. E. Davies. Oxford Univ.
    Press, 1964. (ISBN 0-19-215928-3)

ALCOHOL

There are two aspects of the question of alcohol: its use and its abuse. For articles and books dealing with the problems of

drinking and drunkenness, check the card catalog and/or the periodical indexes. For information and statistics on the use and manufacture of alcoholic beverages, there are three excellent annual
publications. These are published by the industry and are therefore
not unbiased in their approach, but are very useful for statistical
data.

Annual Statistical Review of the Distilled Spirit Industry. Washing-
    ton, D. C.: Distilled Spirit Institute.
Brewer's Almanac: The Brewing Industry in the United States. U. S.
    Brewer's Association.
L. B. I. Facts Book. New York: Licensed Beverage Industries.
    The L. B. I. also publishes several other pamphlets dealing
not only with statistics but also with various aspects of the alcohol
problem and its solution.

ALLERGIES

Librarians should stay as far away as possible from questions involving either legal or medical advice. However, there are
legitimate questions concerning specific diseases which can easily be
answered in various medical dictionaries or handbooks. In case
these do not answer your needs for information on allergies, the
following book is recommended.

Allergy: What It Is and What To Do About It, by Harry Swartz.
    Ungar Press, 1959. (ISBN 0-8044-5899-5)

ALMANACS

The most comprehensive bibliography of almanacs, this is
arranged by state, then chronologically. Selected library locations
are also given.

Almanacs of the United States, by Milton Drake. Scarecrow, 1962.
    2 vols. (ISBN 0-8108-0001-2)

ALPHABET

Questions concerning the alphabet generally fall into one of
two categories. The first type deals with the development of the
alphabet and the various forms it has taken from earliest time to
the present day. Most of these questions can be answered quite
adequately by reference to the articles in a good encyclopedia or the

plates in a good dictionary. Possibly the best encyclopedic article on the subject is in Collier's Encyclopedia. However, if a more detailed discussion is desired, there are several books dealing specifically with the development of the written word.

Alphabets, Ancient and Modern, by J. B. Russell. Wehman, 1945.
Twenty Six Letters, by Oscar Ogg. T. Y. Crowell, 1971. (ISBN 0-690-84115-9)

The other type of question concerning the alphabet is actually about lettering, i.e., various type forms and letters and there are many good books available.

Art Alphabets and Lettering, by John M. Bergling. 9th ed. Bergling, 1967. (ISBN 0-910222-01-0)
Basic Guide to Lettering, by Robert D. Buckley. Chilton, 1951. (ISBN 0-8019-0161-8)

ALTITUDES

For the United States there is no better publication than the Geological Survey Bulletin # 274.

A Dictionary of Altitudes in the United States, compiled by Henry Gannett. I 19.3:274

For altitudes of cities and mountains, check the indexes of the following sources:

World Almanac, Newspaper Enterprise Associates, annual since 1868
Information Please Almanac, ed. by Dan Golenpaul. Dan Golenpaul Associates, annual since 1946.
Rand McNally Commercial Atlas, Rand McNally, annual since 1869.

In addition, any good gazetteer will usually give the altitudes of the place names cited, especially cities and mountains. Particularly good for this are:

Lippincott's New Gazetteer: A Complete Pronouncing Gazetteer or Geographical Dictionary of the World, Repr. of 1918 ed. Finch Press, 3 vols.
Webster's New Geographical Dictionary, rev. ed. Merriam-Webster, 1972. (ISBN 0-87779-146-5)

AMERICAN GUIDE SERIES

No other series of guide books concerning the United States

has approached the American Guide Series in either coverage or value. This series of books, produced by the Federal Writer's Project of the Works Progress Administration as a means of providing work for writers and historians, turned out to be the definitive work on local America. There is scarcely a factual question about an individual state which cannot be answered here. The Scholarly Press has just recently reprinted the entire series:

Alabama, A Guide to the Deep South (ISBN 0-403-02153-7)
A Guide to Alaska, Last American Frontier (ISBN 0-403-62154-5)
Arizona, A State Guide (ISBN 0-403-02155-3)
Arkansas, A Guide to the State (ISBN 0-403-02156-1)
California, A Guide to the Golden State (ISBN 0-403-02157-8)
Colorado, A Guide to the Highest State (ISBN 0-403-02158-8)
Connecticut, A Guide to Its Roads, Lore and People (ISBN 0-403-02159-6)
Delaware, A Guide to the First State (ISBN 0-403-02160-X)
Florida, A Guide to the Southernmost State (ISBN 0-403-02161-8)
Georgia, A Guide to Its Towns and Countryside (ISBN 0-403-02162-6)
Idaho, A Guide in Word and Picture (ISBN 0-403-02163-4)
Illinois, A Descriptive and Historical Guide (ISBN 0-403-02164-2)
Indiana, A Guide to the Hoosier State (ISBN 0-403-02165-0)
Iowa, A Guide to the Hawkeye State (ISBN 0-403-02166-9)
Kansas, A Guide to the Sunflower State (ISBN 0-403-02167-7)
Kentucky, A Guide to the Bluegrass State (ISBN 0-403-02168-5)
Louisiana, A Guide to the State (ISBN 0-403-02169-3)
Maine, A Guide Down East (ISBN 0-403-02170-7)
Maryland, A Guide to the Old Lime State (ISBN 0-403-02171-5)
Massachusetts, A Guide to Its Places and People (ISBN 0-403-02150-2)
Michigan, A Guide to the Wolverine State (ISBN 0-403-02172-3)
Minnesota, A State Guide (ISBN 0-403-02173-1)
Mississippi, A Guide to the Magnolia State (ISBN 0-403-02174-X)
Missouri, A Guide to the "Show Me" State (ISBN 0-403-02175-8)
Montana, A State Guide Book (ISBN 0-403-02176-6)
Nebraska, A Guide to the Cornhusker State (ISBN 0-403-02177-4)
Nevada, A Guide to the Silver State (ISBN 0-403-02178-2)
New Hampshire, A Guide to the Granite State (ISBN 0-403-02179-0)
New Jersey, A Guide to Its Present and Past (ISBN 0-403-02180-4)
New Mexico, A Guide to the Colorful State (ISBN 0-403-02181-2)
New York, A Guide to the Empire State (ISBN 0-403-02151-0)
North Carolina, A Guide to the Old North State (ISBN 0-403-02182-0)
North Dakota, A Guide to the Northern Prairie State (ISBN 0-403-02183-9)
Ohio, The Ohio Guide (ISBN 0-403-02184-7)
Oklahoma, A Guide to the Sooner State (ISBN 0-403-02185-5)
Oregon, End of the Trail (ISBN 0-403-02186-3)
Pennsylvania, A Guide to the Keystone State (ISBN 0-403-02187-1)
Puerto Rico, A Guide to the Island of Boriquen (ISBN 0-403-02869-1)
Rhode Island, A Guide to the Smallest State (ISBN 0-403-02188)
South Carolina, A Guide to the Palmetto State (ISBN 0-403-02189-8)
South Dakota, A Guide to the State (ISBN 0-403-02190-1)

Tennessee, A Guide to the State (ISBN 0-403-02191-X)
Texas, A Guide to the Lone Star State (ISBN 0-403-02192-8)
Utah, A Guide to the State   (ISBN 0-403-02193-6)
Vermont, A Guide to the Green Mountain State (ISBN 0-403-02194-4)
Virginia, A Guide to the Old Dominion (ISBN 0-403-02195-2)
Washington, A Guide to the Evergreen State (ISBN 0-403-02196-0)
West Virginia, A Guide to the Mountain State (ISBN 0-403-02197-9)
Wisconsin, A Guide to the Badger State (ISBN 0-403-02198-7)
Wyoming, A Guide to Its History, Highways and People (ISBN 0-403-02199-5)

AMISH
see
MENNONITES

AMPHIBIANS AND REPTILES

Amphibians and Reptiles of Western North America, by Robert Stebbins.   McGraw Hill, 1954.   (ISBN 0-07-060905-5)
Excellent handbook but limited to amphibians and reptiles found west of the Mississippi.

Familiar Reptiles and Amphibians of America, by Will Barker.
Harper & Row, 1956.   (ISBN 0-06-070301-6)
Although intended for high school use, this is quite authentic and easily used and understood.

Enyclopedia of Reptiles and Amphibians, by J. F. Breen.   Neptune, New Jersey: T. F. H. Publications, 1970.
Undoubtedly the most complete of the many books on the subject.

Field Guide to Reptiles and Amphibians, ed. by Roger Peterson.
Houghton Mifflin, 1958.   (ISBN 0-395-07567-X)
This volume in the famous Peterson guide book series, while quite elementary, is often useful in answering questions of identification and habits.

Snakes of the World, by Raymond L. Ditmars.   Macmillan, 1966.
(ISBN 0-02-53173)
Possibly the most famous of all herpetologists has written the most complete book on all types of reptiles of the world.   Originally published in 1933, it has recently been republished and is the standard for this field.

ANECDOTES

One of the more common questions comes from the person who has to deliver a talk and wants to spice up the presentation with humorous stories or quotations from famous people. You will find several worthwhile references of quotations under the subject heading in the catalog, but the following will give you anecdotes for all occasions. Each one is either arranged by subject or is fully indexed so that you can find the proper story to fit each need.

Complete Speaker's Index to Selected Stories for Every Occasion, by Jacob M. Braude. Prentice Hall, 1966. (ISBN 0-13-164616-8)
New Speaker's Treasury of Wit and Wisdom, by Herbert V. Prochnow. Harper & Row, 1958. (ISBN 0-06-035100-4)
Speaker's Encyclopedia of Stories, Quotations and Anecdotes, by Jacob M. Braude. Prentice Hall, 1971. (ISBN 0-13-824151-1)
Speaker's Special Occasion Book, by The Editors of Quote Magazine. Drake House, 1965.

ANNIVERSARIES
see
HOLIDAYS; WEDDINGS

ANTHEMS, NATIONAL

This is usually a two-pronged question. Usually the first part is "What is the National Anthem of...?" This part is fairly easy to answer. It will be found by looking under the proper country in:

The Statesman's Yearbook, by various editors. St. Martin's Press, annually.

The second part of the question is more difficult but there are two possible sources, once you have determined the title of the desired anthem.

The Song Index and Supplement, An Index to More Than 12,000 Songs in 177 Song Collections... ed. by Minnie E. Sears. Shoe String Press, 1966 repr. of 1934 ed.
This will give a listing of the various anthologies which will contain the desired anthem.
National Anthems of the World, ed. by Martin Shaw, et al. 3rd ed. Pitman, 1969.
This contains most of the national anthems of the world.

ANTHROPOLOGY

The general field of anthropology is such a large one that it encompasses all fields dealing with the development of the races and peoples and all aspects of that development such as mythology, customs, folklore and ethnology. Since each of these subjects is treated separately in this book, only the books on the broad field of anthropology will be listed here.

Origin of Races, by Carleton S. Coon. Knopf, 1962. (ISBN 0-394-43944-9)
Races of Europe, by Carleton S. Coon. Greenwood, 1972. Repr. of 1939 ed. (ISBN 0-8371-6328-5)
Although these two books were written to be used primarily as college textbooks, they are probably the best and most readable sources of information concerning the development of the races. Particularly useful because of their glossaries of anthropological terms and bibliographies.

There are three encyclopedic works which, while not devoted entirely to anthropology, are excellent for answering questions on such topics as tribal taboos, names, worship, family life and mythology. These can be found by references to the general indexes.

The Encyclopedia of Religion and Ethics, ed. by James Hastings. Scribner's, 1908-1927. 13 vols. (Available only on direct order from publisher)
The Encyclopedia of the Social Sciences, ed. by Edwin R. Seligman. Macmillan, 1937. 8 vols. (ISBN 0-02-60913)
The Golden Bough, ed. by James G. Frazer. 3rd ed. St. Martins Press, 13 vols.

ANTIQUES

There are very few subjects which have as many possible approaches as antiques. In fact, it is almost an impossibility even to arrive at a definition that will suit all your users. The references here are highly selective but they will be adequate in most cases.

Any library which receives many questions on this subject should definitely subscribe to the following magazines, both of which are indexed in Readers' Guide and both of which not only cover the broad field of antiques but also list exhibitions and historical background of various pieces.

Antique Magazine, ed. by Alice Winchester. New York: Straight Enterprises. (available on microfilm)
Hobbies: The Magazine for Collectors, ed. by Pearl Ann Reeder.

Chicago, Ill.: Lightner Publishing Company. (available on microfilm)

For lists of other periodicals dealing with antiques, check in Ulrich's International Periodicals Directory (the sub section Antiques under HOBBIES). Here will be listed periodicals covering all aspects of the subject.

To determine possible value or cost of antiques:

Price Guide to Antique Furniture, ed. by John Andrews. Gale, 1973.
Price Guide to Victorian Furniture, ed. by John Andrews. Gale, 1973.
American Bottle Collectors Price Guide, by Donald J. Goodell.
     Tuttle, 1973. (ISBN 0-8048-1098-2)

Recognition of antiques:

Complete Encyclopedia of Antiques, ed. by L. G. Ramsey. Haw-
     thorn, 1962. (ISBN 0-8015-1536-X)
Concise Encyclopedia of American Antiques, ed. by Helen Comstock.
     Hawthorn, 1965. (ISBN 0-8015-1680-3)
Random House Encyclopedia of Antiques, ed. by John Pope-Hen-
     nessey. Random House, 1973. (ISBN 0-394-48811-3)

ANTONYMS
see
SYNONYMS AND ANTONYMS

AQUARIUMS

Under this heading will be found a listing of the aquariums, their location and specialties. If you are looking for information on the establishment of home aquariums, see TROPICAL FISH.

Animals Next Door, A Guide to Zoos and Aquariums of the Americas,
     by Henry Gersh. Fleet, 1971. (ISBN 0-8303-0088-0)
This lists in a readable but informative way all the important zoological gardens and aquariums of the Western Hemisphere.

ARCHITECTURE

For a good discussion of various types of architecture in the United States, among the most useful sources are the various volumes of the AMERICAN GUIDE SERIES (listed under that heading). Each state book contains a separate chapter in which the architecture of of that state is discussed.

American Architects Directory, ed. by Jaques Cattell Press. Bowker,
    1970. (ISBN 0-8352-0281-X)
American Institute of Architects Membership Directory. annual.
        The Bowker publication is to be preferred since it contains
not only biographical information but also things to look for when
selecting an architect. It also lists schools of architecture as well
as state regulations concerning architects. The AIA Directory is
more frequent and therefore more up-to-date if you are only looking
for a specific person or for architects in a specific location.

Illustrated Dictionary of Architecture, by Alfred M. Kemper. Phil-
    lips, 1973. (ISBN 0-81599-197-1)
        A well illustrated dictionary which not only defines and illus-
trates terms used in architecture but also gives a good account of
various historical developments.

Architecture Through the Ages, by Talbot F. Hamlin. Rev. ed.
    Putnam, 1953. (ISBN 0-399-30001-5)
        Simply enough written to be useful even to high school stud-
ents, this is the standard history of architecture. It is particularly
well suited for answering specific questions due to its excellent index.

Architects' and Builders' Handbook, by Frank E. Kidder. 18th ed.
    Wiley, 1931. (ISBN 0-471-47421-5)
        Although fairly old, this remains one of the most valuable
sources for fundamentals. Particularly good for architectural terms
as used in various state building codes.

History of Architecture, by Banister Fletcher. 17th ed. Scribner's,
    1961. (ISBN 0-684-41246-2)
        Excellent for tracing various styles of architecture and for
descriptive discussions of the main characteristics of each style. A
good index makes it easy to locate trends, architects or specific
structures.

Architecture in America, by Wayne Andrews. Atheneum, 1960.
    (ISBN 0-689-00005-1)
        A well illustrated history of American architecture.

What Kind of a House Is That, by Harry Devlin. Parents, 1969.
    (ISBN 0-8193-0315-1)
        Intended for the junior high school level. This is well illus-
trated and will be of great help in recognizing types.

        In addition to these sources, all good encyclopedias have ex-
cellent articles on architecture of various cities and countries.

ARMAMENT

In this section will be listed modern arms and armament including side arms, small arms and weapons systems. For information concerning suits of armor and medieval weaponry see ARMS AND ARMOR. For tanks and other armored vehicles see ARMORED VEHICLES.

Jane's Weapon Systems, by Russell Pretty, ed. Franklin Watts, annually since 1968.
Another of the excellent series originally published by Jane's but currently by Watts. This one analyzes the various weapons systems used by the various countries of the world and up-dates the information annually. For the latest in sophisticated armament, there is no better source.

Small Arms of the World, by Joseph E. Smith. Stackpole, 1973. (ISBN 0-8117-1565-5)
A well illustrated description and instructional manual with excellent directions for firing the major small arms of the world. It describes almost a thousand weapons.

Military Small Arms of the 20th Century, by Ian Hogg. Twentieth Century, 1973. (ISBN 0-695-80406-5)
Similar to the above but limited to those small arms used by military troops. Excellent in its field but less comprehensive than the other book.

Gun Digest, by John T. Amber. 28th ed. Follett, 1974. (ISBN 0-695-80395-6)

ARMED FORCES

For information concerning individual AIRCRAFT, ARMAMENT, ARMORED VEHICLES, or UNIFORMS, see those sections in this book.

INTERNATIONAL

Although most of the references found in this section will deal with the armed forces of the United States, you often will get questions concerning the military potential of other nations. There are two excellent sources for international information.

The Almanac of World Military Power, by Col. T. N. Dupuy, U.S. Army Ret., 3rd ed. Bowker, 1974. (ISBN 0-8352-0730-7)
This is the most comprehensive of the books dealing with the international military potential. For each country of the world is given the necessary factual and statistical information concerning its

political and military situations as well as the strategic problems faced and any military aid pacts or alliances in which it is involved. In addition, statistical tables give breakdowns as to the number of men and types of material available for military actions.

Statesman's Yearbook, ed. by John Paxton, St. Martin's Press, annually since 1864.

Although not intended as a military reference book, this publication analyzes each country of the world. Within each, under the heading of Defense, is an excellent resumé of the size of its armed forces and military equipment.

UNITED STATES

Pay Scales

An often asked question is "What is the latest pay scale for the military services?" This is fairly easy to answer; any of the major almanacs have a chart giving a full outline of pay scales for all ranks and services.

World Almanac and Book of Facts, Newspaper Enterprise Association, annual since 1868.

Look under Armed Forces, U.S. - Pay Scales and Allowances

Information Please Alamanc, ed. by Dan Golenpaul, Dan Golenpaul Associates, annual since 1946.

Look under Armed Forces, U.S. - Pay

Biography

Any major military figure will probably be listed in Who's Who in America but you may be interested in the career of someone who is not yet of that much importance. For officers who have graduated from one of the academies, there is a fairly simple solution: just consult the annual register of graduates of the various academies.

These publications not only list by class rank every graduate of the academy, but also gives a brief biographical account of all of his military service including major assignments, dates of promotions, any medals or honors received, date of retirement and present address.

Register of Graduates and Former Cadets of the U.S. Military Academy. West Point Alumni Foundation, Inc. Annual
Register of Alumni, Graduates, and Formal Naval Cadets and Midshipmen. U.S. Naval Academy, Alumni Association. Annual
Register of Graduates of the U.S. Air Force Academy. U.S. Air Force Academy, Association of Graduates. Annual

Another useful source is:

Aircraft, Engines and Airmen, by August Hanniball. Scarecrow

Press, 1972. (ISBN 0-8108-0430-1)

This is a selective review of the periodical literature, 1930-1939, which indexes many periodicals dealing with aviation. One of its four main sections indexes articles dealing with biographies of fighter pilots. This is sometimes the only source for some items which are not even found in the <u>Air University Index</u>.

General Information

Although it was intended that no out-of-print books would be recommended in this publication, one has to at least be mentioned here since it answers questions of military minutia better than any current publication and should be acquired if it ever is reprinted.

<u>Military Customs and Traditions</u>, by Mark Boatner, McKay, 1956. (op)

In this, one finds the answers to such out of the way facts as "Why does silver outrank gold?" "Why does a Lt. General outrank a Major General?" or "Why is there no "J" company?" Well written, it is handicapped by the lack of an index but is otherwise an excellent addition to any reference section.

Fortunately the naval service has a book still in print which does the same thing for the naval services:

<u>Naval Customs, Traditions and Usage</u>, ed. by Leland P. Lovette. 4th ed. U. S. Naval Institute, 1959. (ISBN 0-87021-411-X)

Dictionaries

Since the understanding of a problem or a group is often dependent upon an understanding of the languages used and since the military jargon is often entirely foreign to the civilian, a dictionary of military terms is often necessary.

<u>Dictionary of United States Military Terms for Joint Usage</u>. Joint Chiefs of Staff. U. S. Government Printing Office, 1968.

This is the official publication of the Joint Chiefs of Staff and as such gives official definitions of terms used in dispatches and press releases.

<u>Naval Terms Dictionary</u>, ed. by John V. Noel, Jr. 3rd ed. U. S. Naval Institute, 1971. (ISBN 0-87021-481-0)

Guides to the Military Life

The following publications are intended as guides for the officers and enlisted men in our armed services. These are professional books designed to give guidance to the career man and cover every phase of his career from induction to retirement, including professional, social and legal aspects. They are of great value in answering any question concerning military service.

Air Force

Air Officers Guide, by Editors of Stackpole Press. Rev. ed. Stackpole, 1968. (ISBN 0-8117-0070-4)
Air Stripers Guide, by Editors of Stackpole Press. Stackpole, 1970.
(formerly Airman's Guide)

Army

Officers Guide, by Editors of Stackpole Press. Rev. ed. Stackpole,
1972. (ISBN 0-8117-1150-1)
New Noncom's Guide, by Editors of Stackpole Press. Rev. ed. Stackpole, 1970. (ISBN 0-8117-1125-0)

Marines

Marine Officers Guide, ed. by Robert D. Heinl, Jr. 3rd ed. U.S.
Naval Institute, 1967. (ISBN 0-87021-367-9)

Navy

Naval Officers Guide, ed. by Arthur A. Ageton. 8th ed. U.S. Naval
Institute, 1967. (ISBN 0-87021-432-2)

ARMORED VEHICLES

Armoured Fighting Vehicles of the World, by Christopher Foss.
Scribner's, 1971. (ISBN 0-684-12573-0)
   Arranged by country and then alphabetically by type of
armored vehicle, this small book provides pictures and technical data
concerning the armored vehicles currently in use. It provides such
information as power unit, armament, weight, range and dimensions.

Armoured Forces, by Richard M. Ogorkiewicz. Arco, 1970. (ISBN
0-668-02334-1)
   This was originally published in 1960 with the title: Armor:
A History of Mechanized Forces. It is an excellent history of the
development of mechanized warfare.

Fifty Famous Tanks, by George Bradford. Arco, 1967. (ISBN 0-
668-01583-7)
   A good pictorial history of the development of tank warfares,
showing pictures and describing the major tanks of history. Good
for pictures but does not give detailed technical data.

Tank Data I, II, III, ed. by Harold E. Johnson and others. We,
Inc., 1967- (I-ISBN 0-911964-06-01; II-ISBN 0-911964-07-X; III-
ISBN 0-911964-24-X)
   Photos and technical data on the tanks of all nations.

Tanks and Armored Vehicles, 1900-1945, rev. ed.   We, Inc., 1970.
    (ISBN 0-911964-16-9)
        This gives the same type of information but limits its cover-
age to vehicles of the Second World War and before.

ARMS and ARMOR

        In this section will be found references to suits of armor and
antique arms, such as swords, blunderbuses, etc.   For modern
ARMAMENT see that heading.
        All the encyclopedias have excellent articles on arms and
armors.   One of the more common questions in this field is identification of various parts of suits of armor.   This is a little harder
to find than it sounds but the following encyclopedias have line drawings which identify each separate piece by name.

Colliers Encyclopedia   (see Armor)
Encyclopaedia Britannica   (see Armor)

        The following books are excellent sources for information
dealing with weapons and their history:

Antique Arms and Armor, by Frederick Wilkinson.   Drake, 1972.
    (ISBN 0-87749-252-2)
Battle Dress: A Gallery of Military Style and Ornament, by Fred-
    erick Wilkinson.   Doubleday, 1971.   (ISBN 0-385-04787-8)
A Short History of Costume and Armor, 1066-1800, by Francis
    Kelly.   Arco, 1973.   (ISBN 0-668-02906-4)
Weapons: A Pictorial History, by Edwin Tunis.   World, 1954. (ISBN
    0-529-03438-7)
        This last title, intended for a high school audience, is one
of the best and most easily understood works.

ARMY
see
ARMED FORCES

ART and ARTISTS

        In this section will be listed the works on the general field
of the arts.   For specific types of art, e.g., PAINTING, SCULP-
TURE, MUSIC, see those subject headings in this book.

ENCYCLOPEDIAS

Encyclopedia of World Art. McGraw Hill, 1959-1968. 15 vols.
This is the outstanding encyclopedia of the arts. It is an
exhaustive survey featuring signed articles on architecture, sculpture, painting and many other artistic fields. Well indexed with
numerous cross-references and many plates in both black and white
and color. This is a first place to look for almost any art reference.

McGraw Hill Dictionary of Art, ed. by Bernard S. Myers. 1969.
5 vols.
Although termed a dictionary, this is more encyclopedic in
nature. All longer articles are signed by specialists in the field
and are well illustrated. Due to its dictionary arrangement there is
no need for an index but there are numerous cross references. It
is a good source for biographic information as well as discussions
of schools and trends. While not a condensation of the Encyclopedia
of World Art, it could be considered as a possible replacement of
that work by smaller libraries which cannot afford the more definitive work.

Praeger Encyclopedia of Art. Praeger, 1971. 5 vols.
Considerably less inclusive than the other two, this one has
about 4000 entries arranged alphabetically. This is a translation
and revision of a standard French work. While articles are quite
short, the work is excellent for bibliographies and illustrations.

INDEXES

American Art Directory, ed. by Jaques Cattell Press, 45th ed.
R. R. Bowker, 1974. Every 3 years. (ISBN 0-8352-0647-5)
This book lists over 2000 museum and art organizations arranged by state and city or by Canadian province and city; for each,
it gives personnel by name, telephone numbers, hours of opening,
budget and art specialties. In addition it lists over 1000 art schools
giving full data needed for enrollment or information. There is also
an index which helps to locate specialized collections such as stained
glass, sculpture, etc.

Art Index, H. W. Wilson, quarterly with annual cumulations since
1929.
This is another in the series of excellent indexes published
by H. W. Wilson. It indexes over 150 periodicals and covers such
fields as archeology, architecture, fine arts, films, etc. Its value
is limited to those libraries having extensive subscriptions to art
publications.

Illustration Index, ed. by Roger C. Greer. 3rd ed. Scarecrow
Press, 1973. (ISBN 0-8108-0568-5)
This is an expansion of the two previous editions of this work
and is an index to popular periodicals and to a few books. Well indexed with references to sources for photographs, charts, paintings
and line drawings.

Dictionary of American Portraits, by Hayward Cirker. Dover, 1967.
(ISBN 0-486-21823-6)
An alphabetical index to portraits of persons important to American history although not limited to native born Americans. It contains over 4000 pictures. Although primarily limited to persons living prior to 1900, presidents of the United States and other important political leaders are included through 1960. Excellent bibliographies are given as well as occupational index.

ART HISTORY

Art Through the Ages, by Helen Gardner. 5th ed. Harcourt Brace
Jovanovich, 1970. (ISBN 0-15-503752-8, HC)
Generally conceded to be the very best work on the subject, this work surveys Western art from its beginning to the present day. Earlier editors included sections on Eastern art and American art but these have been eliminated and the current work concentrates on the art of Europe. It is well illustrated and indexed and is an excellent work.

Story of Art, by Ernst H. Gombrich. 12th ed. Phaidon 1972.
Long a standard in the history of art, this is a well illustrated and well indexed text book which can also be used as an excellent reference source.

BIOGRAPHIES

In this section, general works on artistic biographies will be mentioned. For biographies in specific fields such as SCULPTURE, PAINTING, MUSIC see those subject headings.

Index to Artistic Biography, by Patricia Pate Havlice. Scarecrow
Press, 1973. 2 vols. (ISBN 0-8108-0540-5)
This is an index to biographies of artists. It does not contain the biographies themselves. It indexes 64 works of collected biographies and gives for each artist the names, dates, nationality and type of work in which he was involved.

Who's Who in American Art, ed. by Jaques Cattell Press, 11th ed.
R. R. Bowker Co., 1973. (ISBN 0-8352-0611-4)
This book gives over 6500 persons who specialize in various art related fields in the United States. It includes not only printers, sculptors and illustrators but also museum directors, critics, dealers and patrons of the arts. The book is an alphabetical arrangement in one alphabet of all persons listed but there is a geographic index and a professional classification index.

Who's Who in Art. International Publications Service, biennial since
1927.
Although published in Britain and predominantly British-oriented, this is a good source of information on prominent artists in all fields.

DICTIONARIES

Thesaurus of the Arts, by Albert E. Wier. Gale Publishers, 1974.
   (Reprint of 1943 ed.)
      A dictionary to terms used in all fields of the arts: drama,
music, radio, painting, screen, television, literature, sculpture,
architecture and ballet. Articles are quite brief but have been selected for possible reference value.

Adeline Art Dictionary with Supplement, by Jules Adeline. Ungar,
   1966. (ISBN 0-8044-3015-2)
      A complete index to all terms used in art, architecture,
heraldry, archeology, engraving, etc. , as well as technical terms
used in costumes, armor, pottery, etc.

ASSOCIATIONS

Encyclopedia of Associations, ed. by Margaret Fisk. 8th ed. Gale,
   1973.
      This mammoth work has been published since 1956 and is the
only source of detailed information for many American associations.
It no longer limits its listings to national non-profit organizations
but includes foreign and international groups as well. For each organization the following information is given: address and telephone
number, executive officers, membership, staff and a brief statement
of its history and purpose. This book is arranged into sections by
type of association but is carefully indexed alphabetically by exact
name and by key word within the name.

      Practically every professional group issues a membership di-
rectory. These will be found by looking under the proper subject
heading in this book.
      Often encyclopedias and almanacs give information concerning
specific organizations but the Encyclopedia of Associations is by far
the best source.

ASTROLOGY

      Once again, the library must beware of appearing to endorse
what some consider a pseudo-science, but one cannot avoid an occasional question dealing with man's future and the stars.

Astrology: Your Place Among the Stars, by Evangeline Adams. Dell,
   1930. (ISBN 0-396-04180-9)
      Recognizing that the author takes the subject seriously, this
is probably the best of many available books. She gives clearly the
basic theories on which astrology is based and gives instructions on

the making of simple forecasts.

Astrology for Everyone, by Evangeline Adams. Dodd, 1970. (ISBN
    0-396-04371-2)
        A simplified and up-dated version of her original book.

ASTRONOMY

        Answers to general questions concerning astronomy can be
found in any of the major encyclopedias. All have good articles on
the subject as well as on the major stars and constellations. A
good dictionary will generally answer questions on the major stars
found in the various constellations, but for more detailed information
the following are recommended:

Atlas of the Universe, ed. by Patrick Moore. Rand McNally, 1972.
        This is both an atlas and an encyclopedia. It is profusely
illustrated with charts, photographs and diagrams combined with a
text that is easily understood and interestingly presented. Much of
the material, photographic and textbook, derives from recent space
and moon trips. There are five parts to the Atlas: "Observation
and Exploration of Space, " an "Atlas of the Moon, " an "Atlas of
the Solar System, " and an "Atlas of the Stars. " All are fully indexed, with major features identified. It can be used by all persons
high school and above.

Navigation Aids

American Practical Navigator. U. S. Hydrographic Office, Publica-
    tion #9. U. S. Government Printing Office, published since
    1802.
        This is the premier book for navigational information for use
by sea-going vessels. It was originally published by Nathanial Bowditch but has been a government publication since 1868. It is nevertheless still referred to as BOWDITCH by most navigators and sea-
men.

American Ephemeris and Nautical Almanac for the Year. U. S.
    Naval Observatory. U. S. Government Printing Office, pub-
    lished annually since 1855.
        This is a joint publication of the U. S. Naval Observatory,
the U. S. Nautical Almanac Office and The British Nautical Almanac
Office. It is published annually, giving information for the next two
years concerning the movements of the sun, moon, planets, stars
and other celestial bodies.

Air Almanac, U. S. Nautical Almanac Office. U. S. Government
    Printing Office, 3 times each year.
        Intended to provide all necessary astronomical data needed
for air navigation. Information covers data for one year in advance
of publication.

General Astronomy

The various almanacs all contain sections dealing with astronomical data such as sunrise, sunset, movements of the planets and the solar system, star tables and tide tables.

World Almanac and Book of Facts. Newspaper Enterprise Association, annual since 1868.
Information Please Almanac, ed. by Dan Golenpaul. Simon & Schuster, annual since 1946.

For general information concerning the stars and other heavenly bodies:

Astronomy Explained, by A. E. Fanning. International Publications Service, 1970.
An illustrated introduction to the major aspects of astrology.

Exploring the Heavens, by R. S. Dodson. Crowell, 1964. (ISBN 0-690-28574-4)

Planet, Stars and Galaxies: Descriptive Astronomy for Beginners, by A. E. Fanning. Dover, 1966. (ISBN 0-486-21680-2)
Especially written for the beginning astronomer, it is a guide to the study of the stars.

Pictorial Guide to the Stars, by Henry C. King. Crowell, 1967. (ISBN 0-690-62513-8)

ATHLETICS
see
SPORTS
(Also Individual Sports; e. g., Baseball, Basketball, etc.)

ATLASES

In this section are listed books which review atlases and evaluate them. For actual map questions, see the heading MAPS.

Guide to Atlases - World, Regional, National, Thematic, by Gerard L. Alexander. Scarecrow Press, 1971. (ISBN 0-8108-0255-4)
An alphabetical listing of atlases from all nations published since 1950. An excellent listing of available materials.

International Maps and Atlases in Print, ed. by Kenneth Winch. R. R. Bowker, 1974. (ISBN 0-85935-000-2)
This analyzes the map and atlas output of 700 official and commercial publishing houses that print maps and atlases. It is

arranged by continent, country, region and city. All details of the individual maps and atlases are given along with an informative introduction concerning the best places to obtain maps and atlases.

General World Atlases in Print, compiled by S. Padraig Walsh. 4th
    ed. R. R. Bowker, 1973. (ISBN 0-8352-0562-2)
    A full scale recent analysis of 40 major atlases as well as brief descriptions of over 100 other minor atlases. It makes recommendations of which atlases to purchase and which ones to reject, and gives reasons. It has a chart ranking atlases by size and by comparative cost. An excellent companion to the author's General Encyclopedias in Print.

ATMOSPHERE

Any good encyclopedia will have articles dealing with the atmosphere, and these will generally satisfy the average reader. However, should you want more detailed encyclopedic articles, there are two good scientific encyclopedias for this purpose:

Encyclopaedic Dictionary of Physics, ed. by J. Thewlis, et al.
    Pergamon Press, 1965. 9 vols. 4 supplements.
McGraw Hill Encyclopedia of Science and Technology. 3rd ed.
    McGraw Hill. 1971. 15 vols. and reader's guide. (ISBN 0-07-079798-6)

ATOMIC POWER

Annual Report to Congress of the Atomic Energy Commission.
    Atomic Energy Commission. U. S. Government Printing Office.
    Annual.
    This is the most comprehensive presentation of the year's achievement in the field.

Man and the Atom, by Glenn T. Seaburg. Dutton, 1972. (ISBN 0-525-15099-4)
    An excellent survey of the uses of atomic energy for peaceful projects. Although very popular in style, it is highly reliable. It succeeds fairly well in making complex ideas understandable to the layman.

Atomic Energy Deskbook, by John F. Hogerton. Van Nostrand
    Reinhold, 1963. (ISBN 0-442-15330-9)
    Primarily a dictionary of atomic energy development. Articles vary from simple definitions to major articles.

Sourcebook on Atomic Energy, ed. by Samuel Glasstone. 3rd ed.

Van Nostrand Reinhold, 1967. (ISBN 0-442-02704-4)
The physics of atomic energy explained for the layman.

AUDIO-VISUAL MATERIALS

Organization and Management

Guidelines for Audio-Visual Services in Academic Libraries. American Library Association, 1969. (ISBN 0-8389-5055-8)
Guidelines for Audio-Visual Materials and Service for Public Libraries. American Library Association, 1970. (ISBN 0-8389-
3116-2)

Equipment

ABC's of Audio-Visual Equipment and the School Projectionist Manual, by Phillip Mamino. 2nd ed. State College, Pa. School
Projectionist Club. 1972.
This is probably the most plainly written and easily understood book on the operating of all types of projection equipment.

Audio-Visual Teaching Machines, by Lloyd G. Dorsett. Educational
Technology, 1970. (ISBN 0-87778-009-9)
Audio-Visual Machines, by Raymond L. Davidson. Intext Educational
Publishers, 1969. (ISBN 0-7002-2205-7)
Both of these are intended as texts for audio-visual courses
but either one gives a good description of various types of equipment.

Lists of Materials

Probably the best source of listings of available audio-visual
materials is the Library section of your State Department of Education. Almost every state maintains such lists which are freely sent
to anyone requesting them.
Another excellent source of all sorts of audio-visual materials
is the Educators Progress Service of Randolph, Wisconsin. This
company publishes a series of eight guides to free materials available to schools and libraries. These guides can be purchased as a
unit or separately and each is up-dated annually.

Educators Guide to Free Films. (ISBN 0-87708-031-3)
Educators Guide to Free Filmstrips. (ISBN 0-87708-032-1)
Educators Guide to Free Tapes, Scripts and Transcriptions. (ISBN
0-87708-033-X)
Educators Guide to Free Guidance Materials. (ISBN 0-87708-037-2)
Educators Guide to Free Social Science Materials. (ISBN 0-87708-
036-4)
Educators Guide to Free Science Materials. (ISBN 0-87708-035-6)
Educators Guide to Free Health, Physical Education and Recreation
Materials. (ISBN 0-87708-038-0)

Elementary Teachers Guide to Free Curriculum Materials. (ISBN 0-97708-034-8)

Film Catalog and Supplements, ed. by Reference Department. Baltimore, Md. Enoch Pratt Free Library.
This is a listing of the holdings of an excellent library and therefore a good guide for any library. This catalog has quarterly and annual supplements. ,

AUDITING
see
ACCOUNTING

AUTHORS

There is one series which is a must for every library and which is uniformly good for biographical information concerning authors. It is the "Author Series" published by the H. W. Wilson Company and originally edited by Stanley J. Kunitz (later editions have other editors). Each book in the series is devoted to authors of a particular country, period or type of literature and each contains well written biographies varying in length from 200 to 2000 words and often with photographs of the authors written about.

American Authors. H. W. Wilson, 1938. (ISBN 0-8242-0001-2)
British Authors Before 1800. H. W. Wilson, 1952. (ISBN 0-8242-0006-3)
British Authors of the Nineteenth Century. H. W. Wilson, 1936. (ISBN 0-8242-0007-1)
European Authors, 1000-1900. H. W. Wilson, 1967. (ISBN 0-8242-0013-6)
Junior Book of Authors. H. W. Wilson, 1951. (ISBN 0-8242-0028-4)
More Junior Authors. H. W. Wilson, 1963. (ISBN 0-8242-0036-5)
Third Book of Junior Authors. H. W. Wilson, 1972. (ISBN 0-8242-0408-5)
Twentieth Century Authors. H. W. Wilson, 1942. (ISBN 0-8242-0049-7)
Twentieth Century Authors - First Supplement. H. W. Wilson, 1955. (ISBN 0-8242-0050-0)

Although these are the best written and most desirable collection; by their very nature, they are most selective than many biographical dictionaries of authors. If you do not find the desired authors in those publications check the following:

Contemporary Authors, ed. by Clare D. Kinsman. Gale Research, 1962- .
Projected as a quarterly publication this is a continuing series

of books of biographies of writers of recent books. Almost all authors covered write in English but popular writers in foreign languages are included. For each there is a very brief summary of biographical data as well as a complete listing of all published works and work currently underway.

Critical Dictionary of English Literature and British and American Authors, 3 vols. Gordon Press, 1872. (Also available in reprint edition from Gale Pr.)
    Possibly the most comprehensive of all works on American and British writers, it contains over 45,000 authors who wrote in English before 1900. It tends to have more errors of fact than is desirable but it is often the only source of information on early writers.

Cyclopedia of World Authors, by Frank H. Magill. Harper & Row, 1958. (ISBN 0-06-003720-2)
    Originally a part of Masterplots, this book is a biographical dictionary of the authors whose works are digested in that series. There are about 750 biographies varying in length from 200 to 1000 words.

    Two additional sources which are not actually biographical dictionaries but which are excellent sources for little known authors are the Oxford Companions. These books are designed to provide ready reference for the general reader not only to types of writing but also to individual titles and authors. They are:

The Oxford Companion to American Literature, ed. by James D. Hart. 4th ed. Oxford Univ. Press, 1965. (ISBN 0-19-500565-1)
The Oxford Companion to English Literature, by Sir Paul Harvey. 4th ed. Oxford Univ. Press, 1967. (ISBN 0-19-500163-X)

AUTOGRAPHS

    Many of the biographical dictionaries will give facsimile autographs of biographees along with their portraits, but the most frequent question concerning autographs is their current value and possible sale price.

American Book Prices Current, ed. by Katherine Kyes Leab. Bancroft-Parkman, annual since 1896.
    Part II of this publication gives the latest auction information concerning sales and prices of autographs and manuscripts. Each item is described in detail as to condition, purpose and type. There is a decennial index for easy location of past sales.

    Should your question deal with the hows and whys of autograph collections, the following are recommended:

Big Name Hunting: A Beginner's Guide to Autograph Collecting, by
  Charles Hamilton. Simon & Schuster, 1973. (ISBN 0-671-
  65206-0)
Collecting Autographs and Manuscripts, by Charles Hamilton. University of Oklahoma, 1970. (ISBN 0-8061-0873-8)
  Both are written by America's foremost expert on the subject
and both are easy to read and understand.

AUTOMOBILE LAWS

Digest of Motor Laws, compiled by Cornelius R. Gray. Falls
  Church, Va.: American Automobile Association. Annual.
  This is a summary of regulations governing registration and
operation of passenger cars in the United States, the Canal Zone,
Guam, Puerto Rico, the Virgin Islands and the Provinces of Canada.
Compiled by the legal department of the American Automobile Asso-
ciation.

AUTOMOBILES

Questions about automobiles are mostly of two kinds: the
most common is how to repair certain automobiles, the other concerns identification and specifications of various models.

Repair Manuals

Audels Automobile Guide, 3rd ed. Howard W. Sams Company.
  (ISBN 0-672-23192-1)
Audels Foreign Auto Repair Manual, Howard W. Sams Company.
  (ISBN 0-672-23078-X)
  Audels has long been recognized as the Bible for automotive
engineering and these two books continue the tradition. Each one
analyzes the possible problems and solutions carefully and by means
of careful instruction and illustration explains possible steps to repair.

Chilton's Foreign Car Repair Manual, ed. by John Milton. Chilton
  Book Co. 1971. 2 vols. Vol. I (ISBN 0-8019-5632-3). Vol. II
  (ISBN 0-8019-5637-4).
  For each type of foreign car a detailed outline in words and
pictures explain the necessary repairs and maintenance. Twenty-
two different manufacturer's cars are described. There are separate chapters on "Engine Rebuilding" and "Tune-up and Troubleshooting."

Glenn's Auto Repair Manual, by Harold T. Glenn. Chilton Book Co.,
  1967. (ISBN 0-8019-5147-X)

The book is divided into three sections: (1) troubleshooting, i. e., locating and repairing minor problems; (2) common service procedures, i. e., servicing necessary to all American automobiles; (3) specific instructions for servicing every type of American car. Text and pictures are fully coordinated for ease of understanding. The book is particularly valuable because it gives specifications for every model listed for more than 10 years.

Identification

American Car Since 1775, ed. by Automobile Quarterly. Dutton, 1971. (ISBN 0-525-05300-X)
  The most complete survey of the American Automobile ever published. This has a complete listing of every car manufactured in the United States with a good description and many photographs.

Complete Encyclopedia of Motor Cars, ed. by G. N. Georgano. Rev. ed. Dutton, 1973. (ISBN 0-525-08351-0)
  A photographic history of the motor car arranged alphabetically by name of the car. For each one, the years of manufacture are given as well as a brief history and mechanical specifications. Often it is the only source of pictures of little known automobiles.

World Cars, ed. by Automobile Club of Italy. Herald Books. annual.
  This might be considered a supplement updating the Georgano book. It is arranged by country and then alphabetically by manufacturer. Every car in the world is pictured and data is given concerning price, performance data and basic specifications. (Originally called World Car Catalog.)

AVIATION
see
AIRCRAFT; AIRLINES

AWARDS
see
LITERARY AWARDS
or names of
Individual Prizes such as
NOBEL PRIZES; OSCAR WINNERS, etc.

BALLADS
see
FOLK SONGS

BALLET

The most often asked question concerning ballet is for the plot of the story which a ballet portrays.

Balanchine's New Complete Stories of the Great Ballets, by George Balanchine. Rev. ed. Doubleday, 1968. (ISBN 0-385-05760-1)
Contains the plots for the major ballet productions as well as information concerning first productions, dances, etc. Excellent index.

New Borzoi Book of Ballets, by Rosalyn Krokover. Knopf, 1956. (ISBN 0-394-40844-6)
In addition to plots of 57 ballets, this book has an excellent glossary of ballet terms and many photographs of outstanding dancers.

BANKS AND BANKING

Many current questions concerning banking can be most easily answered by the use of periodical materials. Business periodicals are indexed in:

Business Periodicals Index. H. W. Wilson. Issued quarterly and cumulated annually since 1958.

Moody's Banks and Finance Manual, ed. by Roy H. Krause. New York: Moody's Investor Services, Inc. Annual since 1909.
This is the most complete coverage of financial institutions now being published. It includes data on practically every national, state or private bank in the country; for each bank it gives its history, its officers, number of stockholders and depositors, and its financial situation. This will answer practically any informational question and is generally excellent except for its arrangement; the index must be used to find any information.

Banking Dictionary, by J. Ricci. American Elsevier, 1966. (ISBN 0-444-40473-2)
An international dictionary of banking terms.

Editor and Publisher's Market Guide. Editor and Publisher Co., Inc. Annual since 1924.
The publication is primarily for advertising executives and analyzes the market data for every town in which a daily newspaper is published. For each city, it gives the major banks and financial data.

Encyclopedia of Banking Laws, ed. by Henry J. Bailey. Boston, Mass.: Banking Law Journal, 1964.
A comprehensive digest of Federal and State Banking laws prepared by outstanding attorneys.

Encyclopedia of Banking and Finance, by Glenn Munn. 7th rev. ed.
Boston, Mass.: Bankers Publishing Co. 1973. (ISBN 0-87267-019-8)
An excellent reference manual which lists and defines the terms in the field of banking and finance. It is more than a dictionary in that a full discussion is given to each major topic.

BASEBALL

One of the major fascinations of baseball is the compilation of statistics. They are available in many and varied forms.

All Time Rosters of Major League Baseball Clubs, by S. C. Thompson. A. S. Barnes, 1967. (ISBN 0-498-06403-4)
A listing of the complete roster of every major league baseball club giving the records and achievements of each player each year. This book contains not only the players in the American and National Leagues but those of the old American Association, the Union Association and the outlawed Federal League.

The Baseball Encyclopedia. Macmillan Company, 1969. (ISBN 0-02-57895)
This book is a complete compilation of baseball statistics from 1876 to the date of publication. In addition to the individual records of any person who ever hit or pitched in a major league game, there are year-by-year rosters of each team, giving won and lost records and managers. There is also a listing of all major league records and special achievements as well as a complete record of all World Series and All-Star games.

Baseball's Hall of Fame, by Robert Smith. Rev. ed. Bantam, 1973.
A biographical sketch of each person elected to Baseball's Hall of Fame as well as a brief history of baseball.

Official Baseball Guide, by Charles C. Spink. St. Louis, Mo.: The Sporting News, annual.
An annual survey of major and minor league baseball clubs giving records of all current players and an excellent summary of historical baseball data. This is the best source for the latest baseball rules and changes.

Official Encyclopedia of Baseball, by Hy Turkin. 5th ed. A. S. Barnes, 1970. (ISBN 0-498-07539-7)
Similar to The Baseball Encyclopedia, this one includes much the same information but also gives detailed descriptions and charts for all major league parks.

Official World Series Records from 1903-, compiled by Leonard Gettelson. St. Louis, Mo.: The Sporting News, annual.
Each world series is analyzed, with box scores and a verbal

account of highlights and an excellent compilation of all series records.

BASKETBALL

Basketball's Greatest Games, by Zander Hollander.   Prentice Hall,
   1970.   (ISBN 0-13-072306-1)
Basketball's Hall of Fame, by Sanford Padwe.   Grosset & Dunlap,
   1973.
      Elementary in approach, these two works are good for basic
biographical information of the great basketball players.

Modern Encyclopedia of Basketball, ed. by Zander Hollander, rev.
   ed.   Four Winds Press, 1972.
      An excellent, well illustrated book giving history and develop-
ment of basketball.   Major emphasis placed on the collegiate game
but with a recognition of growing importance of the professional
game.   It contains annual won and lost records for every team as
well as biographical sketches of outstanding coaches and players.

Sports Rules Encyclopedia, ed. by Jess R. White.   Palo Alto,
   Calif.: National Press, 1961.   (ISBN 0-87484-063-5)
      The latest rules of each sport arranged alphabetically by the
sport.

BATTLES

Dictionary of Battles, by David Eggenberger. Thomas Y. Crowell,
   1967.   (ISBN 0-690-23744-8)
Dictionary of Battles, by Thomas Harbottle.   Stein & Day, 1971.
   (ISBN 0-8128-1364-2)
      Both of these books are alphabetical arrangements of battles
of the world and for each battle gives a paragraph outlining partici-
pants, location and results of the battle.

A Guide to the Battlefields of Europe, ed. by David Chandler.   Chilton, 1965.   2 vols.   (ISBN 0-8019-5151-8)
      Arranged by country and then alphabetically by battle, this
work gives all the vital information plus a suggested reading list for
each battle and a brief analysis of the strategy involved often accompanied by maps.

Twenty Decisive Battles of the World, by Sir Edward Creasy.   Revised and expanded by Lt. Col. Joseph B. Mitchell.   Macmillan,
   1964.   (ISBN 0-02-58530)
Decisive Battles of the American Revolution, by Lt. Col. Joseph B.
   Mitchell.   Fawcett-World, 1973.

Decisive Battles of the Civil War, by Lt. Col. Joseph B. Mitchell.
 Fawcett-World, 1970.
        For many years, the definitive book on decisive battles was
Creasy's Fifteen Decisive Battles of the World, which analyzed not
only the battle, its strategies and its leaders but also evaluated it
in terms of effects it had on world history.   Col. Mitchell has revised that book thoroughly and, while not rewriting Creasy, has
added maps and comments to his work as well as adding five new
battles from Gettysburg to Stalingrad.   Col. Mitchell has done similar work in his books on the American Revolution and Civil War.

West Point Atlas of American Wars, ed. by Col. Vincent Esposito.
 Praeger, 1959.   2 vols.
        Prepared by the Department of Military Art and Engineering
of the U. S. Military Academy for their courses in military strategy,
these two volumes are excellent studies of the various campaigns in
which the United States has participated.   For each campaign, there
are detailed day-by-day maps of the developing situation and an excellent textual discussion of daily events.   Volume one covers all
American Wars prior to 1900 and volume two covers 1900-1953.

BEAUTY

Glamour Beauty Book, by Editors of Glamour Magazine. Rev. ed.
 Simon & Schuster, 1966.   (ISBN 0-671-28680-3)
        Contains instruction on make-up, hair dressing, and the
wearing of clothing.   Well illustrated and diagramed.

Charm: The Career Girl's Guide to Business and Personal Success,
 by Helen Whitcomb.   McGraw Hill, 1964.
        More a book on personal grooming and dress than beauty
care.   This is an excellent guide for the young woman.

BEAUTY PAGEANTS

        For a listing of current winners and a list of previous win-
ners, see:

World Almanac and Book of Facts.   Newspaper Enterprise Association, annual since 1868.
        Each year carries a listing of winners of many current con-
tests. These are located by reference to the name of the pageant in
the index.   A complete listing of all previous winners of the Miss
America Pageant is found in the 1972 issue.

Facts on File, ed. by Lester A. Lobel.   New York: Facts on File,
 Inc., weekly with annual cumulation and index.

All major pageants or beauty contests winners are listed in the week of the award.

BEST BOOKS

There are several important annual listings of books which are considered outstanding and which might be considered best books. The following are a few such lists.

Notable Books of the Year, chosen by the Notable Books Council of the Adult Division of the American Library Association.
Best Children's and Young Adult Books of the Year, selected by the Editors of School Library Journal.
National Book Awards, sponsored by the Association of American Book Publishers, American Booksellers, et al.
Pulitzer Prize Awards, sponsored by Columbia University.

For a complete listing of the various notable books and prize winners see:

The Bowker Annual of Library and Book Trade Information. Council of National Library Associations. R. R. Bowker. Annual since 1957.

For listings of outstanding books of the past, see:

Books That Changed the World, by Robert B. Downs. American Library Association, 1956. (ISBN 0-8389-0021-6)
An outstanding librarian analyzes 16 great books and comments upon the lasting effects that they have had on mankind.

How to Read a Book, by Mortimer J. Adler. Simon & Schuster, 1940. (ISBN 0-671-34700-4)
The subtitle of this book is "a lifetime reading plan" and it lists outstanding books from all languages and from over 100 different authors as being outstanding.

The Bible states that of the making of books there is no end and this is equally true of the making of suggested reading lists. They appear with appalling regularity in various library literature. For current "best" lists see that heading in:

Library Literature, an Index to Library and Information Science. H. W. Wilson. quarterly & cumulated every four years since 1921.

BEST SELLERS

Here one will find the books which sold best, not necessarily the best books. For the latter, see BEST BOOKS.

Practically every reputable book review section runs lists of the books, both fiction and nonfiction, which have sold the most copies during the past week. Probably the two best weekly lists are the ones which appear in the following publications:

New York Times Book Review Section. New York Times (newspaper), Sunday Edition.
Publishers Weekly. R. R. Bowker Company. Weekly.

Annual lists of best sellers may be found in:

Bowker Annual of Library and Book Trade Information. Council of National Library Associations. R. R. Bowker. Annual since 1957.
  Listed under "Best Sellers"

World Almanac and Book of Facts. Newspaper Enterprise Association. Annual since 1868.
  Listed under "Books--Best Sellers"

All-time best sellers are to be found in the following:

Golden Multitudes, by Frank T. Mott. Bowker, 1960. (ISBN 0-8352-0051-5)
  Although arranged for quick retrieval of reference facts, this book is very readable and analyzes well the various all-time best sellers and why they sold so well. Dependable for both statistics and opinions.

Seventy Years of Best Sellers, by Alice P. Hackett. Bowker, 1967. (ISBN 0-8352-0085-X)
  This covers the years 1895-1965. It gives a year by year account of best sellers as well as an all-time best seller list. Particularly interesting for its analysis of the events which affected book sales. Excellent index by both author and title.

BIBLE

No attempt will be made here to list or comment on the many versions of the Bible. Every major encyclopedia has good articles on Biblical history. In this series will be found books of Biblical reference, i. e., Concordances, Commentaries, Dictionaries and Biographies.

COMMENTARIES

Commentaries are what their title suggest, comments concerning various passages of the Bible. These are of prime importance to persons wanting additional information about various texts or passages for either Sunday School classes or personal use. Naturally, there are many, and most are aimed particularly at one sect or denomination. For brevity, only the two which are considered best and least biased will be mentioned here.

Interpreter's Bible. Abingdon Press, 1951-1957. 12 vols.
  The most comprehensive commentary currently available, it is a guide to the Bible compiled by 125 scholars. While intended for scholarly research, it is simply enough written for the layman. Each passage of the Bible has the King James version and the Revised Standard version of the text side-by-side on the upper half of the page; the lower half of the page is devoted to a discussion of the meaning of that passage and an explanation of seeming differences in the two texts. Each book of the Bible is introduced by a long signed article by an outstanding theologian.

Abingdon Bible Commentary, ed. by David G. Downey. Abingdon, 1929. (ISBN 0-687-00155-2)
  A much shorter work, also written by Biblical scholars, it comments on all books of the Bible in a non-denominational manner.

CONCORDANCES

A concordance is an alphabetical listing of every word used in a work or writing. There can be concordances of any writer's work. Once again there are many concordances to the Bible, but only the two oldest and best known are listed here. Their references are to the King James and the Standard Revised version.

Young's Analytical Concordance of the Bible, by Robert Young. Rev. ed. Eerdmans, 1955. (ISBN 0-8028-8084-3)
Exhaustive Concordance of the Bible, by James Strong. Abingdon Press, 1958. (ISBN 0-687-40029-5)

DICTIONARIES

Interpreter's Dictionary of the Bible, ed. by George A. Buttrick. Abingdon, 1962. 4 vols. (ISBN 0-687-19274-9)
  Intended as a supplement to the Interpreter's Bible, this is an excellent, well illustrated dictionary which defines terms necessary for Bible study. It incorporates all latest studies such as the Dead Sea Scrolls and other recent findings. It has a section of well drawn colored maps of Bible lands. Indispensable to any Biblical collection.

Dictionary of the Bible, ed. by James Hastings. Rev. ed. Scribner's, 1963. (ISBN 0-684-31052-X)
  For many years the standard Bible dictionary until superseded by the Interpreter's Dictionary of the Bible. It is intended for the layman and general reader but can be equally useful to the theologian.

BIOGRAPHIES

"All The" series of the Bible, ed. by Herbert Lockyer, Zondervan.
    14 vols.
    This series of books is an excellent compilation of lists of
things in the Bible such as all the books of the Bible, all the mira-
cles, etc., but it is particularly good for biographical sketches of
Biblical characters. The following volumes are devoted to biographies.

Book	I.	All the Apostles of the Bible.	(ISBN 0-8013-10052)
Book	IV.	All the Children of the Bible.	(ISBN 0-8013-10051)
Book	VI.	All the Kings and Queens of the Bible.	(ISBN 0-8013-10044)
Book	VII.	All the Men of the Bible.	(ISBN 0-8013-10054)
Book	VIII.	All the Women of the Bible.	(ISBN 0-8013-10038)

All the Women of the Bible, by Edith Deen. Harper & Row, 1955.
    (ISBN 0-06-061810-8)
    A listing of all named women in the Bible with a thorough
discussion of the part they played. In addition there are exhaustive
discussions of background women who, although not named, are important. In addition to these sources, the Biblical dictionaries and
commentaries are good sources for Biblical biography.

BIOGRAPHIES

    This subject is such a broad one that a comprehensive listing
of biographical sources is neither feasible nor desirable here. Biographies of specific types of individuals will appear under that subject heading, e.g., AUTHORS, WOMEN, BASEBALL, etc. In this
section will be listed the most valuable references for general biography, including periodical indexes, indexes to composite books
and biographical dictionaries.
    All good encyclopedias can often be used successfully to find
basic biographical data.

PERIODICAL INDEXES

    The normal indexes such as Readers' Guide, Social Science,
Humanities Index and New York Times Index can be used success-
fully to find periodical biographical information but the single best
source of this type of article is the following:

Biography Index. H. W. Wilson, Co., quarterly with 3 year cumu-
    lations since 1946.
    This index acts as an index to biographical material in more
than 1900 periodicals indexed in other Wilson publications. In addition, it lists materials found in current books of individual and collective biographies as well as biographical articles and obituaries
from the New York Times.

COMPOSITE BOOKS

Essay and General Literature Index. H. W. Wilson Co., semi-an-
nual with 5-year cumulation since 1900.
This is an index to collections of essays and collected works
in many fields of knowledge. Although not primarily biographical in
nature, it is an excellent source of biographical information. It is
indexed in Biography Index; therefore, one does not have to check
both references.

BIOGRAPHICAL DICTIONARIES

General

The McGraw Hill Encyclopedia of World Biography. McGraw Hill,
1973. 12 vols. (ISBN 0-07-079633-5)
Designed to supplement courses of history and political science in colleges and high schools, this work contains over 5000 biographies in the field of world history. Each article averages about
800 words and many may have photographs or portraits of the subject
discussed. This is not only a reliable source book but the format
and illustrations make it a beautiful book as well.

Webster's Biographical Dictionary, ed. by G. C. Merriam Co. Rev.
ed. G. C. Merriam Co., 1972. (ISBN 0-87779-143-0)
The first place to look if you know absolutely nothing about
a person except his name. Published by the G. C. Merriam Co. it
continues in the long tradition of excellent works by that company.
The volume contains 40,000 names which are identified with very
brief biographical notes. While not satisfactory for detailed questions, it is an excellent source for identifying the dates, nationality
and general field of the person desired so that further searching can
be simplified.

Who's Who in the World. Marquis Who's Who, Inc.
A typical Marquis publication giving the bare facts of person's lives in an abbreviated but easily understood form. All bi-
ographees are living and for each is given the name of the person,
the position held, education, marital status, career, civic activities,
religion and any honors or elective offices received. There is a
listing of all published works, and home and business addresses are
given.

American

Current Biography. H. W. Wilson, monthly with annual cumulations
since 1940.
An excellent survey of recent persons in the news, giving in
a very readable way a two- to three-page biography of each. In
most cases, a photograph and bio-bibliography is included. Each
year 300-350 new subjects are written about.

Dictionary of American Biography. Scribner's, 1927-73. 13 vols.

plus 3 supplements. (Available only from the publisher by direct subscription. Not available to the book trade)

This is the standard biographical dictionary to important Americans who died prior to 1945. Each article is signed and many give bibliographies concerning the subject listed. Originally published in 21 volumes by the American Council of Learned Societies, it lists all important persons who have lived in the territory of the present day United States, excluding only British officers serving in America after the Declaration of Independence was signed.

National Cyclopedia of American Biography. New York: White, 1892-1965. 47 vols.

The least selective and therefore the most comprehensive of the American biographical dictionaries. Its strength lies in the number of persons written about; its weaknesses are that the family of the biographee supplies the information in questionaire form and that it is not alphabetically arranged. To find a biographee one has to use the indexes. Often referred to as WHITE'S by reference librarians.

Marquis Who's Who, Inc. of Indianapolis publishes a series of biographical dictionaries dealing with outstanding Americans.

Who's Who in America, Marquis, biennial since 1889.

Over 15,000 names of prominent Americans best known in their own field of endeavor. Contains sketches of non-Americans if they are important to our country, e.g., political leaders of the world.

Who Was Who in America, Marquis. 6 vols.

Historical Volume,	1607-1896.	(ISBN 0-8379-0200-2)
Volume 1	1897-1942.	(ISBN 0-8379-0201-0)
Volume 2	1943-1950.	(ISBN 0-8379-0202-9)
Volume 3	1951-1960.	(ISBN 0-8379-0203-7)
Volume 4	1961-1968.	(ISBN 0-8379-0204-5)
Volume 5	1969-1973.	(ISBN 0-8379-0205-3)

This is actually a supplement to Who's Who In America. Whenever a person who was listed in the current volume dies, his biography is transferred to the next Who Was Who. In that way, one need check only the current volume and the cumulative volumes to find if a person were listed.

Who's Who in the East. Marquis, biennial.
Who's Who in the South and Southeast. Marquis, biennial.
Who's Who in the Midwest. Marquis, biennial.
Who's Who in the West. Marquis, biennial.

Companion volumes to Who's Who In America. These volumes are more inclusive and contain persons of regional as well as national importance. Persons listed in the larger volume are also listed here. In addition, Marquis publishes several who's who-type publications dealing with specific fields of endeavor or accomplishment.

Who's Who in Finance and Industry.   Marquis, biennial.
Who's Who of American Women.   Marquis, biennial.
Who's Who in Science.   Marquis, biennial.
Who's Who in Government.   Marquis, biennial.
Directory of Medical Specialists.   Marquis, biennial.

British

Dictionary of National Biography from the Earliest Time to 1900, ed.
by Sir Leslie Stephen.   Oxford Univ. Press, 1938-1971.   22 vols.
& 7 supplements.
   The outstanding biographical directory of the world.   This is
limited to British notables who lived prior to 1950.   Each sketch is
documented, signed and accompanied by a bibliography.   There is a
Concise Dictionary in 2 volumes which is suitable for the small library and contains 30, 000 biographies of notables who died before
1930.

Modern English Biography, ed. by Frederick Boase.   Barnes &
Noble, 1965.   6 vols.   (ISBN 0-06-490526-8)
   Extremely limited in scope, this is an excellent source book
for relatively minor British personalities who died between 1850-1900.
It will often contain names not found in the Dictionary of National Bi-
ography.   Excellent indexing makes it easy to find pseudonyms, etc.

   For modern living persons, there is a publication similar to
Who's Who in America.

Who's Who.   St. Martin's Press, annual since 1849.
Who Was Who.   St. Martin's Press, 6 vols.
   These seven volumes together constitute a comprehensive biographical dictionary of the British Isles and important world leaders
since 1849.   Emphasis is on the British but world leaders are included.   As in the case of the American work, once a person is
dead, his sketch is moved to the Who Was Who volume.

   There are Who's Who volumes for almost every nation and it
would be hopeless to try and list them all.   The following, though,
may be helpful:

Prominent Personalities in the U. S. S. R. , a biographical dictionary
containing 6015 biographies of prominent personalities in the Soviet Union, by the Institute for the Study of the U. S. S. R.   Scarecrow Press, 1968.   (ISBN 0-8108-0170-1)
Who's Who in France.   Editions Jacques Lafitte, biennial.
International Who's Who.   Europa Publications, biennial.
Who's Who in Communist China.   Rev. ed.   Hong Kong: Union Research Inst. , 1970.

BIOLOGY

Most of your questions dealing with biology will be concerned with specific types of animal life; for those questions refer to specific sections in this book such as BIRDS, FISH, INSECTS, etc. However, there are several good general works with which you should be familiar:

Biological Abstracts. Philadelphia: University of Pennsylvania
Press, annual since 1926.
Prepared under the guidance of the Union of American Biological Societies, this work abstracts and indexes all fields of biology other than clinical medicine.

Encyclopedia of Biological Sciences, by Peter Gray. Van Nostrand-
Reinhold, 1968. (ISBN 0-442-15590-5)
Very comprehensive dictionary of biological terms relating particularly to botany and zoology.

Dictionary of Biology, by Edwin B. Steen. Barnes & Noble, 1972.
(ISBN 0-06-463321-7)
Zoological and botanical terms defined clearly and precisely.

BIRDS

There seem to be almost as many books about birds as there are birds, so the ones listed in this section will be limited to those which can be used for ready reference purposes. This will eliminate many good books concerning the value of birds to the ecology as well as technical treatises on bird physiology.
The most important set of books from the reference point of view is a series by Roger Tory Peterson. This series is well illustrated and the information given is well organized for reference use particularly for identification of various species. Each book deals with the birds of a specific area.

A Field Guide to the Birds, by Roger Tory Peterson. 2nd ed. Houghton-Mifflin, 1968. (ISBN 0-395-08083-5)
This book is limited to the identification of all birds East of the Mississippi.

A Field Guide to the Birds of Texas and Adjacent States, by Roger
Tory Peterson. Houghton-Mifflin, 1963. (ISBN 0-395-08087-8)
A Field Guide to Western Birds, by Roger Tory Peterson. 2nd ed.
Houghton-Mifflin, 1963. (ISBN 0-395-08085-1)
How to Know the Birds, by Roger Tory Peterson. Houghton-Mifflin,
1962. (ISBN 0-395-08090-8)

The above listed set will answer most of your bird identification questions but several others should be mentioned.

Audubon Land Bird Guide: Small Land Birds of Eastern and Central
North America from Southern Texas to Central Greenland, by
Richard H. Pough. Rev. ed. Doubleday, 1951. (ISBN 0-385-
06804-2)
A comprehensive illustrated guide to all the common and un-
common birds of the area. Intended primarily for young people.

Audubon Water Bird Guide; Water, Game and Large Land Birds, by
Richard H. Pough. Doubleday, 1951. (ISBN 0-385-06806-9)
A comprehensive illustrated guide to game and water birds.
Intended primarily for the teenager.

Birds of America, by John J. Audubon. Dover Press, 1967 (Repr.
of 1844 ed.). 7 vols.
A reprint of possibly the most famous of American publications on birds by America's foremost printer of nature subjects.
Excellent pictures but less helpful in identification than many other
books.

Birds of Europe, by Bertel Bruun. Western Publications, 1971.
(ISBN 0-307-49251-6)
Birds of Hawaii, by George C. Munro. Rev. ed. C. E. Tuttle,
1960. (ISBN 0-8048-0063-4)
Birds of Mexico; A Guide to Field Identification, by Emmett R.
Blake. University of Chicago, 1953. (ISBN 0-226-05640-6)
The above three are dependable guides to birds of various
parts of the world and are well illustrated. This is, as indicated
above, a very brief selection of the many such books available.

BLACKS

In this section will be found the general works dealing with
the black experience and state of life in the United States. For information concerning specific blacks, e.g., MUSICIANS, ATHLETES,
EDUCATORS, etc., see those subject headings.

Bibliography of the Negro in Africa and America, by Monroe N.
Work. Octagon, 1966. (ISBN 0-374-98759-9)
An updating of the author's previous work in which an effort
was made to furnish detailed information concerning all phases of
the present day life of the Black in America. It is necessarily a
selective bibliography but is about the best work of this nature available, particularly for the earlier items.

Black Almanac, by Alton Hornsby, Jr. Rev. ed. Barron. Annual.
This is a successor to the Negro Yearbook, originally published by the Tuskegee Institute. It publishes annually statistics and
articles dealing with the economic, cultural and civic activities of

the Black with special emphasis on recent events.

Negro Almanac, ed. by Harry A. Ploski.   New York: Bellwether,
    1971.
        This book published in three editions, all identical except for
title.   The other two titles are AFRO-USA, Reference Work on the
Black Experience in America, in one volume, and a five-volume set
entitled Reference Library of Black America.   This is the single
most comprehensive source of information on Black Americans.

BOATS AND BOATING

        There are three aspects of boats and boating: i. e. Selection,
Operation and Maintenance.   For ideas on naming and selecting
boats, the following two titles are useful:

Motorboat, Yacht or Canoe--You Name It, by Jean E. Taggart.
    Scarecrow, 1973.   (ISBN 0-8108-0661-4)
        A guide to suggested names for your craft giving examples
of what other owners have done.

Your First Boat: How to Choose It, How to Use It, by David Klein.
    Funk & Wagnall, 1967.   (ISBN 0-308-90010-3)
        A brief discussion of the type of boats available with sugges-
tions on how to choose the right one for your purpose.

        For information on operation and maintenance of boats, see:

Basic Seamanship and Safe Boat Handling, by Blair Walliser. Double-
    day, 1962.   (ISBN 0-385-05038-0)
        Elementary information for proper and safe handling of all
boats.   Excellent resumé of the rules of the seaways as they affect
each type.   Contains detailed data on the handling of all types of
boats.

Boatmen's Handbook.   Motor Boating, 1971.   (ISBN 0-910990-06-9)
        A handbook for the care and maintenance of all types of
motorboats with suggestions as to their proper use.   Contains a
guide to buying boats and equipment.

Complete Illustrated Book of Boating, by E. Zadig.   Prentice Hall,
    1972.   (ISBN 0-13-160143-1)
        Illustrated guide to the making, sailing and navigation of all
types of small craft.   Good list of boating equipment available.

Encyclopedia of Pleasure Boating, by Arthur Liebers.   Rev. ed.
    A. S. Barnes, 1973.   (ISBN 0-498-01178-X)
        A very comprehensive guide to all types of pleasure craft
both power and sail.   It gives data and instruction not only on navigation and handling but also for maintenance and repairs.

Your Guide to Boating: Power and Sail, by John Bohannan.   Barnes
   & Noble, 1965.   (ISBN 0-06-463238-5)

BONDS
see
INVESTMENTS

BOOK PRICES

   There are two common types of questions concerning book
prices; one is for current books--how much do they cost?, who published them?, etc.; the other is for information concerning the value
of books to collectors.
   For current books, one naturally turns to the regular sources.
The more common of these are:

Books in Print. R. R. Bowker, annual.   4 vols.
Publisher's Trade List Annual.   R. R. Bowker, annual. 6 vols.
Subject Guide to Books in Print.   R. R. Bowker, annual. 2 vols.
   The three publications, while separates, should still be considered as a unit.   The three together provide an accurate, easily
used and understood bibliography of publications currently available
in the United States.   The Publisher's Trade List Annual is a compilation of publisher's catalogs bound in a uniform set.   It does not
contain every publisher but comes as close as is possible.   Books
in Print was formerly an index to the PTLA but now provides the
price, publisher, author and ISBN number for almost any book currently in print.   The Subject Guide is useful in cases where you are
searching not for a specific book but for books on a specific subject.

   For books not yet published, check:

Forthcoming Books, Now Including New Books in Print.   R. R.
   Bowker, 6 times per year.
   This might be considered a supplement to the above-listed
books since it contains publishers' forecasts of their output for 5
months in advance.   It gives the same bibliographic data found in
the permanent volumes.

   Other countries have similar listings.   For example see the
following:

British Books in Print, A Reference Catalog of Current Literature.
   London, England.   Annual.   2 vols.

   Principal sources of prices of books for collectors include:

American Book Prices Current, ed. by Katherine Kyes Leab.   Bancroft-Parkman, annual.

This is a record of all the books, manuscripts and autographs sold at the principal book auctions of the United States and represents the probable latest sale value of books with a collector's value. There are cumulative indexes about every ten years to simply finding desired items.

Bookman's Price Index, A Guide to the Values of Rare and Other Out of Print Books, by Daniel F. McGrath. Gale Research Co., annual since 1964.

Listings in this annual are based on descriptions and pricings as listed in dealer's catalogs. Arrangement is alphabetical by author if known; otherwise by title.

The Used Book Price Guide. Kenmore, Washington: Price Guide Publishers, annual since 1962. (Five-year cumulative edition, 1967-1972, available.) (ISBN 0-911182-72-1)

The books listed herein are not actually collector's items but are the prices asked for used books. Often you can find books listed here that will never be listed in the auction or collectors' catalogs.

BOOKS - COLLECTING

Under this heading, books about book collecting will be listed. For prices of out-of-print books and collectors' items see BOOK PRICES.

American Book Trade Directory, ed. by Helaine Mackeigan. R. R. Bowker, biennial since 1915.

Valuable to the book collector because it lists the specialities of book dealers and auctioneers.

Book Collecting: A Beginners Guide, by Seumas Stewart. Dutton, 1972. (ISBN 0-525-06968-2)
How To Buy and Sell Old Books, by L. Freeman. Century House, n. d.
Primer of Book Collecting, by John T. Winterich. 3rd ed. Crown Publishers, 1966.

These three books are excellent introductions to the hobby of book collecting and each identifies types of books, gives hints as to how to recognize editions and other data needed for the collector.

The Literature of Book Collecting, ed. by Robert W. Vail. New York: Finch Press, 1936.

This is the outstanding bibliography of literature dealing with book collecting. Although now quite dated, the materials listed represent the best on the subject. It was collected and prepared by the Washington Square College Book Club of New York University.

BOOKS - PLOTS AND CHARACTERS

Here will be found plots and characters for works of fiction and poetry. For plots of plays, see PLAYS - PLOTS. Since plots are often discussed in reviews of books, a check might be made in the section BOOKS - REVIEWS for that type of coverage.

PLOTS

Masterpieces of World Literature in Digest Form, ed. by Frank
    Magill. 1952-1969. 4 vols.
       Originally published as Masterplots in several different formats, this edition combines all previous publications into one alphabet. This is the most comprehensive of the many compilations of book digests and for every work digested gives the type of work, the author, the time and place involved and the date of first publication. There is a short outline of the plot and a critique of the work as well as a list of the principal characters.

Masterplots Annual Volumes, ed. by Frank Magill. Salem Press,
    annual since 9154.
       This might be considered a supplement or continuation of the permanent volume and gives for each new book the same type of information.

Thesaurus of Book Digests, ed. by Hiram Haydn. Crown Publish-
    ers, 1949.
       This contains very brief summaries of books arranged by titles of book. There is also an author index and an index to characters. In some cases where an author is remembered for the strength of his work rather than an individual title, he is discussed by name rather than by work.

Reader's Digest of Books, by Helen Rex Keller. Macmillan, 1936.
    (ISBN 0-02-56171)
       Originally published as Vol. 29 of the Warner Library of the World Best Literature, it has been reprinted many times. (The whole Library of the World's Best Literature was reprinted in 1972 by Scarecrow Press in a 6-volume Mini-Print edition.) Keller gives plot digests of outstanding works, both fiction and non-fiction from all parts of the world. It is alphabetically arranged by title but unfortunately in two alphabets with no distinct division of the two. Care must be taken to check both portions of the book.

Oxford Companion to American Literature, ed. by James D. Hart,
    4th ed. Oxford Univ. Press, 1965. (ISBN 0-19-500565-1)
Oxford Companion to English Literature, ed. by Paul Harvey. 4th
    ed. Oxford Univ. Press, 1967. (ISBN 0-19-500163-X)
       These are not intended as a source for plot outlines but can be used for very brief accounts of some otherwise hard to locate items.

CHARACTERS

Cyclopedia of Literary Characters, ed. by Frank N. Magill. Harper
& Row, 1964. (ISBN 0-06-003991-4)
    This also may appear under the title Masterplots Cyclopedia
of Literary Characters. It is arranged by the title of the work and
for each work gives the principal characters and a description.
There is an index by character and by author.

Dictionary of Fictional Characters, by William Freeman. Dent, New
York: The Writer, 1963. (ISBN 0-87116-024-2)
    This lists in alphabetical order over 20,000 fictional charac-
ters from all segments of world literature since the invention of
printing. It covers not only novels and short stories but poems and
plays as well.

BOOKS - REVIEWS

Book Review Digest. H. W. Wilson Co., monthly with annual compilation since 1905.
    This is both an index to book reviews and an abstracting
service for book reviews. Each year approximately 4000 book reviews are cited giving for each one the publication, its date and an
abstract of the book review. It also indicates the number of words
in the review. This helps to evaluate the possible worth of the review for your use. About 100 periodicals are indexed regularly but
occasionally other periodicals are included for special materials.
Indexes all books receiving two or more reviews.

New York Times Book Review. Arno Press. Annual vols. from
1896 to date.
    This is a reprint of the book reviews which appear in the
weekly New York Times Book Review section. This is undoubtedly
the most complete newspaper book review section and provides an
excellent overview of the literature of our times. There is an index
available for the whole set.

Book Review Index, Gale. Bimonthly with annual cumulations, 1965-
1968, 1972-
    Most comprehensive of all book review citations. Includes
complete indexing to all reviews in 230 periodical, i.e., 60,000 reviews per year. Excellent source for books receiving only one review in obscure sources.

BOTANY

    In this section will be those items dealing with the broad field

of Botany. For specific subjects such as PLANTS, FLOWERS, etc.,
see those headings.

Biological Abstracts, Philadelphia, Pa.: Biological Abstracts, 1926-
A comprehensive abstracting and indexing service in the field
of Biology. There is excellent coverage of botanical subjects.

Biological and Agricultural Index. H. W. Wilson, 1964-
A cumulative subject index in all fields of biology and agriculture.

Gray's Manual of Botany, by Asa Gray. 8th ed. Van Nostrand-
Reinhold, 1950. (ISBN 0-442-22250-5)
This has a subtitle, "a handbook of the flowering plants and
ferns of Central and Northeastern U. S. and Canada, " which describes and gives basic data on over 8000 species of plant life with
many line drawings and cross references from common to scientific
names.

Botanical Names for English Readers, ed. by Randal H. Alcock.
Gale, 1973 (Repr. of 1931 ed.).
Glossary of Botanic Terms with Their Derivation and Accent, by
Benjamin D. Jackson. 4th rev. ed. Hafner, 1960 (Repr. of
1928 ed.). (ISBN 0-02-84711)
These are two excellent dictionaries to botanical terms in
common usage.

BOUNDARIES

Boundaries, Areas, Geographic Centers and Altitudes of the United
States and the Several States... by Edward M. Douglas. 2nd
ed. U. S. Geological Survey (Bulletin # 817), 1931. (I 19. 3:
817)
Historical data on the various additions to the territory of the
United States with historical maps showing boundary changes as well
as the routes of the various explorers in American history. Particularly good for such things as length of seacoast, cost of acquisitions, and lowest and highest elevations in each state.

BOWLING

Bowler's Manual, by Lou Bellisimo. 2nd ed. Prentice-Hall, 1969.
(ISBN 0-13-080499-1)
This is an official publication of the American Bowling Congress and gives, in addition to the fundamentals of bowling techniques, a full explanation of all the official rules of play along with
lists of outstanding bowling achievements.

Bowling For All, by Joe Falcaro. 3rd ed. Ronald Press, 1966.
A champion bowler discusses the sports and illustrates with
word and picture the proper techniques.

BOXING

In this section are given books dealing with boxers, boxing
records and rules of the ring. For books dealing with how to box
see that heading in your card catalog.
For a mere listing of current champions by weight class and
for lists of champions in each class over the years, the almanacs
are good sources.

Information Please Almanac, ed. by Dan Golenpaul. Dan Golenpaul
Associates, annual since 1946.
Under BOXING in index.

World Almanac and Book of Facts. Newspaper Enterprise Association, annual since 1868.
Under BOXING in index.

Heavyweight Champions, by John Durant. Rev. 5th ed. Hastings
House, 1971. (ISBN 0-8038-3030-0)
A biographical history of the heavyweight class in boxing giving a full treatment to each of the holders of the title and his contribution to the sport.

Official Boxing Rules. New York. Amateur Athletic Union of the
U. S. Annual.
This gives the latest amateur rules as well as the current
champions in each division.

Who's Who in Boxing, by Bob Burrill. Arlington House, 1974.
(ISBN 8-87000-232-5)
A biographical directory to the fighters, promoters and managers currently operating on the fight scene. Excellent for current
information but its future value will depend upon how often and how
well it is updated.

BOY SCOUTS

Boy Scout Encyclopedia, by Bruce Grant. Rev. ed. Rand McNally,
1965. (ISBN 0-528-82144-X)
Although not an official publication of the Boy Scouts of
America, it has been written under their direction and approved by
the association. There are articles on all facts of scouting in the
United States.

Scout Handbook, by Frederick L. Hines. 8th ed. Boy Scouts of
    America, 1972. (ISBN 0-8395-6500-3)
    Originally entitled Handbook for Boys, this is the official
publication of the Boy Scouts and gives all types of data on scouts
and scouting. Although of prime interest to Boy Scouts, its many
articles on camping, woodcraft, etc. can be of benefit to almost
everyone.

BRANDS ON CATTLE

Hot Irons, by Owen Arnold. Cooper Square, 1972 (Repr. of 1946
    ed.). (ISBN 0-8154-0416-6)
    An entertaining but highly informative book which discusses
the whys and hows of cattle branding as well as giving illustrations
of the more famous brands and their history.

Symbols, Signs and Signets, by Ernst Lehner. Dover, 1950. (ISBN
    0-486-22241-1)
    Although not entirely devoted to cattle brands, this book is a
collection of thousands of symbolic designs that are used in the
graphic arts. There is very little text. The prime value is the
black and white drawings of various symbols. Among other signs
given are many cattle brands.

BRIDGE

    Most books on bridge deal with one particular system of bid-
ding or of play and therefore cannot really be recommended for reference purposes. There are three, however, which do not limit
themselves to a single system or style of play. These three are
equally good at explaining rules, brdige conventions and the many
systems of bidding. Each defines, in an easily understood way, the
many intricacies which have kept bridge an almost universally en-
tertaining pastime.

Official Encyclopedia of Bridge, ed. by Richard Frey. Rev. ed.
    Crown Publishers, 1971.
    This is the sanctioned publication of the American Contract
Bridge Leagues.

Contract Bridge Complete, by Ernest W. Rovere. Simon & Schuster,
    1973. (ISBN 0-671-21437-3)
Charles H. Goren's New Contract Bridge in a Nutshell, by Charles
    H. Goren. Rev. ed. Doubleday, 1972. (ISBN 0-385-00740-X)

BRIDGES

This section lists reference sources for information on individual bridges, not facts on how to design or construct them.

Bridges Over Navigable Waters of the United States. U. S. Army
  Corps of Engineers. U. S. Government Printing Office, 1961.
  (D103: 2:B76)
  Gives location, owner, type of bridge, clearance, date of construction and type of traffic use for every bridge in the United States crossing navigable waters.

Famous Bridges of the World, by David B. Steinman. Dover, 1953.
  (ISBN 0-486-20161-9)
World's Great Bridges, by H. Shirley-Smith. Rev. ed. Harper &
  Row, 1965. (ISBN 0-06-006300-9)
  Both these books give similar information concerning the bridges mentioned. They give such data as the date of construction, the designer and engineer if known, the overall length and height as well as a brief history of the bridge and its impact on world history.

BUDDHISM

A Dictionary of Buddhism, by T. O. Ling. Scribner's, 1972. (ISBN
  0-684-12763-6)
  An English language translation of Buddhist terms and an explanation of many facets of the Buddhist terms and the religion.

Gospel of Buddha, by Paul Carus. Rev. ed. LaSalle, Ill.: Open
  Court Publ. Co., 1973. (ISBN 0-87548-228-7)
  An American translation of the basic teachings of Buddha with an explanation of necessary terms and meanings.

In addition to these books, the following multivolume religious encyclopedias have excellent articles giving not only the basic beliefs but the mythology and practices as well.

The Golden Bough, a Study in Magic and Religion, by James G.
  Frazer. St. Martin's, 13 vols. (Also available in condensed one-volume set, Macmillan) (ISBN 0-02-54098)
The Mythology of All Races, ed. by John Arnott MacCulloch. Cooper
  Square, 1932. 13 vols. (ISBN 0-8154-0144-2)

BUDGET - GOVERNMENTAL

The Budget of the United States for the Fiscal Year..., Bureau of

the Budget. U. S. Government Printing Office, annual since 1921.
(PrEX 2. 8)
    This is the complete operating budget of the United States for
the fiscal year.   It gives the recommendation concerning both income and expenditures.   For most libraries this is more information
than is desired and a pamphlet, The Budget in Brief (Pr EX 2. 8/2),
will answer most questions.   In addition to this, budget hearings concerning any appropriations for government expenditure are also
available from the Superintendent of Documents.

Statesman's Yearbook, ed. by John Paxton.   St. Martin's Press,
    annual since 1864.
    Brief summaries of the budgets is given in each national
description.

Book of the States.   Council of State Government, biennial since
    1935.
    This is the standard reference book concerning state govern-
ment and gives all the pertinent data concerning each state including
information on taxation and expenditures.   This will not give a detailed breakdown of state budgets.   If you need a more specific listing, each state government issues a budget statement.

Municipal Yearbook.   International City Manager's Association, an-
    nual since 1934.
    Although this will not give budgets for individual cities, it
does give excellent summary information for the United States and
for average cities of various sizes throughout the country.

BUDGETS - PERSONAL
see
PERSONAL FINANCE

CALENDARS

    For questions concerning specific holy days or festivals see
subject headings HOLIDAYS or FESTIVALS.
    For a discussion of the history of the calendar and possible
calendar reform:

Three Hundred Sixty Five Days: The Story of our Calendar, by
    Keith G. Irwin.   T. Y. Crowell, 1963.   (ISBN 0-690-82322-3)

    The more common questions concerning the calendar, though,
are ones concerning on what day Easter falls, on what day of the
week was a specific date in a specific year.   These are easily answered by checking under PERPETUAL CALENDAR and EASTER in
the index of either of the two major almanacs.

Information Please Alamanc, ed. by Dan Golenpaul. Dan Golenpaul
    Associates, annual since 1946.
World Almanac and Book of Facts. Newspaper Enterprise Associa-
    tion, annual since 1868.

CAMPING

There are three aspects of camping for which you will need
answers: problems of camping, equipment needed and where are the
campgrounds?

GENERAL INFORMATION

Fell's Guide to Camping and Family Fun Outdoors, by Nancy Cleaver.
    Fell Publishing Co., 1970.
Guide to Family Camping, by George S. Wells. Stackpole, 1973.
    (ISBN 0-8117-2021-7)
Modern ABC's of Family Camping, by G. S. Wells. Stackpole, 1967.
    (ISBN 0-8117-1042-4)
    These are only three of many volumes dealing with the joys
and tribulations of camping and all three are excellent for introduc-
ing the neophyte to camping activity.

EQUIPMENT

Consumer's Guide Camping Equipment and Recreational Vehicle Re-
    port, by Editors of Publications International, Ltd. Doubleday,
    1973. (ISBN 0-385-04734-7)
How to Select, Buy and Enjoy a Motor Home, Van, Camper, Tent
    Top or Tent. Beverly Hill, Calif.: Trail-R-Club of America,
    1970. (ISBN 0-87593-097-2)
    Either of these books gives a good discussion of the pros and
cons of each type of camping gear and suggestions of what to look
for and what to avoid in initial purchase.

There are two periodicals which are almost "musts" for the
camper. They have articles not only about camping in general but
are excellent for information concerning tests on new materials and
equipment.

Trailer Travel, ed. by Paul Fought. Highland Park, Ill.: Woodall
    Publ. Co., monthly since 1935.
    Oriented towards the camper with a recreational vehicle, it
tests and compares regularly all such vehicles and trailers as well
as giving general camping information.

Better Camping, ed. by Catherine E. McMullen. Highland Park,
    Ill.: Woodall Publishing Co., monthly since 1960.
    Devoted to the tent camper, it frequently tests such items as
lanterns, tents, sleeping bags etc. as well as giving general camping
information.

CAMPSITES

Woodall's Trailering Parks and Campgrounds, by Editors of Wood-
      alls. Simon & Schuster. Annual.
      The most comprehensive of the campground guides. This is
published by Woodall's and contains in addition to the normal information concerning facilities, restrictions and location of each campground, the Woodall rating of from one to four diamonds. Excellent
source for finding the campground you want. Contains telephone
numbers for advance reservations.

Campground Guide for Tent and Trailer Tourists, by Jerry Patter-
      son. Wakefield, Kansas: Campgrounds Unlimited. Annual.
Rand McNally Campground and Trailer Park Guide, by Editors of
      Rand McNally. Rev. ed. Rand McNally, 1973. (ISBN 0-528-
      84155-6)

CARD GAMES

Hoyle Up-To-Date: Official Rules for All Important Games, ed. by
      Albert H. Morehead. Grosset and Dunlap, 1970. (ISBN 0-448-
      01984-1)
      An updating of the world's most famous book on card games,
this book gives the official rules of all important card games. In
addition to official rules, hints are given as to proper play and
strategy as well as a brief history of each game and a glossary of
card-game terminology.

      For information concerning the rules and play of BRIDGE see
that heading.

CAREERS

      There are two principal questions concerning careers: "What
career should I undertake?" and "How do I get a job?" Both aspects will be considered here.

SELECTING A CAREER

Careers, Research Monographs. Chicago, Ill.: Institute of Re-
      search. Revised as needed.
      This is a set of over 300 selected careers. For each career
there is a pamphlet describing the career selected, its benefits and
its weakness. This is an important aspect in that it does not try to
sell the career but to describe it fairly and clearly. It tells the
necessary educational preparation needed as well as personality or
physical attributes which would help in the career. Although revised

quite often, the user must be warned that salary quotations are usually far below the current rates due to rapid inflation. Each monograph is separately bound, attractively printed and illustrated. There are almost 2000 individual jobs discussed in the full set of careers.

Federal Career Directory, A Guide for College Students. United
    States Civil Service Commission, annual. (CS 1.7/4 C18)
    This is a recruiting brochure intended to attract worthwhile college students into a field of public service. The directory presents specific information about Federal careers for college graduates. It is an invaluable source of information for any young person considering Federal Service. It not only describes in detail many Federal positions and the qualifications needed but also tries to orient the possible employee into what his relationship to other government agencies would be. In addition, it has an index of jobs listed in relation to college majors.

Dictionary of Occupational Titles. 3rd ed. U. S. Bureau of Labor.
    Employment Service, 1965. (L7. 2:OC1/95)
Occupational Outlook Handbook. Bureau of Labor Statistics. (L2. 3:)
    These two publications should be considered together. The Dictionary is an alphabetical dictionary of occupations, providing uniform names for all jobs of a similar nature with a description of each job. More than 36,000 job titles are given. The Handbook is a comprehensive source of occupational and industry career information.

Lovejoy's Career and Vocational School Guide, ed. by Clarence E.
    Lovejoy. Simon & Schuster, 1973. (ISBN 0-671-21451-9)
    This is a comprehensive guide to the field of vocational education giving not only job descriptions but also lists of training programs and schools including home study courses that will prepare you for your selected vocation. For each school is given full information including tuition, faculty, graduation requirements and possibility of financial help.

SUMMER EMPLOYMENT

Directory of Overseas Summer Jobs and Vacation Work, National
    Directory Service. Annual since 1969.
Summer Employment Directory. National Directory Service. Annual
    since 1952.
    These two publications list summer jobs both at home and overseas for high school and college students as well as teachers and other seasonal workers. Each one is divided by state or country and then by type of position.

GETTING THE JOB

Applying For a Job--A Self-Study Guide for Students, by Patricia
    M. Rath. Interstate, 1968.
    A guide to the student on preparing for the job interview,

with hints on how to dress, prior study needed and conduct while in the employer's office.

How To Get a Better Job, by Austin Marshall. Hawthorn, 1964. (ISBN 0-696-65450-4)
    Gives hints as to professional advancement. When to consider moving and when not to, as well as instructions on the job application and interview.

Why and How to Prepare an Effective Job Resume, ed. by Juvenal L. Angel. Rev. ed. World Trade Publishers, 1972.
    Based on the study of 10,000 job resumes, this book provides a complete guide to the preparation of your own job application as well as providing easily adapted resumes from practically every professional or occupational field.

CARTOGRAPHY
see
MAPS

CARVING OF MEATS

Art of Carving, by Editors of House and Garden. Simon & Schuster, 1963. (ISBN 0-671-05390-6)
    There are detailed diagrams for the carving of almost every type of meat and poultry.

CATS

Cat Training, by Margrit Lippmann. Neptune, N.J.: TFH Publications, 1973.
    Based on the mistaken idea that one can train a cat to do anything that it does not want to do, this book gives guidance in housebreaking, feeding etc.

International Encyclopedia of Cats, ed. by G. N. Henderson. McGraw Hill, 1973. (ISBN 0-07-028163-7)
The Complete Cat Encyclopedia, ed. by Grace Pond. Crown Publishers, 1972. (ISBN 0-517-50140-6)
    These two encyclopedias of feline information both give the history and development of all breeds of cats as well as information concerning cat diseases, cat breeding and cat training.

Cats: An Intelligent Owner's Guide, by G. N. Henderson. Transatlantic, 1966.

A well organized guide book to feeding, caring for, exercising, mating and showing of cats.   There is a section on different breeds of cats.

CATTLE

For a discussion of various breeds of cattle giving their distribution in various parts of the world and giving good pictures and description of various breeds, see one of the following books.

American Cattle: Their History, Breeding and Management, by
    Lewis F. Allen.   Wilmington, Del.: Scholarly Resources, Inc.,
    1973 (Repr. of 1868 ed.).   (ISBN 0-8420-1471-3)
Cattle of North America, by John E. Rouse.   Univ. of Oklahoma,
    1973.   (ISBN 0-8061-1023-6)
World Cattle, by John E. Rouse.   Univ. of Oklahoma, 1970. 2 vols.
    (ISBN 0-8061-0864-9)

For discussion of diseases of cattle see one of the following:

Special Report on the Diseases of Cattle, by Drs. Atkinson, Dickson, et al.   Rev. ed.   U S. Dept. of Agriculture, Bureau of
    Animal Industry, 1942.   (A 4. 2: C29/6/942)
Veterinary Handbook for Cattlemen, by J. W. Bailey, 4th ed.
    Springer Publications, 1972.   (ISBN 0-8261-0284-0)

CAVES

Amateur's Guide to Caves and Caving, by David R. McClurg. Stackpole, 1973.   (ISBN 0-8117-0094-1)
    Discusses history and geology of caves as well as their locations with a guide on how to explore them.   Well illustrated with a good glossary of speleological terms.

Caverns of the World, by Alonzo W. Pond.   Grosset & Dunlap, Inc.,
    1969.   (ISBN 0-448-26114-6)
Celebrated American Caves, ed. by Charles E. Mohr.   Rutgers
    Univ. Press, 1955.   (ISBN 0-8135-0241-1)
    These two discuss the important cave and cavern discoveries, giving for each one a brief history of the cave, how it was discovered, the total depth and length of the underground portion and in some cases, pictures of outstanding formations.

Visiting American Caves, by Howard N. Sloane.   Crown Publishers,
    1966.
    This is a comprehensive guide to all American caves open to the public either for spelunking or by guided tour.

CENSUS

Bureau of the Census, Fact Finder of the Nation.   U. S. Bureau of
    the Census.   U. S. Government Printing Office, 1965. (C3. 2:
    C33/13/965)
        An excellent though brief history of the development of the
    Bureau of the Census and a discussion of the methods used in cen-
    sus taking, the type of information provided and special services of
    the census.

Statistical Abstract of the United States.   U. S. Bureau of the Cen-
    sus.   U. S. Government Printing Office, annual since 1878.
    (C3. 134)
        The findings of the Bureau of the Census are so great that
    most smaller or medium sized libraries could not hope to contain
    the many volumes which are published after each decennial census
    but this publication is an excellent abstract of all the statistical in-
    formation derived from the census.   In this one work are found sta-
    tistics on the political, social and economic conditions of the United
    States.   Statistics are given for several years in each issue so that
    one does not have to consult every issue for continuing statistical
    data.

Catalog of the Bureau of Census Publications.   U. S. Bureau of the
    Census.   U. S. Government Printing Office, quarterly with an-
    nual cumulations since 1946.   (C3. 163/2)
        This publication supersedes and up-dates the 1950 publication,
    A Catalog of U. S. Census Publications, 1790-1945.   It list by sub-
    ject all current publications available from the Census Bureau.

CERTIFICATION OF TEACHERS

Requirements for Certification for Teachers, Counselors, Librarians
    and Administration for Elementary, Secondary Schools and
    Junior Colleges, ed. by Elizabeth Woellner.   Univ. of Chicago
    Press, annual since 1935.
        A state arrangement in which are listed the latest minimum
    official requirements for each type of educator.

CHAMPIONS (IN SPORTS)

        For a detailed account and history of previous sports, e. g.,
    BASKETBALL, BASEBALL, etc.   For current or recent champions,
    see a good almanac.

Information Please Almanac, ed. by Dan Golenpaul.   Dan Golenpaul

Associates, annual since 1946.
World Almanac and Book of Facts, Newspaper Enterprise Association, annual since 1868.

CHECKERS
see also
GAMES

Win at Checkers, by Millard Hopper. Dover, 1956. (ISBN 0-486-20363-8)
There is a mistaken belief that checkers is a less complicated and therefore an inferior game to chess. This book dispells that idea by discussing the strategy and planning necessary to master the play at checkers.

CHEMICAL ELEMENTS

The most common question on chemical elements is for information concerning the symbols used, the atomic number, the atomic weight and the balance of the various elements. The easiest and quickest method of finding this information is by use of the periodic table of the elements. All good encyclopedias include articles under Elements and all have charts giving this information.
For the periodic table in the traditional 8-tier format see:

Collier's Encyclopedia, ed. by William D. Halsey. Crowell Collier Educational Corporation. 24 vols.
World Book Encyclopedia. Field Enterprise Educational Corp. 22 vols.

The following encyclopedias do not have the traditional table, but contain excellent articles and charts giving all essential information.

Encyclopedia Americana. American Corporation. 30 vols.
This is the most complete chart giving, in addition to named information, such items as % of earth's crust, size of the atom and the ion, the melting point, the boiling point, and date of discovery and discoverer.

Encyclopedia Britannica. Encyclopedia Britannica. 30 vols.

In addition to these there are several very good books about elements and their properties. Only one will be mentioned here.

Building Blocks of the Universe, by Isaac Asimov. Rev. ed. Abelard, 1961. (ISBN 0-200-71099-0)

A highly popularized account of the various elements with a full discussion of the properties of rock. Written for high school use, it still is an excellent introduction to the subject. It also contains a traditional periodic table.

CHEMISTRY

Once again, the field of chemistry is such a large one that it will be broken down into various types of reference sources.

ABSTRACTS AND INDEXES

Chemical Abstracts. Easton, Pa.: American Chemical Society, semi-monthly with annual cumulations since 1907.

This is the most comprehensive abstracting and indexing of the entire field of chemical literature. More than 3000 periodicals are abstracted and any information can be found by the use of the excellent index.

Applied Science and Technology Index. H. W. Wilson Co., monthly with annual cumulation since 1958.

This is a subject index to English language periodicals dealing with the applied arts including chemistry. Periodicals to be indexed are selected by vote of the subscribers and the list contains most of the important practical journal on chemistry as well as other subjects.

BIOGRAPHY

American Men and Women of Science, ed. by Jaques Cattell Press. 12th ed. R. R. Bowker, 1971. 8 vols.

This work is divided into two types of biographical sketches. The first six volumes deal with the Physical and Biological Sciences and contain the biographies of outstanding persons in the chemical field. The second section of the 12th edition deals with the Social and Behavioral Sciences. These publications select persons who because of their achievements, research activity or position are important to the physical and biological sciences. For each person included the normal biographical information is included in a brief tabular form.

Dictionary of Scientific Biography, ed. by Charles C. Gillespie. Scribner's, 1970. 12 vols.

Only 8 volumes of this mammoth work have thus far been published but when completed it will represent the most complete biography work in the field of science. The biographies are in paragraph rather than tabular form and run from 300 to 3000 words in length. Each one is signed and many carry bibliographies.

World's Who's Who in Science, ed. by Allen G. Debus. Marquis-

Who's Who, 1968. (ISBN 0-8379-1001-3)

This is a volume of the Marquis Biographical Library and as such carries the usual information in the same format as the other Who's Who In America volumes.

DICTIONARIES

Concise Chemical and Technical Dictionary, ed. by Harry Bennett. 2nd ed. Chemical Publishing Co., Inc., 1973. (ISBN 0-8206-0026-1)

Literally thousands of chemical terms are defined in technical but easily understood terms. Meant for students of chemistry, it identifies not only chemical terms but terms in related fields as well.

Hackh's Chemical Dictionary, ed. by Julius Grant. 4th ed. Mc-Graw Hill, 1969. (ISBN 0-07-024064-7)

Excellent chemical dictionary which identifies not only chemical terms but many from such fields as physics, biology, mechanics and astrophysics as well. It is good for pronunciations and for the use of diagrams and tables in its explanations.

ENCYCLOPEDIAS

Encyclopedia of Chemistry, ed. by Clifford Hampel. 3rd ed. Van Nostrand Reinhold, 1973. (ISBN 0-442-23095-8)

An amazingly complete one-volume encyclopedia of chemical terms and developments, this would be a worthwhile acquisition even for the small or medium sized library.

Encyclopedia of Chemical Technology. Wiley Interscience, 1963-1972. 25 vols, supplement and index.

This mammoth work is the most comprehensive and probably the most useful large publication in the field of chemistry. It deals not only with theoretical chemistry but the practical applications of all fields of chemistry, industrial, medical and engineering. Although written in extremely readable language and style, it is an excellent resource book.

HANDBOOKS

Handbook of Chemistry and Physics, ed. by Robert C. Weast. Cleveland, Ohio: Chemical Rubber Co., annual since 1919.

Often referred to as the CRC Tables, this is the most comprehensive group of statistical mathematical and general scientific tables now in print. Section "A" is devoted to mathematical tables in logarithms, sines, cosines, square roots, Fourier series, etc. Section "B" is devoted to the elements and inorganic compounds; Section "C," organic compounds; Section "D," general chemical tables; Section "E," general physics constants; and "F," miscellaneous tables such as viscosity of liquid and gases, surface tensions, hardness scales, density of liquids, etc.

Biochemists' Handbook, ed. by Cyril Long.   Van Nostrand Reinhold,
1961. (ISBN 0-442-04869-6)
   The aim of this book is to present, in as concise form as
possible, factual biochemical information of all kinds. Much of the
information is given in tabular form and the data is quantative
rather than opinionated. It will serve as a source of information
to teachers as well as practicing biochemists. Each article is
signed by the expert compiling the data.

CHESS
see also
GAMES

   There are many books on how to play chess, chess strategy
and best games by various players. Many of these are too far advanced and complicated for the beginning or intermediate chess player.

How To Be A Winner At Chess, by Fred Reinfeld.   Doubleday, 1954.
(ISBN 0-385-01430-9)
   This is a quite elementary text book giving detailed explanations of moves and strategy, from the most simple to the more
complicated.

Official Chess Handbook, ed. by Kenneth Harkness.   McKay, 1972.
(ISBN 0-679-13027-6)
Official Chess Rulebook, ed. by Kenneth Harkness.   McKay, 1970.
(ISBN 0-679-13028-4)
   These two books are sanctioned by the United States Chess
Federation and give the latest rules as well as current developments
in international and national chess scenes. The handbook has an ex-
cellent section on chess history and famous players.

CHILDREN'S LITERATURE

   Once again the field is so large that it would be entirely impossible to cover it adequately in the space provided in this book.
Therefore, this is a highly selective collection of references for the
answering of most of your questions.
   One is dependent to a large extent on periodicals for information on publications and the following should be consulted regularly.

Horn Book Magazine, About Children's Books and Reading, ed. by
Paul Heins. Horn Books, Inc., bimonthly 1924.
   This magazine is devoted to children's literature in its entirety. It is primarily a book reviewing medium but each issue does
discuss various writers, illustrators or history. Absolutely the best
but not the most comprehensive publication in the field.

School Library Journal, ed. by Lillian N. Gerhardt. R. R. Bowker
   Co., monthly (September to May) since 1954.
   This was formerly included as a part of the Library Journal
issue for the 15th of each month but is now a completely separate
magazine. Devoted primarily to articles emphasizing current children and school library problems, it is nevertheless an excellent
source of signed book reviews. This is probably the most extensive
book review coverage available in the juvenile field and the reviews,
written by practicing librarians, represent a more realistic approach
than some.

   Children's books are also regularly in the New York Times
and other newspaper book columns.

   Bibliographies of recommended children's books include:

Children's Catalog, 12th ed. H. W. Wilson, 1971. (ISBN 0-8242-
   0438-7)
   This, another of the excellent Wilson catalogs, lists 5119
titles selected and recommended for young readers. These are four
annual supplements planned through 1975 which will add approximately
2000 titles. The catalog is arranged by Dewey Decimal Classification number and for each book is given bibliographic information including suggested cataloging and classification and a brief annotation
of the book with indications of possible grade level.

Books for Children as Selected and Reviewed by The Booklist and
   Subscription Books Bulletin. American Library Association,
   annual since 1966.
   These annual publications of the American Library Association
provide an excellent bibliography of suggested titles for each year
and all are in print since 1966. For titles listed there are full annotations, classification and indexing.

Books for Elementary School Libraries, An Initial Collection, ed. by
   Elizabeth D. Hodges. American Library Association, 1969.
   (ISBN 0-8389-0069-0)
   Over 3000 well annotated books are recommended as a pos-
sible initial collection for the school library both new and old titles
are included with full bibliographic and cataloging information.

   There are many general histories of children's literature
available but the following can be highly recommended:

Children and Books, by May Hill Arbuthnot. 4th ed. Scott Fores-
   man, 1972.
   This book is designed for classes in children's literature but
is an excellent work on the history and importance of children's literature. It answers such questions as: "What kind of books do
children like?" and "How can we get the child to read?" It discusses not only the content of books but their authors and illustrators as well. There are excellent bibliographies in all fields.

For a complete listing of Newberry and Caldecott winners, see:

Bowker Annual of Library and Book Trade Information. Council of National Library Associations. R. R. Bowker Co., annual since 1957.

CHRISTIANITY

History of Christianity, by Kenneth S. Latourette. Harper & Row, 1953. (ISBN 0-06-065030-3)
    A brief history of Christianity made even more helpful for reference purposes by an excellent index.

History of the Christian Church, by Philip Schaff. AMS Press (Repr. of 1930 ed). (ISBN 0-404-10500-9) 7 vols.
    This for many years has been the most detailed and painstakingly researched of all church histories. Although published originally in 1889, it still has great reference value.

    Although no effort will be made to cover the individual beliefs and teachings of the various denominations, the following book is important for church history.

Handbook of Denominations in the United States, ed. by Frank S. Mead. 5th ed. Abingdon, 1970. (ISBN 0-687-16568-7)
    This gives brief impartial accounts of the various denominations of the United States. For each one is given a brief history, a summary of doctrines, church officers and statistics as to membership.

CHRISTMAS
see also
HOLIDAYS

Christmas: An American Annual of Christmas Literature and Art, ed. by Randolph E. Haugan, Minneapolis: Augsburg Press, annual since 1930.
    An oversized annual devoted entirely to the religious customs, symbols and beliefs celebrated within the United States. Excellent color illustrations not only enhance the appearance of the book but add to its reference value as well. It does not include mythical or legendary accounts such as St. Nicholas or Santa Claus because the editor feels they are not Christian in origin.

Christmas, Its Origins and Associations, Together With Its Historical Events and Festive Celebration During Nineteen Centuries:

Its Origin and Associations, by William F. Dawson. Gale, 1968 (Repr. of 1902 ed.).

An excellent history of the origin and development of various Christmas legends and customs. This one will tell about Santa Claus, decorations and the Christmas tree.

1001 Christmas Facts and Fancies, by Alfred C. Hattes. 2nd ed. Dodd, Mead, 1944. (ISBN 0-396-00061-4)

Excellent for development of Christmas traditions especially as it is celebrated around the world.

There will be chapters dealing with Christmas and Christmas customs in each of the books on Holidays and Festivals.

CHRONOLOGY

In this section will be found lists and tables which place historical, social and literary events in their chronological setting. Both annual and general chronologies are cited, although the more important listings are those of a retrospective nature.

ANNUAL CHRONOLOGIES

Britannica Book of the Year, ed. by William Benton. Encyclopedia Britannica. Annual.

Under "Chronology of Events" there is a day-by-day recording of major news events of the year. Although Britannica is cited here, every major encyclopedic yearbook has such a chronology.

Facts on File Yearbook, an Indexed Record of World Events, ed. by Lester A. Sobel. Facts on File, Inc. Annual since 1941.

While not actually a chronology, this publication answers the same purpose. It is a compilation of the weekly issues and as such, arranges events in the order in which they occur. There is an excellent index for finding specific events.

Information Please Almanac, ed. by Dan Golenpaul, Dan Golenpaul Associates. Annual since 1946.

A day-by-day summary of news stories and world events found under "News Chronology of 1972. " _World Almanac_ also has a chronology but its arrangement detracts from easy use.

GENERAL CHRONOLOGIES

Dictionary of Dates, by Helen R. Keller. Hafner, 1971 (Repr. of 1934 ed.). (ISBN 0-02-84760)

Although this set lacks an adequate index, it is useful for finding a chronological history of any country. The countries are arranged alphabetically under continents; within each country, listings are chronological by year. Following each country's listing is a list of kings or rulers for that country. Now dated but excellent for the period up to 1930.

Encyclopedia of World History, ed. by William L. Langer. 5th ed.
    Houghton Mifflin, 1972. (ISBN 0-395-07886-5)
    This is a chronologically arranged history of the world based on the famous work by Ploetz, An Epitome of History. It is arranged by historical period and then alphabetically by continent and then by country. Dates, names and events are printed in bold type to make them stand oût from the text. An appendix carries lists of world leaders, kings and presidents for each country.

CIRCUS

Circus: From Rome to Ringling, by Marian Murray. Greenwood
    Press, 1973 (Repr. of 1956 issue). (ISBN 0-8371-6259-9)
    Excellent history of the circus from the earliest spectaculars down to the present day. Well written, it gives a good verbal history of the Greatest Show on Earth.

    Should more information be desired on any phase of circus activity, there is an excellent bibliography dealing with the circus.

The Circus and Allied Arts: A World Bibliography, 1500 to the Pre-
    sent, ed. by Raymond T. Stott. International Publ. Service,
    1958-1971. 4 vols.
    This is a bibliography of writings on the circus and allied arts from the year 1500 to 1970. Quite comprehensive, it is based on the holdings of the British Museum, La Bibliothèque Nationale and the Library of Congress as well as other sources.

CITIES

    Since every major encyclopedia carries articles dealing with the major cities of the world, no listing will be made of individual encyclopedias. In like manner, many books have been written about individual cities. These can be found by checking your card catalog.

The Municipal Yearbook. Washington, D. C.: International City-
    Management Assn. Annual since 1934.
    This is the single best source for answering questions concerning municipal governments and cities. It is an annual compilation of articles and statistical data dealing with all phases of city management and government. It covers current trends, issues and current activities, municipal finance, manpower and public safety. In addition, it has many statistical charts showing latest information and salaries paid, departmental budgets, etc. There is also a di-

rectory of city officials for every municipality over 5000 in the United States.

County and City Data Book. Bureau of the Census. U. S. Government Printing Office. Publ. every 5 years.

The best possible source of statistical data concerning the various counties and cities of the United States, compiled by the Bureau of the Census. It is a statistical abstract of information gathered about every municipality and county in the United States and is replete with charts, diagrams and maps to make these statistics more meaningful. For each city, there are 148 columns of statistics ranging from population density to mean average temperature and rainfall. What can be expressed statistically about a city can be found here.

Editor and Publisher's Market Guide. Editor and Publisher Magazine Annual since 1924.

This is an annual supplement of the Editor and Publisher Magazine and as such is intended for advertisers to give them a good overview of the markets involved. This overview also gives an excellent picture of the city. For every major metropoliton unit in the United States and Canada, there is a listing giving location, transportation facilities, population, households, banks, principal industries, payrolls and paydays, climate, type of water, major retail outlets and newspapers.

Great Cities of the World, ed. by William A. Robson. Sage Publications, 1972. 2 vols.

This book is divided into two sections. Section One deals with a general discussion of the great city of today and its problems and advantages. Section Two is an alphabetical arrangement of cities from Amsterdam to Warsaw. Each article is from 30 to 50 pages in length and is written by a native of the city discussed. Each chapter has a map of the city as well as information concerning its history, its present government and how it evolved, its party politics, taxation and budget and possible future developments.

See the section on AMERICAN GUIDE SERIES for listings of guides to the United States. Each state volume has sections on the major cities of that state as well as mention of almost every hamlet or village. For nicknames of cities, see NICKNAMES.

CITIZENSHIP
see
NATURALIZATION; VOTING RIGHTS

CIVIL RIGHTS

A Catalog of Civil Rights, by Milton Konvitz. Columbia University
Press, 1961. (ISBN 0-231-02258-1)
A history of the civil rights gains, losses and statements over
the century from the Civil War to the present day. Neither over-
enthusiastic nor bleakly pessimistic, it gives a reliable accounting
of programs and activities in all fields of civil rights activities.

Civil Rights: A Current Guide for the People, Organizations and
Events, by John Adams. R. R. Bowker Co., 1970. (ISBN 0-
8352-0405-7)
This booklet has descriptive paragraphs about individuals and
organizations involved in the civil rights movement. It was originally intended as a background guide to CBS commentators but has
been expanded for the general public. It contains a record of voting
on Congressional bills and a chronology of key events in the civil
rights movement to September, 1970. A good bibliography and index
and an excellent listing of leading black figures of the present.

Civil Rights Reader, by Leon Friedman. Walker & Co., Inc. 1967
(ISBN 0-8027-0060-8)
This is a collection of documents beginning with the President's Report in 1947 and coming up through the beginning of 1967
with statements from Moynahan, Bayard Rustin and others. It not
only documents the achievements of the movement but points the way
for future activity.

Law and Political Protest: A Handbook to Your Political Rights
Under the Law, by Tom Dove. Chicago, Ill.: World Without
War Publications, 1970. (ISBN 0-912018-08-9)
Intended as an outline of what can and cannot be done in the
process of peaceful protest.

CIVIL WAR
see
U. S. HISTORY - CIVIL WAR

CLIMATE

Climate and Man. Dept. of Agriculture. U.S. G.P.O., 1941 (A 1.10:941)
This was the 1941 Yearbook of Agriculture and concerns the
relationship between climate and weather and crops. The findings
are documented by tables and maps which give detailed information
on climate in all parts of the United States.

Climate, Present, Past and Future, by Hubert H. Lamb. Barnes
& Noble, 1972. (ISBN 0-416-70160-4)

A history of climatic changes in the world from the ice age to the present, with an educated guess as to future developments.

Climatic Atlas of the United States, by the U. S. Environmental Data Service, Seale, 1973.
Charts and maps make this an easily understood description of weather conditions in all parts of the United States.

Introduction to Climate, by Glenn T. Trewartha.   4th ed. McGraw-Hill, 1968.   (ISBN 0-07-065148-5)
An excellent introductory volume to the study of climatology. It discusses the reasons for climate differences and changes in the weather, not only in the United States but around the world.   It has excellent maps.

CLOCKS AND WATCHES
see also
ANTIQUES

American Clocks and Clockmakers, by Carl William Dreppard.   Enlarged ed.   Boston, Mass.: Branford, 1958.   (ISBN 0-8231-3001-0)
Excellent historical background on American clockmakers and their clocks, with a bibliography and glossary.

The Clock Book, by William Nutting.   Ann Arbor, Mich.: Finch Press (Repr. of 1924 ed.).
A comprehensive history of the making of clocks in the United States, with a good listing of various makers.

History of Clocks and Watches, by Kenneth Welch.   Drake Publications, 1972.   (ISBN 0-87749-242-5)
Well illustrated history of various watch and clockmakers of the world.

Old Clocks and Watches and Their Makers, by Frederick J. Britten.   British Book Centre, 1973 (Repr. of 1932 ed.).   (ISBN 0-8277-1549-8)
The subtitle reads "A Historical and Descriptive Account of the Different Styles of Clocks and Watches of the Past in England and Abroad. "   The book contains a list of nearly 14, 000 makers and a glossary of technical terms, hallmarks and a bibliography.

Watchmakers and Clockmakers of the World, by G. H. Baillie.   Wehman, 1963.
This is a comprehensive alphabetical directory of the world's horologists.   It gives the name, place, type of watch or clock and other brief information for over 35, 000 different clock and watchmakers.   Primarily limited to makers before 1825, it does list prominent makers of a later date.

CLUBS

For lists of various fraternal or other clubs see the heading ASSOCIATIONS. For information concerning the governing or chartering of clubs see PARLIAMENTARY PROCEDURE.

COAL

Bituminous Coal Facts. Washington, D. C.: National Coal Association, biennial since 1954.
Graphs and charts combined with factual data concerning all phases of the coal producing industry. Each issue has several special articles dealing with specific coal-related subjects in addition to the strictly factual and statistical material.

Commodity Year Book, ed. by Henry Jiler. Commodity Research Bureau, Inc., annual since 1939.
This publication gives prices and production statistics for each of the various commodities needed for our national welfare. Under Coal, one finds statistics on world coal production as well as salient statistics on the bituminous coal industry of the United States. There are also summary statistics for each coal-producing state with statistics as to coal reserves and probable future uses.

Minerals Yearbook. Bureau of Mines. U. S. Government Printing Office, annual since 1932. (I 28. 37)
Summary of both anthracite and bituminous coals by state and region as well as analysis of coal reserves available can be found under the heading Coal.

Potential for Energy Conservation. Emergency Preparedness Office. U. S. Government Printing Office, 1973. (Pr Ex 4. 2 En 2/2)
A discussion of the possible substitution of coal for scarcer fuels.

Natural Resources for U. S. Growth, by Hans S. Landsbery. Peter Smith, 1963.
Trends in Natural Resource Commodities, by Neal Potter. Johns Hopkins Press, 1962. (ISBN 0-8018-0536-8)
These two books compliment each other. Trends in Natural Resource Commodities gives statistics of price, output, consumption and employment in industries including coal which deal with our natural resources from 1870-1957. Natural Resources for U. S. Growth, originally published by Johns Hopkins as a companion work entitled Resources in American Future, gives patterns and availability of various resources, including coal, for the years 1960-2000.

COATS OF ARMS
see
HERALDRY

COINS

Although coin questions come in two varieties--identification or evaluation--they usually can be answered from the same sources.

Appraising and Selling Your Coins, ed. by Jack Friedburg.   8th ed.
    New York: Coin and Currency Institute, 1973.   (ISBN 0-87184-208-4)
    Limited primarily to U. S. coins, this book gives hints on the recognition, evaluation and source of possible sales for coin collectors.

Coins of the World, 1750-1850, by William D. Craig.   2nd ed.,
    Western Pub., 1972.
    Lists and describes all coins issued by almost every country during the period 1750-1850.   It gives pictures of many of the coins and present market value.

Fells International Coin Book, by Charles J. Andrews.   5th ed.
    Frederick Fell, 1973.   (ISBN 0-8119-0051-7)
Fell's United States Coin Book, by Charles J. Andrews.   7th rev.
    ed.   Frederick Fell, 1970.   (ISBN 0-8119-0058-4)
    These two books do for coins what the Scott Stamp Catalogs do for stamps.   They identify, evaluate and price them.   These two books usually present as nearly an accurate appraisal as can be found.

Illustrated Encyclopedia of World Coins, by Burton Hobson.   Double-
    day, 1970.   (ISBN 0-385-03020-7)
    Coins from all parts of the world and from all periods of history arranged by country and then chronologically.   Excellent illustrations make identification easy.

Treasury of the World's Coins, by Fred Reinfeld.   Sterling, 1967.
    (ISBN 0-8069-6005-1)
    A book intended for the beginning collector.   It gives an excellent history of coinage as well as hints on the maintenance of the collection and identification of famous coins.

Encyclopedias all have articles dealing with the history of coinage under the heading Numismatics.

COLLEGE COSTS

With continually rising costs of college education, an important question is "How can I pay the bill?"

Lasser's Thirty-Three Ways to Meet Spiraling Cost of a College Education, by J. K. Lasser Tax Institute. Simon & Schuster, 1969. (ISBN 0-346-11917)

Barron's Handbook of Junior and Community College Financial Aid, by Nicholas Proia. Barron, 1971. (ISBN 0-8120-0402-7)
These two books are prepared by well known business management firms and are excellent sources of ideas for financial aid.

Lovejoy's Scholarship Guide, by Clarence Lovejoy. Rev. ed. Simon & Schuster, 1964. (ISBN 0-671-43120-X)
Now quite dated, this still remains one of the more comprehensive guides to undergraduate scholarships.

COLLEGES AND UNIVERSITIES

No book or group of books can take the place of the individual college catalog since it gives the latest and most up-to-date information concerning fees, tuitions, requirements for entrance and graduation and other data. Every library should have a collection of college catalogs for use by their users. However, the following books will also be useful.

College Names, by Albert Keiser. Twayne Publishers, 1952.
What does the name signify? For whom was it named? Why is it named that?

Accredited Higher Institutions. Office of Education, U. S. Supt. of Documents. Irregularly published, usually every four years.
This lists all colleges and universities which are accredited by recognized regional, state or professional accrediting agencies.

American Universities and Colleges, ed. by Otis Singletary. 11th ed. American Council on Education, 1973. (ISBN 0-8268-1211-2)
An alphabetical listing by states of every accredited senior institution in the United States. Basic information for evaluating each institution is provided. Good index and many excellent supplementary tables and articles.

College Blue Book. 14th ed. New York: CCM Information Corporation, 1972. 4 vols.
Over 3600 colleges and universities of the United States are fully described giving all needed information concerning each college. The information is in four volumes. Vol. 1, U. S. Colleges--Narrative Descriptions; Vol. 2, U. S. Colleges--Tabular Data; Vol. 3, Degrees offered, by College and Subject; Vol. 4, Occupational Information.

Comparative Guide to American Colleges, by James Cass. Harper
    & Row, 1972. (ISBN 0-06-010668-9)
    Attempts to answer that impossible question: where does a
college rate? Naturally a definitive answer is impossible but this
book does give an evaluation of each school along with the normal
institutional data.

Lovejoy's College Guide, by Clarence E. Lovejoy. 11th ed. Simon
    & Schuster, 1970. (ISBN 0-671-20648-6)
    Gives much the same information as found in the American
Universities and Colleges but is slightly more up to date.

COLOR

    There are two aspects of the question of color: the scientific
and its use in decoration.

The Science of Color. Optical Society of America, 1963. (ISBN 0-
    9600380-1-9)
    The scientific approach to the question of color. This dis-
cusses the various optical effects and is illustrated with many plates
in color as well as graphs and charts.

Decorating With Color, by Carleton Varney. Des Moines, Iowa:
    Creative Home Library, 1972. (ISBN 0-696-18600-4)
    This discusses the effects of various colors on moods,
warmth, etc. in decorating. Contains charts for mixing and match-
ing various colors and designs.

COMMODITIES

Commodity Yearbook, ed. by Harry Jiler. Community Research,
    Inc., annual since 1939.
    For each of the various commodities needed for our national
welfare, there are statistics of production, both national and world-
wide, as well as summary statistics about every facet of production
and use in the United States. There also is a projection of possible
future use.

Minerals Year Book. Bureau of Mines. U. S. Supt. of Documents,
    annual since 1932. (I 28. 37:)
    This is the basic annual compilation concerning the various
mineral industries of the United States and its effect on other countries of the world. A good analysis of the present and future situation for each mineral.

Natural Resources for U. S. Growth, by Hans S. Landsberg. Peter

Smith, 1963.
Trends in Natural Resource Commodities, by Neal Potter. Johns
   Hopkins Press, 1962. (ISBN 0-8018-0536-8)
   These two books were authorized by The Resources for the
Future, Inc. and were both originally published by Johns Hopkins
Press. The first-mentioned gives patterns of production and availability of various resources for the years from 1960-2000. The
second book gives a historical view of the commodity production and
use from 1870-1960. The two together give a comprehensive view
of America's past, present and projected future needs and uses of
commodities.

COMMUNISM

Soviet Foreign Relations and World Communism: A Selected, Anno-
   tated Bibliography, ed. by Thomas T. Hammond. Princeton
   Univ. Press, 1965. (ISBN 0-691-08714-8)
   This bibliography is divided into three sections. Part I is
Soviet Foreign Relations by chronological periods; Part II, Soviet
Foreign Relations by country or area; and Part III, Soviet Ideology,
the comintern and military power. Good index to authors and titles
but none to subject.

Communism in the United States, a Bibliography, ed. by Joel Seid-
   man. Cornell University Press, 1969. (ISBN 0-8014-0514-9)
   A bibliography of books dealing with communism within the
United States.

Fifty Years of Communism, 1917-1967, by G. F. Hudson. Basic
   Books, 1968. (ISBN 0-465-02381-9)
   A primer of communist history, intelligently written and
easily understood recording successes and failures of the Soviet
Communist state.

What We Must Know About Communism, by Henry Overstreet.
   Norton, 1958. (ISBN 0-393-05277-X)
   This is a survey of Marxist principles and practices both in
the Russian Revolution and in today's world. It points out with
bitter clarity the significance of Communist policies on the United
States today and in the future.

COMPOSERS

Great Composers: 1300-1900, ed. by David Ewen. H. W. Wilson
   Co., 1966. (ISBN 0-8242-0018-7)
Composers Since Nineteen Hundred, ed. by David Ewen. H. W. Wil-
   son Co., 1969. (ISBN 0-8242-0400-X)

Popular American Composers, ed. by David Ewen. H. W. Wilson
Co., 1962. (ISBN 0-8242-0040-3)
Popular American Composers, First Supplement, ed. by David Ewen.
H. W. Wilson Co., 1972. (ISBN 0-8242-0436-0)
These four make up the "Biographies of Composers" series
of the H. W. Wilson Company. They have continued their fine tra-
dition of reference works and each volume presents well written bi-
ographical sketches and often pictures of the individual composer.
There are bibliographies and indexes to various compositions.

Milton Cross' New Encyclopedia of the Great Composers and Their
Music, by Milton Cross. Doubleday, 1970. 2 vols. (ISBN 0-
385-03635-3)
Excellent short biographies of the world's greatest composers
combined with a brief discussion of the type of music and often of
individual pieces.

Composers of Yesterday, a Biographical and Critical Guide, by
David Ewen. Scholarly Press (Repr. of 1937 ed.). (ISBN 0-403-
01551-0)
Composers of Tomorrow's Music, by David Ewen. Dodd, Mead,
1971. (ISBN 0-396-06286-5)

CONDUCTORS

International Gallery of Conductors, by Donald Brook. Greenwood
Press, 1973 (Repr. of 1951 ed.). (ISBN 0-8371-4767-0)
Biographical sketches of the great conductors of the world
with a discussion of their strengths, weaknesses and lives; many
photographs.

Great Conductors, by Harold C. Schonberg. Simon & Schuster, 1967.
(ISBN 0-671-28953-5)
Modern conductors and their orchestras are discussed, telling about individual styles and temperaments which affect the music
they conduct.

CONGRESS - U. S.

Biographical Directory of the American Congress, 1774-1971. U. S.
Government Printing Office, 1971.
A biographical dictionary of every person who served in the
U. S. Congress from the Continental Congress through the ninety-
first congress of the United States. Often the only source of information on little known Representatives or Senators. In addition to
biographical information, there is a listing of the cabinets of every
president since George Washington and a listing of the members of

each Congress throughout our history.

Official Congressional Directory, U. S. Government Printing Office.
    One per Congressional session.
    Includes a biography of each current member of Congress, a
list of state delegations, committee assignments, directors of offices
of various Congressmen, directory of homes, Washington and office
address of each one, directories of the executive and judicial
branches of government as well as international organizations,
foreign and U. S. Diplomatic Corps and the members of the Press
Gallery. One important feature is a listing of maps of various congressional districts.

Constitution of the United States... Standing Rules of the Senate.
Constitution of the United States... Standing Rules of the House of
    Representatives.
    These two are known as the Senate Manual and the House
Manual respectively, and each contains the standing rules, orders,
laws and resolutions affecting the individual house. In addition,
each manual has the Declaration of Independence, the Articles of
Confederation etc.

CONSERVATION

Conservation Yearbook. Department of the Interior. U. S. Supt. of
    Documents. Annual since 1965. (I 1. 95)
    Outlines the problems confronting a rapidly growing America
in guarding and preserving our natural resources, land, air, water
and people. This annual publication seems to have replaced the annual report of the Department of the Interior.

Conservation in Action. Fish and Wildlife Service. U. S. Supt. of
    Documents. Irregularly since 1947.
    These are popular well illustrated booklets dealing with vari-
ous types of conservation measures.

CONSTITUTIONS

NATIONAL

    There is no dearth of places in which the U.S. Constitution can be
located. Every good encyclopedia will have articles on the Constitution which give the entire text. Only three less obvious sources
will be mentioned here for the National Constitution.

Documents of American History, by Henry Steele Commager. 8th ed.
    Appleton Century Crofts, 1968. (ISBN 0-390-20367-X)

A compilation of the important documents in the history of the United States. Full text not only of the Constitution, the Declaration of Independence, the Mayflower Compact but all others as well. A must for every library.

Random House Dictionary of the English Language, by Editors of Random House. Random House, 1966. (ISBN 0-394-40087-9)
An excellent dictionary; this has more than a dictionary function. Its special features include texts of the Constitution and the Declaration of Independence as well as many other unexpected dividends for a home dictionary.

The Constitution of the United States of America; Analysis and Interpretation. U. S. Government Printing Office, 1964.
The full text of the constitution with annotations of all constitutional cases decided by the Supreme Court of the United States until June 1964.

STATE

Book of the States. Lexington, Ky.: Council of State Governments. Biennial since 1934.
Each issue gives constitutional developments for the biennium as well as basic constitutional data for each state. Complete texts of the constitutions are not given.

Constitutions of the United States: National and State, by Columbia University Legislative Drafting Research Fund. Oceana Press, 1967.
Has complete texts of the U. S. Constitution and for every one of the 50. states, including all amendments and changes in effect through 1965.

FOREIGN

Constitutions of Nations, ed. by Amos J. Peaslee. Rev. 3rd. ed. The Hague, Netherlands: Martinus Nijhoff, 1965-69. 4 vols.
The full text of each national constitution is given as supplied by the Foreign Ministries of the various countries, which also supplied the summary discussions and histories that accompany the constitution. The countries are arranged first by continent and then alphabetically by country. Of interest also is the fact that the national seal precedes each national constitution.

CONSUMER PRICE INDEX
see
PRICES

CONTESTS

Fell's Official Guide to Prize Contests and How to Win Them, by
Allen Glasser.   Frederick Fell, 1963.   (ISBN 0-8119-0054-1)
   A basic guide to various types of prize contests with hints on
proper steps to take to have a chance at winning.   The contests are
legitimate but the pitfalls many.   This book gives instructions to insure that you will not eliminate yourself.

COPYRIGHT

   The very best place to find official information concerning
copyright laws and practices is the Copyright Office of the Library
of Congress.

Compendium of Copyright Office Practices.   Copyright Office, U. S.
Govt. Printing Office.   Irregularly published.
   "A general guide to Copyright Office practices in representative situations arising in the conduct of registration and related functions of the office.   The compendium contains definitions and examples of registrable material, discusses common copyright problems, and indicates the action the Copyright Office will take in such
cases.   Some parts of the compendium have not yet been completed,
and the practices and policies of the Copyright Office are subject to
review and modification in the light of new developments and experi-
ences; thus additions, deletions, and revisions will be made from
time to time. "

How to Secure Copyright, by Richard Wincor.   2nd ed. Oceana, 1957.
(ISBN 0-379-11021-0)
   A step-by-step analysis of the way to protect your manuscript
and to receive a copyright safely.

Manual of Copyright Practice for Writers, Publishers and Agents, by
Margaret Nicholson.   2nd ed.   Oxford University Press, 1956.
(ISBN 0-19-500040-4)
   This is really a handbook for the obtaining of a copyright.
It is organized by type of publication and gives sample forms and a
question and answer section that anticipates almost every possible
question.   It contains not only the text of the U. S. Copyright law but
also the Berne Convention and the Universal Copyright Convention.
Easily understood and well indexed.

COSTUME

Bibliography of Costume, by Hilaire Hiler.   Benjamin Blom, 1967

(Repr. of 1939 ed.).

A dictionary catalog of 8000 books and periodical articles on the history and theory of costumes.

Book of Costume, by Millia Davenport. Crown Publishers, 1964.
Although limited to the historical period prior to 1850, this is an important source of information on costumes. Particularly good illustrations, many in color, are mainly reproductions of contemporary paintings of the costume period. There are about 3000 illustrations.

Costume Throughout the Ages, by Mary Evans. 3rd ed. Lippincott, 1950. (ISBN 0-397-00019-7)
Typical regional costume from all parts of the world and all periods are presented with full but small illustrations. A distinct effort is made to relate costume to the historical period and cultural development of the peoples involved. Excellent bibliographies and lists of pictures available.

History of American Costume 1607-1870, by Elizabeth McClellan. Tudor Publishing Co. Repr. of 1937 ed. (ISBN 0-8148-0135-8)
Well illustrated, this studies the development of American costume from Colonial days through the Civil War period. Coverage is given to Spanish and French settlements in Florida and Louisiana as well as to the English settlers. Well indexed.

In addition to the above named sources, every encyclopedia, especially World Book, has interesting articles, often well illustrated, on the development of costumes and their history. The National Geographic Magazine is also an excellent source of pictures of costumes from many places around the world.

COUNTIES

The best single source for answering statistical questions concerning counties of the United States is the following:

County and City Data Book. Bureau of the Census. U. S. Govt. Printing Office. Published every five years.
Presents 144 items of statistical data for each county in the United States, from size and population density to educational level of inhabitants and mean annual temperature.

For historical information, see the state volume in the American Guide Series. Each volume has historical articles on counties, cities and sections.

COWBOYS

American Cowboy: The Myth and the Reality, by Joe B. Frantz.
  University of Oklahoma Press, 1968 (Repr. of 1955 ed.). (ISBN
  0-8061-0330-2)
       The stories, the legends and the facts of the American cow-
boy are woven into a scholarly but still easily read book. It quotes
liberally from contemporary sources to give a good background of
Western culture.

Humor of the American Cowboy, by Stan Hoig. University of Nebraska Press, 1970. (ISBN 0-8032-5719-8)
       The stories told around the campfires were often ribald,
sometime downright off color, but always funny. This book presents
many of the stories sufficiently softened to appear in public print.

Western Words: A Dictionary of the American West, by Ramon F.
  Adams. University of Oklahoma Press, 1968. (ISBN 0-8061-
  0807-X)
       This is the language not only of the cowman but also of the
trapper, the hunter and the gold prospector. Although not as thorough as Mathew's Dictionary of Americanisms it is much more readable and definitions are spiced with the tales of the Old West. More
than 2500 words are defined, and in many cases sources for expressions are given.

CRIME AND CRIMINALS

Uniform Crime Reports for the United States, by U. S. Federal
  Bureau of Investigation. U. S. Govt. Printing Office, publication
  varies, usually annual since 1930. (J1. 14)
       The cover title of this official report of the Federal Bureau
of Investigation is Crime in the United States. "This publication
contains an analysis of crime in the United States, including statistical tables of offenses known, arrests, persons charged and dis-
posed of, and police employee data. The Uniform Crime Reports
provide information for a wide range of users, the police, legisla-
tors, courts, corrections, social scientists and the general public. "

Crime and Delinquencies Abstracts, by the U. S. National Institute of
  Health. U. S. Government Printing Office. Annual. (HE20. 2420)
       Intended to meet the needs of individuals working in the field
of crime and delinquency for comprehensive and rapid information
about new developments and research results, this bibliography contains citations to the current literature on crime and delinquency,
as well as brief abstracts. Also included is a compilation of current on-going projects concerned with the prevention, control, and
treatment of crime and delinquency.

American Correctional Association Directory: State and Federal Correctional Institutions in the United States of America, Canada,
  England and Scotland. The Association. Annual since 1955.
      A directory of members of American Correctional Association.

Crimes That Shook the World, by Richard Hirsch. Books for Libraries (Repr. of 1949 ed.). (ISBN 0-8369-8064-6)
      Ten stories of crimes of violence dealing with political
assassinations, spies and kidnappings. One could wish for a wider
coverage but these are excellent.

CROSSWORD PUZZLES

Constructing Crosswords, by William J. Harrison. Exposition
  Press, 1968. (ISBN 0-682-46873-8)
      The how-to-do-it book of making puzzles with beginner's dia-
grams and progressing to more difficult puzzles.

Unabridged Crossword Puzzle Dictionary, by Albert F. Sisson.
  Doubleday, 1963. (ISBN 0-385-02843-1)
      This is possibly the best and most detailed of the many cross-
word puzzle dictionaries currently on the market. Similar to any
thesaurus, this one is also arranged to make the location of specific
letter arrangements easily located.

CURRENT EVENTS

      Under this heading will be found summaries of recent events,
i. e. , the things that took place last week or last month. For long
range events, see CHRONOLOGY.

Facts on File, an Indexed Record of World Events, by Lester A.
  Sobel. Facts on File, Inc. , weekly with annual cumulations
  since 1941.
      This is without a doubt the premier source for current events
material. It is a reference service which publishes a 20-page
weekly digest of the news with regular cumulative subject indexes
which aid in finding wanted materials. The news digest covers all
facets of news events, such as deaths, headlines, politics, medicine,
science, crime--anything one might find in a daily paper. Since it
quickly places the accurate date of current affairs, it can be used
as a supplementary index to the local newspaper.

Deadline Data on World Affairs. McGraw Hill Publications, bi-
  weekly since 1956.
      This is a basic chronology of important events in the field of
international relations. It is published on 5" x 8" cards which are

up-dated every other week. There are cards for each commercial
or military alliance (SEATO, European Common Market, etc.) and
for each country or subdivision; the up-dated cards give the latest
political or military events. Excellent for an overall view of recent
events leading up to the current situation. This pinpoints the actual
date of any happening and the local newspaper can supply a more
detailed account.

CUSTOMS

There are two possible questions under this heading. For
customs and duties, i.e., taxation, see TAXATION; for social customs, see HOLIDAYS, FESTIVALS, or MANNERS AND CUSTOMS.

DANCE

Dance Encyclopedia, by Anatole Chujoy. Simon & Schuster, 1967.
(ISBN 0-671-22586-3)
Encyclopedia articles about every form of the art of the dance,
written and signed by experts. These articles include biography,
dance forms, types and terminology all in one alphabet. Excellent
bibliography of both books and recordings.

Dance in Society, by Frances Rust. Humanities Press, 1969.
An analysis of the relationship between the social dance and
society from the middle ages to the present day.

World History of the Dance, by Curt Sachs. Norton, 1963. (ISBN
0-393-00209-8)
Originally published in Germany, this is an excellent historical account of the development and meaning of the dance around the
world.

DATES
see
CHRONOLOGY

DEBATES AND DEBATING

The premier publisher in the field of books for debaters and
debate topics is the H. W. Wilson Company which has built up an
impressive array of debate materials.

Building the Contest Oration, by Ezra C. Buehler. H. W. Wilson, 1965. (ISBN 0-8242-0008-X)
Gives in detail the procedures in preparing, building and delivering contest orations, with an analysis and evaluations. Also discusses the validity of the whole debate procedure.

Competitive Debate: Rules and Techniques, by George McCoy Musgrave. 3rd ed. H. W. Wilson, 1957. (ISBN 0-8242-0010-1)
The rules of debate along with customs and procedures are listed. Case presentation, cross examination, strategy and administration are also examined. There is an excellent 16-page bibliography.

How to Debate: A Textbook for Beginners, by Harrison B. Summers. 3rd ed. H. W. Wilson, 1963. (ISBN 0-8242-0019-5)
The elements of the theory of debate are given in simple, easily understood language and the various steps of a debate are discussed. The book gives examples on forms to be used, logical preparation of evidence, timing, etc.

The Reference Shelf. H. W. Wilson. 6 vols. per year.
In this series each title is devoted to a different topic of current interest and each book is divided into the pros and cons of the arguments involved, with summary conclusions and excellent bibliographies. The sixth volume each year is Representative American Speeches, which gives the full texts of important speeches delivered during the year and full biographic data on the speech maker. Of particular interest to the debater is a special issue of the Reference Shelf entitled The Debate Index which was published as number 3 of volume 36 (1964), (ISBN 0-8242-0081-0). This is a selective index to books and periodical articles which will be helpful to debaters.

DECLARATION OF INDEPENDENCE

Texts of the Declaration of Independence can be found in every good encyclopedia or almanac but the following book is devoted to the reproduction of texts of important American documents and should be in every library.

Documents of American History, by Henry Steele Commager. 8th ed. Appleton-Century Crofts, 1968. (ISBN 0-390-20367-X)
In addition to the text of every important document, this has a brief introductory passage giving the setting and background for the document.

DECORATIONS AND MEDALS

American Badges and Insignia, by Evans S. Kerrigan. Viking,

1967.   (ISBN 0-670-11702-1)
American War Medals and Decorations, by Evans S. Kerrigan.
Viking, 1971.   (ISBN 0-670-12101-0)
   Together these two books provide a comprehensive guide to
all military badges and insignia worn by the United States Armed
Forces.   Each badge or insignia is pictured in black and white and
described fully in the accompanying text.   There are 1100 black and
white illustrations and eight plates showing 100 ribbons in full color.

Orders and Decorations of All Nations, by Robert Warlich.   Washington, D. C.: Quaker Press, 1973.
   An excellent summary of all current and recent decorations
and orders awarded by all nations of the world.   In 360 pages,
there are 1100 black and white illustrations and eight pages of full
color.   Excellent supplementary text makes identification easy.

Ribbons and Medals, Naval Military, Airforce and Civil, by H.
Taprill Dorling.   New ed. London: George Philip & Son, 1960.
(ISBN 0-540-00192-9)
   Intended primarily to provide a means whereby the ordinary
person may recognize most of the ribbons and medals worn by
members of the Armed Forces.   British in orientation, it is a good
source of information on medals and decorations of all nations.
Most medals are pictured in black and white drawings.   It would be
better if color plates could have been provided but each one is fully
described by color in the accompanying text.   Excellent index facili-
tates use.

DEMONS

Devils and Demons: A Dictionary of Demonology, by J. Tondriau.
New York: Pyramid Publications, 1972.
   An alphabetical dictionary arrangement of the demons of the
world giving preferred and variant names and spelling as well as
the personalities of each demon.   There is a good discussion of
demonology.

Dictionary of Angels: Including the Fallen Angels, by Gustov Davidson.   Free Press, 1967.   (ISBN 0-02-90694)
   Although devoted primarily to good angels this alphabetical
arrangement includes evil angels as well.   For each name, the
original source is given as well as a summary of the powers of
that angel or demon.   Beginning on page 352, there is a listing of
all the fallen angels and, if known, what his/her position was prior
to the fall.   In the appendix there are several interesting invoca-
tions, spells, etc., such as exorcism, a love spell, a spell for the
manufacture of a magic carpet and other such useful things.

Encyclopedia of Religion and Ethics, ed. by James Hastings.   Scribner's, 1908-1927.   13 vols.   (Sold only by publisher on direct

order; not available through book trade.)
This important work on religion includes articles on all religions of the world and is particularly good for primitive beliefs and customs. Information concerning demonology or individual demons can be found through the index.

Mythology of All Races, ed. by John A. MacCulloch. Cooper Square, 1932. 13 vols. (ISBN 0-8154-0144-2)
This is an important encyclopedia for any mythological information. There is an excellent general index in which one can find materials dealing with the demons of any part of the world, individual demons or with demonology in general.

New Catholic Encyclopedia, ed. by The Catholic University of America. McGraw Hill, 1967. (ISBN 0-07-010235-X)
A specialized encyclopedia dealing with the same subjects covered by a general encyclopedia but with a Catholic interpretation of events and happenings. It is especially good for medieval church, literary and historical events. Volume 4 has a good dissertation on Demons and Demonology.

DENOMINATIONS

Handbook of Denominations in the United States, ed. by Frank S. Mead. 5th ed. Abingdon, 1970. (ISBN 0-687-16568-7)
Brief important accounts of the various denominations of the United States. For each one is given a brief history, a summary of doctrines, church officers and statistics of membership.

DICE
see also
GAMES

Scarne on Dice, by John Scarne. Rev. ed. Stackpole, 1962. (ISBN 0-8117-1510-8)
The world's foremost authority on various games of chance gives hints on strategy to be followed in winning at dice games. Equally important to the dice player is his summary of things to watch for in order to check whether your opponent may be cheating.

DICTIONARIES
see
REFERENCE BOOKS

DIGESTS OF BOOKS
see
BOOKS - PLOTS

DIPLOMATS

Biographic Register. U. S. Department of State. U. S. Govt.
Printing Office. Annual since 1870. (S1. 69:)
Concise biographic information on the personnel of the Department of State and other Federal agencies in the field of foreign
affairs. Biographies are included of all Ambassadors, Ministers,
Chiefs of Missions, Foreign Service Officers and Civil Service employees above the grade of GS-12. In addition to regular State Department personnel, biographies are included for key personnel in
the Peace Corps, U. S. Information Service, etc.

Diplomatic List. U. S. Department of State. U. S. Government
Printing Office. Varied frequency since 1887; currently monthly.
(S1. 8:)
This is a complete listing of all the foreign Diplomatic Corps
accredited to Washington. For each country is given the address of
the Embassy, any national holidays regularly observed by that Embassy and a full listing by name and address of the Ambassador and
principal members of his staff. There is an order-of-precedence
chart for protocol purposes.

Foreign Service List. U. S. Department of State. U. S. Govt.
Printing Office. Quarterly since 1965. (S1. 7)
Although printed since 1928, this has only fairly recently
been put on a regular quarterly schedule. It lists U. S. Diplomatic
representatives to foreign countries arranged by country. There is
a complete listing of all geographic locations, addresses and telephone numbers of foreign service posts around the world.

International Yearbook and Statesman's Who's Who, ed. by John V.
Yates. London: Burke's Pearage. Annual since 1953.
There are two sections to this book. Section I is devoted to
an analysis of the nations of the world, giving for each country the
political, economic, educational and statistical information. The
second section is a biographical section that gives sketches of world
leaders in government, church, commerce, industry and education.

Statesman's Yearbook, a Statistical and Historical Annual of the
States of the World, ed. by John Paxton. St. Martin's Press.
Annual since 1864.
A brief but reliable annual giving statistical and descriptive
information about nations of the world and particularly their governments. For each country is given the ruler and term of office, a
resumé of the constitution, its area, population, programs for educational and social welfare, defense, justice and any pertinent in-

formation which can be given concisely. It gives lists of consular and diplomatic offices for each country and their locations; and for the U. S. and Great Britain gives names of the diplomatic officers to and from that country. This is as nearly a "must" reference book as can be found for any library.

DISASTERS

For information on recent disasters see heading CURRENT EVENTS. For listings of major disasters throughout our history, i. e., floods, tidal waves, earthquakes, fires, assassinations, railroad wrecks, plane crashes, explosions or any other events that take large toll of lives, both major almanacs have several pages devoted to DISASTERS.

Information Please Almanac, ed. by Dan Golenpaul. Dan Golenpaul Associates. Annual since 1946.

World Almanac and Book of Facts. Newspaper Enterprise Associates. Annual since 1868.

DISTANCES

Distances Between Ports. Naval Oceanographic Office. U. S. Government Printing Office, 1965. (Reprinted 1971) (CD203. 22: 151/971)
A table of distances between the major ports of the world by sea.

Rand McNally Commercial Atlas. Rand McNally Co. Annual since 1872.
A commercial atlas of the United States with all the usual atlas information and fine maps of each state of the U. S. and each province of Canada. Has distance tables for railroad distances within the U. S., a mileage and driving time map of the U. S., Mexico and Canada, and charts giving airline distances between world cities and steamship distances between major ports. There is also an excellent world map showing time zones.

Standard Highway Mileage Guide. Rand McNally, 1970.
This book is intended as a supplement to the Rand McNally Road Atlas and other Rand McNally publications. This one is an alphabetical mileage guide showing distances between U. S. cities. There are black and white maps to vicinities and to states but its prime purpose is for determining distances.

World Almanac and Book of Facts. Newspaper Enterprise Associates. Annual since 1868.

Has charts showing airline and automobile distances as well as distances between world ports.

DIVORCE

As warned in an earlier section, the librarian's function does not extend to the point of offering legal advice. This is the responsibility of the attorneys-at-law but you will get questions concerning DIVORCE and can supply direct answers so long as you do not venture advice.

The best source for local divorce laws is the Code of Laws for your particular state, which is generally published by the State Legislature. This will give the legal basis on which divorces can be granted. There is however a small book which summarizes divorce laws succinctly and clearly.

Marriage, Divorce and Adoption Laws of the U. S., by Editors of Gould Press. Gould Press, 1973. (ISBN 0-87526-645-4)

For statistics on divorce, see the following:

Vital Statistics of the United States, by U. S. Division of Vital Statistics. U. S. Government Printing Office, annual since 1937.
This appears in four volumes; volume 4 is devoted to data concerning marriage and divorce for each state and locality of the nation.

Statistical Abstracts of the United States, by the U. S. Bureau of the Census. U. S. Government Printing Office, annual since 1878. (C3. 134)
An abstract of the Federal census, this publication is bursting with statistics. There are comprehensive data dealing with the incidence of marriage and divorce.

DOCUMENTS
see also
GOVERNMENT PUBLICATIONS

Probably the best source for contemporary documents is the New York Times which prints in their entirety almost all important documents as they appear. For other contemporary documents, see:

Historic Documents, ed. by William B. Dickinson, Jr. Congressional Quarterly, Inc., annual since 1972.
This is a new service by Congressional Quarterly, Inc. intended to present in a readable and easily found form the texts of the important documents each year. The book is arranged chrono-

logically so that a document is easily found if you know the date.
If you do not, there is a comprehensive table of contents and a subject index. The index will be cumulative each year with a five-year
eventual cumulation. This first volume is excellent for American
documents but ignores the rest of the world.

HISTORICAL DOCUMENTS

Documents of American History, ed. by Henry Steele Commager.
8th ed. Appleton-Century-Crofts, 1968. (ISBN 0-390-20367-X)
    Undoubtedly the prime source of documentary history of the
U. S. readily available to the small or medium sized library. This
presents all the important documents dealing with U. S. history in a
chronological order with an excellent index. Should be in every library. Each document is introduced with a brief history giving its
historical and social setting.

Documentary Source Book of American History, 1606-1926, ed. by
William McDonald. B. Franklin, 1969 (Reissue of 1926 ed.).
(ISBN 0-8337-2163-1)
    Complete texts of most documents dealing with American his-
tory although many are excerpted to present the opinion and ideas
rather than entire text. Neither as complete or as comprehensive
as Commager.

Documents on American Foreign Relations, ed. by Richard Stebbins.
Simon & Schuster, annual since 1939. (Recent volumes by
Simon & Schuster, earlier by Harper & Row)
    From 1938-1952 these were edited by the World Peace Found-
ation in Princeton, N. J., and since that time by the Council on
Foreign Relations. An excellent source for recent documents such
as presidential messages, speeches, reports, resolutions, etc. Good
index to all aspects of American foreign relations.

Documents on International Affairs, varied editors. Oxford University Press, annual since 1929.
    Intended as a supplement to the Survey of International Affairs
published by the Royal Institute of International Affairs in London,
this is a collection of treaties and other important papers related to
international affairs. Although an excellent source the coverage lags
from four to five years behind the date of publication.

DOGS

    There are many books dealing with various types and breeds
of dogs. There would not be room in a book this size to list even
a small number of them so coverage here will be on the general
books dealing with dogs. Many encyclopedias have articles with
plates showing pictures of dogs as well as entries under the names
of the various breeds.

Complete Dog Book, ed. by American Kennel Club. Doubleday, 1969.
(ISBN 0-385-04675-8)
This is the "Bible" of the dog world, edited and authorized
by the American Kennel Club. It gives a history and the standards
of each breed admitted to the American Kennel Club. It is revised
regularly and gives information on well over 100 different breeds of
dogs recognized by the A.K.C. In addition to history and standards
for breeds, it has a glossary of terms, pictures of breeds and a
complete listing of dog breeding clubs in America.

Dog Owner's Encyclopedia, by Brian Vesey-Fitzgerald. British Book
Center, 1972. (ISBN 0-8277-0930-7)
A general guide to all aspects of dogs as pets, answering
questions concerning health grooming and training.

Dog Obedience Training Guide, by Fred Otte, Jr. Collier-Macmillan, 1962. (ISBN 0-02-06349)
Although very basic in its approach this is a quite good guide
to general dog care and training. The original title, Teach Your
Dog to Behave, describes its approach very well. It is well illustrated and gives not only instruction in methods of dog training but
describes useful equipment as well.

Dog Psychology: The Basis of Dog Training, by Leon F. Whitney.
2nd ed. New York: Howell Book House, Inc., 1971. (ISBN 0-
87605-520-X)
It is the belief of the author that the secret of dog training
lies in understanding how the dog thinks. This book then delineates
the idea of dog psychology and applies it to training the dog.

DRAMA

There are many approaches to the subject of drama. For
ease in use, this section will be devoted to studies of the drama as
an art form and to its history. For plots of drama, see PLAYS -
PLOTS.

Dramatic Bibliography, by Blanch M. Baker. Haverstown, Pa.:
Richard West, 1973.
A reprint of a standard bibliography giving an annotated list
of books on the history of the drama and stage as well as criticisms
of their productions. Excellent source book for historical materials.

Annals of the New York Stage, by George C. Odell. AMS Press,
1970. 15 vols. (Repr. of 1927 set). (ISBN 0-404-07830-3)
An excellent history of the theatre in New York City from its
earliest beginnings to 1927. Good indexes and references to original
sources make this an excellent reference tool for finding playwrights,
actors and plays produced in New York.

Development of the Theatre: A Study of Theatrical Art from the
Beginnings to the Present Day, by Allardyce Nicoll.   5th ed.
Harcourt Brace, 1967.   (ISBN 0-15-125327-7)
    A history of the theatre with emphasis on the British stage
from the time of Shakespeare to the modern times.   Well illustrated with pictures of theatres and playbills, this is an excellent
work.

    In addition to these sources, you can find good articles deal-
ing with drama and the theatre in the following books.

Cambridge History of American Literature.   3 vols. in 1.   Macmillan, 1943.   (ISBN 0-02-52093)
    Has two chapters dealing with the development of the drama
in America along with a good bibliography.

Cambridge History of English Literature.   15 vols.   Cambridge-
University Press, 1903-33.
    Many chapters dealing with drama during different periods of
English literature; with excellent bibliographies.

DRESS
see
COSTUME

ECOLOGY
see also
BIOLOGY; BOTANY; PLANTS, etc.

The Ecological Glossary, ed. by J. R. Carpenter.   Stechert-Hafner,
1971 (Repr. of 1938 ed.).
    This is the standard dictionary of ecological terms.   It ident-
ifies nearly 3000 terms and gives reference to the individual sources
in which they are originally found.

Ecology in Theory and Practice, ed. by Jonathan Benthall.   Viking
Press, 1972.   (ISBN 0-670-28839-X)
    This is a collection of lectures on various phases of the eco-
logical problems facing our world today.   While they bear very little
relationship to each another, taken as a whole they present an excellent layman's presentation of the interaction of man and his en-
vironment.

ECONOMICS

The many aspects of economics are so varied that only the

general subject can be covered here. For economic applications to various fields see the specific subject heading desired, such as AGRICULTURE, BANKS AND BANKING, ADVERTISING, etc.

Once again due to the size of the subject, this section is sub-divided by form. In addition to the items below, many books in the general subject will be found by referring to the card catalog.

BIBLIOGRAPHY

Cumulative Bibliography of Economic Books. Gordon, 1965-1972. 2 vols.

This is an annotated bibliography of books dealing with economics published in the last 20 years. Volume one covers the years 1954-1962; volume two, 1963-1970.

International Bibliography of Economics. Published by UNESCO (UNIPUB), 1961. 9 vols.

An official publication of UNESCO, this is an extensive bibliography of books in all languages dealing with the field of economics.

Sources of Business Information, ed. by Edwin T. Coman, Jr. 2nd ed. University of California Press, 1964. (ISBN 0-520-00257-1)

Although needing revision and updating, this is one of the best discussions of reference books of value to the business man. It lists not only books but periodical and pamphlet materials as well in all fields of business endeavor. A good index makes this an easy book to use.

INDEXES

Business Periodicals Index. H. W. Wilson Company. Quarterly with annual cumulations since 1959.

This is a cumulative subject index of English-language periodicals in the fields of accounting, advertising, public relations, banking, communications, finance, labor and related fields. Periodicals to be indexed are selected by vote of subscribers.

Index to Economic Journals, by the American Economic Association. Irwin, 1969. 10 vols.

An excellent index to economic journals, this indexes by author and title articles in the English language in the major economic journals of the world. It has one major shortcoming: the time-lag between the date of the articles and the date of the publication of the index varies from three to five years, making the material often out of date before indexing.

DICTIONARIES

A Dictionary of Economics, by Harold S. Sloan. 5th ed. Barnes & Noble, 1970. (ISBN 0-06-463266-0)

This dictionary is almost encyclopedic in nature and contains definitions and explanations of almost 3000 economic terms. Many cross references make it easy to relate those terms to relevant laws and regulations.

A Dictionary of Economic Terms, ed. by P. A. Taylor. Rev. ed. Routledge and Kegan, Paul, 1968. (ISBN 0-7100-2986-1) Although definitely British in orientation, this provides a rather short listing of economic terms.

ATLASES

Economic Areas of the United States, by Donald J. Bogue. Free Press, 1961. (ISBN 0-02-90440) Extensive tables, charts and maps combined with long textual preparation for each area of the United States make this a good source for statistical information on the commercial and industrial potentials of the country.

Oxford Economic Atlas of the World. 4th ed. Oxford University Press, 1972. (ISBN 0-19-894106-4) This is intended to meet the needs of economists, geographers and those engaged in international trade. It is in two parts. Part I is a collection of maps showing world distribution of commodities and Part II is a statistical index to countries showing the importance of the various commodities to the economic health of each country.

HANDBOOKS AND STATISTICS

Business Executive Handbook, by Stanley M. Brown. 4th ed. Prentice-Hall, 1953. A concise, easily understood handbook to business mathematics, letters, selling, advertising, business meetings and allied subjects.

Business Management Handbook, by Jacob Kay Lasser, 3rd ed. McGraw-Hill, 1968. (ISBN 0-07-036555-5) This is a handbook of methods and policies applicable to all areas of the business community. It is particularly useful in the field of tax laws and interpretations. It has a good index.

Overseas Business Reports, by the U. S. Bureau of International Commerce. U. S. Govt. Printing Office, 1962- (C1.50:) This series of often up-dated pamphlets on various countries of the world gives basic market and investment information on the foreign countries of the world. It describes economic and commercial conditions as well as outlining procedures for doing business with individual nations, including taxation and trademark regulations. Issued and reissued as market conditions dictate.

Survey of Current Business. U. S. Office of Business Economics. U. S. Govt. Printing Office, monthly since 1921. Presents in comprehensive statistical charts and graphs with accompanying text the latest information on current business trends in the United States.

EDUCATION

Once again, this is a large subject which could not be covered in merely one section. See also such educational subjects as AUDIO-VISUAL MATERIALS, COLLEGES AND UNIVERSITIES, etc.

BIOGRAPHY

American Men and Women of Science, ed. by Jaques Cattell Press.
  12th ed. R. R. Bowker Co. , 1971-73. 8 vols. (ISBN 0-8352-9347)
  This mammoth work is divided into two sections. Vols. 1-6 cover "The Physical and Biological Sciences" and vols. 7-8 the "Social and Behavioral Sciences. " Together they have biographies of 160, 000 scientists. It gives the usual Who's Who type of information plus the specialties of various men and women listed. It gives full name and address, position held, degrees and honors and memberships of each person.

Leaders in Education, by Jaques Cattell Press. 4th ed. R. R.
  Bowker, 1971. (ISBN 0-8352-0434-0)
  This companion volume to American Men and Women of Science has biographical sketches of over 15, 000 educators prominent in all branches of education. It gives the annual Who's Who type of information; i. e. date and place of birth, parents, marital status, education, position, honors, publications and present address.

Who's Who in American Education, ed. by Robert C. Cook. Hatties-
  burg, Miss.: Who's Who in American Education, biennial since 1929.
  "A biographical directory of eminent living university and college professors, superintendents and principals of schools, state and national school officials, librarians and miscellaneous educators" (Subtitle). This gives the normal Who's Who type of tabular biographical data.

DICTIONARIES AND ENCYCLOPEDIAS

Dictionary of Education, by Carter V. Good. 3rd ed. McGraw-Hill,
  1974. (ISBN 0-07-023720-4)
  This work was prepared under the direction of Phi Delta Kappa, the National Honorary Fraternity for Education, and is the most scholarly of the many dictionaries of education available. It was compiled with the assistance of many specialists and was reviewed by many more, so that the terms selected for inclusion not only represent the important words in the field but the definitions are those acceptable to a wide range of educators. Almost 25, 000 terms are defined and pronunciation given for difficult words. Names of persons and institutions are excluded unless they are closely related to a method or movement in the field of education.

Encyclopedia of Education, ed. by L. C. Deighton. Macmillan, 1971.
  10 vols.

This is a complete educational encyclopedia with more than a thousand articles on all facets of education, each one signed by an expert with a bibliography. It is excellent for movements, systems and products used in education. There is an excellent index which makes locating small items easy.

Encyclopedia of Educational Research, ed. by C. W. Harris. 4th ed. Collier-Macmillan, 1969. (ISBN 0-02-18483)
Although alphabetically arranged this is actually neither a dictionary nor an encyclopedia but a collection of articles which summarize and criticize research that has been done in all fields of education. It is particularly good for its bibliographies. It was prepared by the American Educational Research Association and one might consider The Review of Educational Research (Washington, D. C.: American Educational Research Association, quarterly since 1931) as a supplement and updating of this publication.

Cyclopedia of Education, ed. by Paul Monroe. Gale Research Association, 1968 (Repr. of 1928 ed.). 5 vols.
Placed last because of its age, this was at one time the very best encyclopedic work in the field of education and although now very out of date, it remains an excellent source of historical and biographical information. All articles are signed and most have good bibliographies. Its use today is primarily for research in educational developments but it is a worthwhile addition to any educational library.

HANDBOOKS

Handbook of Research on Teaching, ed. by Robert Travers, 2nd ed. Rand McNally, 1963. (ISBN 0-528-61824-5)
This is a project of the American Educational Research Association and is designed to give the serious student of education summaries of research projects in the field. Extensive bibliographies accompany each of the articles and almost every article is signed. It contains material on grade levels, teaching areas and subject fields.

Handbook on International Study for U. S. Nationals. Institute of International Education, 1970. (ISBN 0-87206-029-2)
This is a fully indexed and descriptive list of educational programs in foreign countries which are open for American students. It also includes possibilities for exchange study and summer schooling.

INDEXES

Current Index to Journals in Education. Macmillan, monthly with annual cumulations.
This is a monthly catalog and index to journals and periodical literature in the field of education.

Education Index. H. W. Wilson Co., monthly with annual cumulations since 1929.

This is a cumulative author and subject index to educational materials in the English language. It is primarily a periodical index but it also indexes yearbooks, proceedings and some monographs dealing with education. Periodicals to be indexed are selected by subscribers' votes based on the reference potential of the publication.

Research in Education. U. S. Department of Health, Education and Welfare. Office of Education, monthly since 1966.

This is a monthly abstract journal that announces recently published research and research related reports in the field of education. For each article or monograph listed, an abstract is given citing the Office of Education number. All Educational Research Information Center (ERIC) publications are listed and are available on microfiche or on paper.

STATISTICS

Digest of Educational Statistics. U. S. Department of Health, Education and Welfare, Office of Education. U. S. Govt. Printing Office, annual since 1962.

This is an abstract of statistics from the many publications of the Dept. of Health, Education and Welfare dealing with both public and private education in the U. S. It covers all levels--elementary, secondary, and higher education--as well as Federal programs and vocational education programs. It is made more useful by a good index and many useful tables.

MISCELLANEOUS

The Office of Education and other agencies publish many works in all fields of education. For a selective listing of their many publications see #31 of the Price Lists of Government Publications, available at no charge from the U. S. Superintendent of Documents, U. S. Government Printing Office.

ELECTIONS

The raw statistics concerning elections in this country can be found in the various almanacs and a quick summary of the election can be located by consulting the New York Times or Facts on File for the period. For a more comprehensive look at election results, the following are recommended.

America Votes, ed. by Richard Scammon. Washington, D. C.: Congressional Quarterly, biennial since 1952.

In these volumes all the basic data concerning American elections are brought together and one can build a picture of the changes since 1952 in political philosophy and behavior of the American people. It analyzes not only presidential elections but congressional and gubernatorial elections as well. It also gives complete list of persons receiving votes in the presidential election regardless of how few are received.

National Party Platforms, 1840-1968, ed. by Kirk H. Porter. 4th ed. University of Illinois Press, 1970. (ISBN 0-252-00137-0)
Until 1840, there were actually no written party platforms on which the candidate ran. This is a compilation of the texts of the major party platforms for each national election since that time. In addition to the platforms there is a brief introductory statement setting the social and political scene of the times.

A Statistical History of the American Presidential Elections, by Svend Peterson. Frederick Ungar, 1963. (ISBN 0-8044-1729-6)
This contains 133 statistical compilations including number of votes and percentages for each candidate by state and by election. It also lists for each election a state summary of the history of each political party from the Whigs onward. There is a complete list of candidates who have competed for the office from 1789 through the 1960 election.

For a good narrative account of the last four presidential campaigns, see the following books. Each of them takes an individual campaign and covers the various candidates, conventions and campaigning right through the election night. They often read like science fiction or a novel but Mr. White has done his research well and, after reading one of his books, you know the reasons why one candidate won and the other lost.

Making of the President, 1960, by Theodore White. Atheneum, 1961. (ISBN 0-689-10191-7)
Making of the President, 1964, by Theodore White. Atheneum, 1965. (ISBN 0-689-10292-5)
Making of the President, 1968, by Theodore White. Atheneum, 1969. (ISBN 0-689-10293-3)
Making of the President, 1972, by Theodore White. Atheneum, 1973. (ISBN 0-689-10553-3)

ELECTRICITY

Handyman's Electrical Repairs Handbook, by Robert Hertzberg. Arco. 1959. (ISBN 0-668-00827-X)
A how-to-do-it book for the repair of minor appliances and electrical problems. It is well illustrated and easily understood so that the nonelectrician can perform many minor repairs easily. Diagrams and charts add greatly to its usability.

N. F. P. A. Handbook of the National Electrical Code, ed. by Frank Stetka. 2nd ed. McGraw Hill, n. d. (ISBN 0-07-06147-1)
This is based on the national code sponsored by the National

Fire Protection Association and covers such topics as wiring, design, methods and materials to be used. This will be good for general regulations but the user should also have available the local and state building codes.

New Electric Science Dictionary, by Frank D. Graham. Audel's, 1965. (ISBN 0-672-23051-8)
    An alphabetical dictionary used in the field of electricity and electrical engineering.

ENCYCLOPEDIAS

General Encyclopedias in Print, 1973-74: A Comparative Analysis, by S. Padraig Walsh. 9th ed. R. R. Bowker, Inc., 1973. (ISBN 0-8352-0646-7)
    This is intended to provide a practical guide in the choice of an encyclopedia. The material presented is as accurate and as current as possible. For each encyclopedia there is a detailed analysis of the encyclopedia and how well it achieves its avowed purpose and serves the audience it addresses. For each work, there is given the publisher, the current price, the purpose and age suitability, its publishing history, its arrangement, its contributors and its accuracy as well as its physical make up. It gives also a list of places in which each work is recommended and an excerpt from the Subscription Books Bulletin Review if it was reviewed there. This is an excellent book to put in the hands of the questioner who wants to know which encyclopedia he should buy for his family.

ENGINES

Aircraft

Aircraft, Engines and Airmen, by August Hanniball. Scarecrow Press, 1972. (ISBN 0-8108-0430-1)
    This is a selective review of the periodical literature, 1930-1969, indexing many periodicals dealing with aviation. It is divided into four parts: articles dealing with aircraft, with aircraft engines, with biographies of fighter pilots and with Air Forces. There are indexes by aircraft names, manufacturers of aircraft symbols and engine names and symbols. This sometimes provides the only indexing of some items not even found in the Air University Index.

Jane's All The World's Aircraft, ed. by John W. Taylor. Franklin Watts. Annual since 1909.
    This annual pictures all the aircraft of the world with full specifications and data concerning armament, range, size and equipment. There is a section devoted entirely to the aircraft engine which gives all pertinent data.

Automobile

There is no single book which does for automobiles what Jane's does for aircraft. For automobile engines see AUTOMOBILES.

Railroad

Jane's World Railway's. McGraw Hill, annual since 1958.
A survey of railways of the world describing their routes, equipment and management. There is a section devoted entirely to the locomotive engine.

ENGLISH LANGUAGE

Dictionary of Modern American Usage, by Herbert W. Horwill. 2nd ed. Oxford University Press, 1944. (ISBN 0-19-869109-2)
Dictionary of Modern English Usage, by Henry W. Fowler. 2nd ed. Oxford University Press, 1965. (ISBN 0-19-500153-2)
These two books should be considered together since they both deal with usage of the English language. The Fowler book is British -oriented and the Howell book American but both deal with the current language and its use. Together they make up a primary source of information concerning basic grammar and usage. Entries are in alphabetical order and opinions are bolstered by liberal use of quotations. These are reference books which can be read for pleasure.

Manual of Style. 12th ed. revised. University of Chicago Press, 1969. (ISBN 0-226-77008-7)
This book, first published in 1906, is the oldest of the style manuals but continuous revisions have kept it amazingly modern. Intended primarily for research writers, it answers almost any question concerning the preparation of manuscripts or papers. It not only gives the usual information concerning footnotes and bibliographies but also includes information about proofreading, spelling, punctuation and other points of grammar. This is a must for any serious library.

Style Manual. Rev. ed. U. S. Government Printing Office, 1967. (G. P. I. 2)
This style manual is of immense value to anyone engaged in writing. It contains information on capitalization, spelling, punctuation, use of italics and other aspects of the publishing business. It is particularly good for often mispelled words and punctuation.

ENGRAVING AND ENGRAVERS

History of Engraving and Etching, by A. M. Hind. Peter Smith,

1914.   (ISBN 0-8446-2256-7)
    Although quite old this is still the best history of engraving and covers the art form from the fifteenth century to 1914.   It is particularly good for its bibliographies and its index to engravers. There is also a classified list of engravers by type of work produced.

History of Prints and Print Making from Dürer to Picasso, by F. Salamon.   McGraw Hill, 1972.   (ISBN 0-07-054460-3)
    This is not nearly as inclusive as the Hind book but it is up-to-date and covers 20th century engravers and their works.   It is intended primarily as a guide for collectors but it does give a good historical background and lists of engravers and their works.

Bryan's Dictionary of Painters and Engravers, ed. by George Williamson.   5 vols.   Kennikat, 1971 (Repr. of 1905 ed.).   (ISBN 0-8046-0052-X)
    This is the most comprehensive biographical dictionary devoted to painters and engravers.   It lists not only the major work of each engraver but in many cases gives the location as well. Volume 5 has six pages devoted to monograms used by painters and engravers.

American Engravers Upon Copper and Steel, by Mantle Fielding.   B. Franklin, 1964 (Repr. of 1917 ed.).   (ISBN 0-8337-1124-5)
American Engravers Upon Copper and Steel, by David Stauffer.   B. Franklin, 1964.   2 vols.   (ISBN 0-8337-3378-8)
    Together these books present a definitive history of copper and steel engraving in the United States.   Each one has biographical sketches of engravers and a checklist of engravings arranged by name of engraver.   The Fielding book is intended as a supplement to the Stauffer book.

ENTOMOLOGY
see
INSECTS

EPIGRAMS
see
QUOTATIONS; ANECDOTES

ETHNOLOGY

Dictionary of Races or Peoples, by United States Immigration Commission.   Gale Research, 1969 (Repr. of 1911 ed.).
    This dictionary is intended as a study of the peoples primarily

inhabiting those lands from which most of our immigrants come. Over 600 subjects are popularly rather than scientifically presented, most of them quite short. It covers all important areas but specific emphasis has been given to Europe. There are four pages of bibliography.

Ethnological Bibliography of North America, by George F. Murdock. 3rd ed. New Haven, Conn.: Human Relations Area Files Press, 1960. (ISBN 0-87536-201-X)
    A selective bibliography, classified and arranged by areas and within each area by the tribes or groups in that area. It includes both periodical and monograph materials dealing with all primitive and historical cultures. More than 17,000 titles are cited.

Ethnographic Atlas, by George F. Murdock. University of Pittsburgh, 1967. (ISBN 0-8229-3114-1)
    An ethnological atlas of the world, showing the distribution of the world's peoples clearly. It covers tribes and ethnic groups, language areas and prehistory. It is a generally useful complement to other books on the subject.

Handbook of American Indians North of Mexico, ed. by Frederick W. Hodge. Rowan, 2 vols. (ISBN 0-87471-004-09)
    This reprint of the 1912 Bulletin #30 by the U.S. Bureau of Ethnology remains the very best source of information concerning the Indian tribes of North America. It contains a descriptive list of tribes, confederacies, racial stocks and settlements of all Indians North of Mexico. In addition, it has biographies of many major Indian leaders, bits of history and legend, customs and languages. Especially interesting is a glossary of Indian terms which have been accepted into the English language.

Strange Customs, Manners and Beliefs, by Alpheus H. Verrill, Books for Libraries, 1946. (ISBN 0-8369-1199-7)
    Particularly good for dress, ornaments, food, medicines and rituals such as burials and marriage, this is a popularly written account of many strange customs of primitive peoples from all parts of the world.

ETIQUETTE

    The subject of etiquette touches every aspect of our daily lives and every profession and occupation has its own social rules and regulations. For etiquette in the ARMED FORCES, see that heading; for protocol and diplomatic etiquette, see DIPLOMATS. Also the etiquette of different countries is often mentioned in books about the social life and customs of those countries.
    There are two major books in America which together form the Bible of Etiquette.

Emily Post's Etiquette, edited by Elizabeth L. Post. 12th ed. Funk
and Wagnalls, 1969. (ISBN 0-308-10038-7)
Amy Vanderbilt's Etiquette, by Amy Vanderbilt. Rev. ed. Doubleday, 1972. (ISBN 0-385-03915-8)
Of the two, the Post book remains the more strait-laced and
conservative guide to conventional manners while Vanderbilt tends to
be more modern in her approach. Both, though, are excellent for
answering any question concerning the proper thing to do at the
proper time. No library would be complete without at least one
and preferably both of these books.

Wedding Etiquette Complete, by Marguerite Bentley. Manor Books,
1972. (ISBN 532-00123-125)
Everything you would want to know about weddings. It lists
all types, both formal and informal, and outlines not only the ceremony but the preparation for the wedding and the entertainments that
come before and after it. There are samples of invitations, announcements and thank you notes.

ETYMOLOGY

Few other languages in the world have as rich a background
of development as the English language, particularly as it is spoken
in the United States. The English of the British Isles is itself a
conglomerate of Germanic and Latin sources, while American English
has assimilated even more terms.
Almost every dictionary gives some basic background on our
word origins and etymology, so only specialized dictionaries will be
mentioned here.

The Oxford English Dictionary, ed. by J. A. Murray. Oxford University Press. 13 vols. (ISBN 0-19-861101-3)
This is the source of information on the background history
of words in the English language. It is the most scholarly dictionary available and while not perhaps too useful for every-day use, it
is excellent for etymology and derivations. The citation for each
word usually includes quotations showing the first use of that word
in printed form. It also delineates the history of the word with
changes of pronunciation and meaning throughout its history.

Dictionary of American English on Historical Principles, ed. by Sir
William Craigie. University of Chicago Press, 1938-1944.
(ISBN 0-226-11741-3)
This might be called the "son of the OED" in that it is the
most comprehensive dictionary dealing with the etymology of American English. It explains meanings and indicates date of first use,
with quotations dated and arranged chronologically. There are symbols to indicate whether the word was used first in England or here
in this country. The use is limited slightly by the fact that it covers
only the period prior to 1900 and, while colloquialisms are listed,

slang terms are not unless they are from a very early date or are of historical importance.

Dictionary of Americanisms on Historical Principles, by Mitford
McLeod Mathews. University of Chicago Press, 1951. 2 vols.
(ISBN 0-226-51011-5)

Although more limited in coverage than the Craigie book in that it deals only with terms which originated in the United States, it also brings the coverage of new words coined and foreign words adopted up to 1950; in that way it acts as a supplement to Craigie. Definitions are arranged chronologically and often contain illustrated quotations and pictures. Usually only the preferred pronunciation is given.

Dictionary of American Slang with a Supplement, by Harold Wentworth. T. Y. Crowell, 1960. (ISBN 0-690-23602-6)

A necessary adjunct to Craigie and Mathews since it is a comprehensive compilation of slang terms, many of which will not be included in either a standard or an etymological dictionary. It includes army terms, prison words and general slang in common usage, giving derivations and variant meanings. There have been some complaints about its use in high schools because of its inclusion of scatological definitions.

EVOLUTION

It is assumed that anyone asking questions concerning Evolution is already familiar with The Origin of Species by Charles Darwin, so that that book will not be listed here. Since there are still religious connotations inherent in this question, three books are listed which represent pro, con and neutral positions.

Evolution and the Christian Doctrine of Creation, by Richard H.
Overman. Westminster Press, 1969. (ISBN 0-664-20768-5)

This is an interesting argument concerning the possible compromise between Christianity and the evolutionary theory but without deviating one step from the idea of creation by God. Many scientists and many Christians will disagree with Overman's conclusions but the book is readable and provocative.

Three Billion Years of Life, by Andre de Cayeux. Stein and Day,
1970. (ISBN 0-8128-1349-9)

This translation from the French attempts to interpret evolutionary evidence and theories in such a way as to be acceptable to the Christian layman. Cayeux believes in evolution but not the Darwinian version. He believes that it was not a matter of random selection but rather of divine guidance. Even if one disagrees with his conclusions, there is an excellent glossary of evolutionary terms which will be of help to the non-scientific layman.

Understanding Evolution, by Herbert J. Ross. Prentice-Hall, 1966. (ISBN 0-13-935908-7)
   An excellent short book which better than many recent publications gives a historical overview of the whole question of evolution. It explains in simple terms the biology, genetics and geological evidence supporting the Darwinian theory. This is a solid, reliable introduction to what has always been a fascinating but seldom understood subject.

EXAMINATIONS AND TESTS

   There are many examinations and tests which persons have to take and for which they would like to do preliminary study. Most frequently asked for are Civil Service and College Entrance examinations. Others include general intelligence tests and achievement tests administered by educators.

   The Arco Publishing Company has an entire series of Arco Civil Service Test Tutors which covers practically every form of Civil Service employment.
   The following are study outlines for general preparation for Civil Service Tests. In addition there are 155 individual job titles for which study guides are available. To find these see the Arco Publishing Company catalog. Since all the following are from Arco, only the titles, dates and ISBN numbers will be given.

Civil Service Handbook. 4th ed. 1965. (ISBN 0-668-00040-6)
Federal Service Entrance Examinations. 8th ed. 1972. (ISBN 0-668-00528-9)
General Entrance Series. 1969. (ISBN 0-668-01861-1)
General Test Practice for 92 U.S. Jobs. 6th ed. 1971. (ISBN 0-668-00011-2)
Homestudy Course for Civil Service Jobs. 1965. (ISBN 0-668-01587-X)

   Arco also comes to the assistance of the person wanting to prepare for college entrance and achievement tests. The College Entrance Examination Board claims that such study is not productive of better grades but it certainly does not detract.

The College Board Examination, by Martin McDonough. Arco Publishing Co., 1972. (ISBN 0-668-02623-5)
College Entrance Tests, by David Turner. Arco Publishing Co., 1968. (ISBN 0-668-1858-5)
College Level Examination Program (CLEP), by David Turner. Arco Publishing Co., 1972. (ISBN 0-668-02574-3)

   In addition to the Arco series, the National Learning Corporation of Plainview, New York has a series which is quite beneficial.

College Level Examination Series, by Jack Rudman.   Plainview,
      New York: National Learning Corporation.   (ISBN 0-8373-5300-
      9)
      Includes:
      College Proficiency Examination.   (ISBN 0-8373-5400-5)
      Graduate Record Examination.   (ISBN 0-8373-5200-2)
      High School Equivalency Test.   (ISBN 0-8373-5107-4)

Mental Measurements Yearbook, ed. by Oscar K. Buros. Gryphon
      Press.   Varied dates.
      1st edition, 1938.   (ISBN 0-901674-12-4)
      2nd edition, 1942.   (ISBN 0-910674-13-2)
      3rd edition, 1949.   (ISBN 0-910674-03-5)
      4th edition, 1953.   (ISBN 0-910674-04-3)
      5th edition, 1959.   (ISBN 0-910674-05-1)
      6th edition, 1965.   (ISBN 0-910674-06-X)
      7th edition, 1972.   (ISBN 0-910674-11-6)   2 Volumes.
      This work is both a reviewing service and a bibliography.
It is divided into two sections.   The first lists tests available, with
a brief history of the tests and their use in education; the second
lists books on testing.   The reviews of both books and tests, written
by noted educators, present varying opinions on the worth or validity
of the tests reviewed.

FACTS

These questions usually deal with such things as where did
an event take place, who invented what, or where or what is the
highest, deepest, etc. that man has gone.

Facts on File, a Weekly World News Digest With A Cumulative In-
      dex.   Facts on File, weekly with annual cumulation since 1940.
      This is a weekly publication of news events with biweekly in-
dexes.   Excellent for location of dates things happened.   Winners
of prizes, beauty awards, etc.   Excellent indexing.

Famous First Facts, by Joseph N. Kane.   3rd ed.   New York: H.
      W. Wilson, 1964.   (ISBN 0-8242-0015-2)
      A compilation of the first time things happened in the United
States, such as "when was the first ice cream cone invented?"   It
is well indexed by years, by days of the week and month, by personal names and by geographical location.   The main body of the
book is alphabetical by "first fact" desired.

Guinness Book of World Records, by Norris McWhirter.   Rev. ed.
      Sterling, 1972.   (ISBN 0-8069-0006-7)
      Originally printed by the Guinness Stout Manufacturers and
distributed to pub owners in Britain under the title, Guinness Book
of Superlatives, this rapidly became so popular that the name was
changed and it was made into a commercial publication.   Includes

all sorts of superlatives, i.e. highest, lowest, longest, shortest, etc. Arranged by broad subject heading with a good index.

FAIRY TALES

Every children's library will have a generous supply of books of fairy tales for the young reader. The problem is to locate within a collection the individual fairy tale desired.

Index To Fairy Tales, Myths and Legends, ed. by Mary H. Eastman. Faxon, 1926. (ISBN 0-87305-088-2) Suppl. 1, 1937. Faxon. (ISBN 0-87305-061-4) Suppl. 2, 1952. Faxon. (ISBN 0-87305-082-7)

This is a title index to the best known and most loved fairy stories, myths and legends, with cross references from lesser used titles to the usual ones. It indexes more than 800 different collections containing fairy stories, myths and legends. Particularly good for the children's librarian but of interest to anyone interested in folk tales.

Time for Fairy Tales, Old and New, by May Hill Arbuthnot. Lothrop, 1961.

An anthology of folk and fairy tales collected by an expert on children's literature. The selection is masterful but of more importance are the introductory chapters discussing origins and history of the development of fairy tales and the use of these stories with modern day children. There are bibliographies of stories from all lands and a good title and author index.

FELLOWSHIPS AND GRANTS

Foundation Directory, ed. by Marianna O. Lewis. 4th ed. Columbia University Press, 1971. (ISBN 0-87954-000-1)

A compilation of detailed information on 5,454 foundations of the United States listing each one by state and city, and with supplementary indexes to their fields of endeavor and operations. The foundations listed all have assets of over a half million dollars and each makes grants totalling more than $25,000 per year. Each grant is identified by donor, purpose, field of interest and method of application.

Foundation Grants Index, ed. by Lee Noe. Columbia University Press, 1973. (ISBN 0-231-03803-8)

A comprehensive listing of grants available from private foundations; giving full information of monies available, fields covered and methods of locating and applying for grants.

The Grants Register, Postgraduate Awards for the English Speaking World, ed. by Roland W. Turner. St. Martin's Press, biennial since 1972.
"The Grants Register aims to provide exhaustive, current information about awards·to graduates and advanced scholars from Australia, Canada, Ireland, New Zealand, South Africa, The United Kingdom and the United States. The book lists scholarships and fellowships at all levels of graduate study..."--Foreword. The number of entries totals more than 1,300; for each, full information is given on how to qualify, how to apply and length of availability.

Graduate and Professional School Opportunities for Minority Students. 5th ed. Princeton, N. J.: Educational Testing Service, 1973.
Gives full tabular information on schools and professions offering particular programs of help for minority students. It gives information on date of application, eligibility and all pertinent details for eligible students. It is arranged in two parts, by type of graduate school and by graduate program to be pursued within the school.

Scholarships, Fellowships and Loans, ed. by Norman Feingold. Bellman, 1972. (ISBN 0-87442-005-9)
Possibly the most complete collection of information concerning all types of graduate and undergraduate financial aid. Only volume 5 is currently in print. This is unfortunate since each volume, although complete within itself, does not always repeat information from other volumes.

FESTIVALS
see also
HOLIDAYS

Book of Festivals, by Dorothy G. Spicer. Gale, 1969 (repr. of 1937 ed.).
The most comprehensive of the books dealing with festivals, it is particularly good for those with religious significance. The major religious festivals are described and their religious significance given. There are tables for the date of the celebration of Easter and other moveable feasts, and a good bibliography.

Festivals of the Jewish Year, by Theodor Hubert Gaster. Peter Smith, 1962 (Reprint of 1953 ed.). (ISBN 0-8446-2113-7)
The most important festivals of the Jewish year are discussed with special attention paid to similar celebrations in other religions. There is a good bibliography.

Festivals of Western Europe, by Dorothy G. Spicer. Wilson, 1958. (ISBN 0-8242-0016-0)
This contains good descriptions of the major festivals of all the countries of Western Europe with the exception of Great Britain.

It gives historical and religious significance as well as methods of celebrating. There is an index to festivals by name and by locations as well as a glossary of terms used.

Festivals U. S. A. and Canada, ed. by R. Meyer. Rev. ed. Washburn, 1967.
 This is devoted to strictly American festivals such as Thanksgiving, Independence Day, etc. but is not limited to religious celebrations. Good for historical facts as well as for description of various celebrations.

FILMS
see
MOTION PICTURES

FIREARMS
see also
ARMAMENT

Firearms Dictionary, by R. A. Steindler. Stackpole Press, 1970. (ISBN 0-8117-0614-1)
 More than 1800 words, phrases, and items of nomenclature related to guns and firearms are defined. It includes both English and foreign words. It has 200 plates and drawings to help explain the definitions.

Gun Digest, by John T. Amber. Follett, annual since 1956.
 An annual publication which concentrates on American firearms but does list some imports. It is particularly good for shotguns and hunting rifles.

Small Arms of the World, by Joseph E. Smith. Rev. ed. Stackpole, 1973. (ISBN 0-8117-1565-5)
 A well-illustrated, descriptive and instructional manual with excellent directions for firing the major small arms of the world. It describes and gives directions for almost a thousand weapons.

FIRST AID

First Aid Textbook. American Red Cross. 4th edition. Doubleday, 1957. (ISBN 0-385-09805-7)
 An official publication of the American Red Cross, this is a short but extremely useful book in which emergency treatments are accurately and simply explained with charts and illustrations to support the text.

FISH

Most of the major encyclopedias have good articles on the subject but Collier's Encyclopedia and World Book have several pages in color of various fishes. The third edition of Webster's New International Dictionary also has an excellent color plate with 25 different fish illustrated.
Possibly the most reliable and prolific publisher in the field of fish and wildlife is the U. S. Fish and Wildlife Service. For a listing of many of their publications see:

Price List # 21. Fish and Wildlife. U. S. Government Printing Office. (Entire set of price lists available free upon request.)

Living Fishes of the World, by Earl S. Herald. Doubleday, 1961. (ISBN 0-385-00988-7)
This is a comprehensive listing of most of the world's fish arranged by systematic classification and illustrated with many plates, most of which are underwater and many in color. For each fish is given the natural habitat, range, adult size and length of life as well as its commercial possibilities.

Freshwater Fishes, by Juraj Holcik. International Publications Service, 1970.
An illustrated guide to the freshwater fishes of the world.

Fishes of the World in Color, by Hans Hvass. Dutton, 1965. (ISBN 0-525-10577-8)
Excellent for identifying fish. Combines guide book-type writing with color plates.

Game Fishes of the United States, by G. Brown Goode. Winchester Press, 1972 (Reprint of 1879 ed.). (ISBN 0-87691-085-1)
This recent reprint is the most comprehensive book dealing with game fish of the North American continent. For each fish is given a full description including geographical distribution, maximum size and length of life. Well illustrated with black and white pictures.

FISHING

This subject can be divided into two parts, i. e. , commercial and sports fishing. Once again, the U. S. Fish and Wildlife Service is possibly your best source of information for both aspects of the question (see Price List # 21. Fish and Wildlife, available from the U. S. Government Printing Office free of charge, for a general listing of materials available).

COMMERCIAL FISHING

Commercial Fisheries Abstracts. U. S. Fish and Wildlife Service.
U. S. Government Printing Office. Monthly.
Commercial Fisheries Review. U. S. Fish and Wildlife Service.
U. S. Government Printing Office. Monthly since 1939.
Fishery Bulletin. U. S. Fish and Wildlife Service. U. S. Govern-
ment Printing Office. Irregular since 1881.

These three publications of the Fish and Wildlife Service give
an up-to-date and comprehensive survey of commercial fishing in the
United States. The Abstracts are from 90 journals dealing with important developments in the fishing industry and are intended for the
serious student. The Review gives current information on production, marketing and statistics as well as latest government regulations. The Bulletins are monographs dealing with specific investiga-
tions and have good bibliographies.

Future of the Fishing Industry of the United States, ed. by Gilbert
DeWitt. University of Washington Press, 1968. (ISBN 0-295-
95204-0)

A good analysis of the current status of the fishing industry
as well as an analysis of future possibilities. Good bibliographies.

SPORTS FISHING

Angler's Guide to Fresh Water Sport Fishes of North America, by
Edward C. Migdalski. Ronald Press, 1962.
Angler's Guide to Salt Water Game Fishes: Atlantic and Pacific, by
Edward C. Migdalski. Ronald Press, 1958.

These two books together might almost be considered an encyclopedia of sports fishing. They give information concerning the
various equipment for both fresh and salt water fishing and instructions as to its use. There is a full discussion of types of game
fish and types of baits and lures to be used in fishing for each.
There are many tables and charts.

Fisherman's Handbook, by John Power. Scribner's, 1972. (ISBN
0-684-12845-4)

This is written as a reference book and not for continual
reading, but what it loses in literary style it makes up in factual
data. It lists and describes the major game fish of the United
States, gives data on natural and artificial baits, and tells where to
fish at what time of the year. It gives guides not only to state and
local parks but to national parks as well. It has a section on equipment both for boats and for fishing tackles, and a glossary to explain the use of terms. Especially good for its comprehensive listing of state fishing laws.

New Fisherman's Encyclopedia. Rev. ed. Stackpole Press, 1963.
(ISBN 0-8117-0645-1)

A volume in Stackpole's Outdoor Reference Library, this is a
large volume that answers almost any underwater questions. It
identifies and tells where to find both fresh and salt water fish, what

gear and methods to use in taking them, and gives hints on boats
and other equipment. Excellent illustrations.

FLAGS

Once again, all major encyclopedias and dictionaries will
have plates in color of the flags of the world.

Flag Book of the United States, by Whitney Smith. Morrow, 1970.
A Story of American Flags, by W. W. Wannamaker. Columbia,
    S. C.: State Printing Co., 1972. (ISBN 0-911432-18-3)
    Either of these books will provide accurate information con-
cerning the development of the American flag and the various standards which have flown over our country. Both are well illustrated
and fully documented with good indexes. The Smith book is better
for flags of the individual states and the Wannamaker book is excellent in its section dealing with flags of the Confederacy. The
Wannamaker book is much the more emotional of the two.

Flags of the World, by E. M. Barraclough. Rev. ed. Warne, 1969.
    (ISBN 0-7232-1338-0)
    For each country of the world, there is a description and
discussion of the current flag as well as an historical account of
various flags used by that country. Full color illustrations make
identification easy. The chapter on the United States has plates of
state flags as well as the history of the national standard.

International Flag Book in Color, by Christian Pederson. Morrow,
    1971.
    Although written for the elementary school audience and
therefore inadequate for adult research, this book is excellent for
flag identification due to its full color illustration and arrangement.

FLOWERS

Both cultivated and wild flowers are considered in this section. Most encyclopedias will have brief articles about various
species under the common name of the flower. In addition, your
card catalog will have many entries under specific types, e. g.,
Roses, etc.

Complete Guide to Garden Flowers, by Herbert Askwith. A. S.
    Barnes, n. d. (ISBN 0-498-09591-6)
    This covers all phases of flower life and culture. It gives
descriptions of various flowers with their geographical limitations
and type of soil or fertilizers needed. It lists when and where to
plant each type of flower and at what time of year one can expect

each to bloom, so that plans can be made to always have plants in flower. There is a good glossary of gardening terms.

Field Guide of American Wild Flowers, by F. Schuyler Mathews.
Putnam, 1966. (ISBN 0-399-10282-5)
Excellent for identification--good description and pictures.

Field Guide to Wildflowers of Northeastern and North-Central North
America, by Roger Peterson. Houghton-Mifflin, 1968. (ISBN
0-395-08086)
Another of the "Peterson Guides," this one pictures and de-
scribes most of the wildflowers of the northern half of the United
States. Excellent for identification.

Flower Gardening, a Primer, by James Wilson. Van Nostrand Reinhold, 1970. (ISBN 0-442-09529-5)
A beginner's book on flower gardening. Quite elementary in
approach, it does give hints on times to plant or prune, and on how
to prepare the earth.

One Thousand One Questions Answered About Flowers, by Norman
Taylor. Dodd, Mead, 1963. (ISBN 0-396-04855-2)
This is possibly the most ambitious of all books about flowers
in that it tries to anticipate possible questions and give answers to
any possible problem.

Quick-key Guide to Wildflowers, by David Archbald. Doubleday,
1968. (ISBN 0-385-09184-2)
This is a good key to wildflower identification, arranged by
easily recognized characteristics of each plant.

Recognizing Flowering Wild Plants, by William C. Grimm. Stackpole, 1968. (ISBN 0-8117-1398-9)
An illustrated identifying guide to wildflowers common to the
United States. It gives information on geographic location, hints for
identification and times of blooming for each variety.

Wild Flowers of America, ed. by Harold W. Rickett. Crown, 1963.
Over 400 of the more common (but also including some rare)
flowers are described with detailed information concerning location,
blooming, color, etc. Especially useful because of many plates in
color and a glossary of specific terms.

FOLK MUSIC

Although not exactly synonymous, folk music and folk dance
are usually treated in the same sources. Both aspects will therefore be considered in this section.

American Folksong and Folklore, a Regional Bibliography, by Alan

Lomax. Scholarly Press, 1942. (ISBN 0-403-01615-0)
This is an annotated bibliography arranged by type of work,
i. e., song, dance and worship songs found in both books and periodicals. It also includes folk tales of America.

Folksingers and Folksongs in America, by Ray M. Lawless. Rev.
ed. Hawthorn Books, 1965. (ISBN 0-696-60665-8)
A comprehensive encyclopedia concerning the folk music of
America. It contains biographies and criticisms of individual singers
as well as bibliographies of published works and information on recordings. It also lists various folk festivals, folklore societies, etc.

Folk Dancing: A Guide for Schools, Colleges and Recreational
Groups, by Richard Kraus. Macmillan, 1962. (ISBN 0-02-
36630)
Intended as a text for classes in the folk dances, this is a
well illustrated and easily understood description and instruction for
various folk dances from around the world.

America Sings, by Carl Carmer. Knopf, 1950. (ISBN 0-394-
90902-X)
The stories and songs of our country's development. This is
a combination of the folk stories and folk songs from America's
past. It includes not only the words to the songs but the music as
well, with background notes on their history.

American Ballads and Folk Songs, by John Avery Lomax. Macmillan, 1934. (ISBN 0-02-57415)
The largest single collection of American folk songs and ballads, collected by America's foremost authority on the folk music of
America. In most instances, the tunes as well as the words are
given and in cases of variant tunes or words, both versions are
given. This is the best source available for this information.

FOLKLORE
see also
FAIRY TALES

Funk and Wagnall's Standard Dictionary of Folklore, Mythology and
Legend, ed. by Maria Leach. Funk and Wagnalls, 1972. (ISBN
0-308-40090-9)
An updating of what has become a standard work, this book
makes up for what it lacks in literary presentation by its highly
accurate presentation of the facts of folklore. Written by experts
in all fields, it is arranged alphabetically by subject and includes
ethnological background by countries, specific characters, names of
legends, folk tales, etc. It is particularly good for identifying gods
and goddesses. Although limited, the bibliographies given are very
good.

The Golden Bough, by Sir James Frazer. St. Martin's Press. 13
   vols. (Also available in one-volume abridged edition from Macmillan). (ISBN 0-02-54098)
   One of the two editions should be in every library because
they present an excellent interpretation of the development of belief
and customs through the ages. For most libraries, the one-volume
edition will be adequate.

Motif-index of Folk-Literature, ed. by Stith Thompson. University
   of Indiana Press, 1955-58. 6 vols. (ISBN 0-253-33887-5)
   This classifies and defines the motifs which pervade the traditional folk literature. Each recurring theme is identified by type
of story or ballad or folklore involved, as well as by country and
place. It does give some locations of the stories but is primarily
an index for motifs.

Treasury of American Folklore, ed. by Benjamin A. Botkin. Crown
   Publishers, 1944.
   This covers every aspect of Americn folklore from humor
through serious superstitions. It contains stories, ballads, legends
of all the heroes, badmen, demigods and villains of America's past.

FOODS

   This section does not deal with the preparation of foods. This
aspect of the subject is covered very well in a variety of cookbooks
and every library should have a collection of cookbooks. Since such
a collection should represent the needs of a particular locale, no
specific cookbooks are recommended here.
   The U. S. Department of Agriculture is vitally interested in
providing information on good nutrition and food and has several
Yearbooks of Agriculture devoted to the subject. These are well
written with signed articles by experts in the field of nutrition and
food. All have extensive bibliographies and good indexes.

   Food and Nutrition.   1959.   Cat. # A 1. 10:959
   Protecting Our Food   1966.   Cat. # A 1. 10:966
   Food For Us All.   1968.   Cat. # A 1. 10:969

   Another important book on the subject of food is the following:

Encyclopedia of Food, by Artemus Ward. Peter Smith, 1923. (ISBN
   0-8446-1464-5)
   Although originally published in two volumes, only volume one
has been reprinted at this time. Volume two consisted primarily of
illustrations. One usually does not associate a humorist with a serious work of reference value but in this case Ward has edited an
excellent work. About 2000 alphabetically arranged entries deal with
every aspect of different foods and ways of preparing them. There

is a glossary of food terms, as well as a multi-lingual dictionary in six languages.

Funk and Wagnall's Cook's and Diner's Dictionary. Funk and Wagnalls, 1969. (ISBN 0-308-40034-8)
  This is the most comprehensive book dealing with terms in the fields of cooking, nutrition, wine and other culinary fields. Excellent for answering questions which require just a definition of terms.

FOOTBALL

Collegiate Football, U. S. A., 1869-1973, by John McCallum. Mc-
  Graw-Hill, 1973. (ISBN 0-07-044801-9)
  The official publication of the National Football Foundation, this gives a loving history of the game of football including the evolution of the football rules. There is a complete roster, through the 1972 season, of the College Football Hall of Fame, including both players and coaches with a brief biographical sketch of each person. There is also a complete listing of NCAA teams with their won and lost records for the past twenty years and a history of the various bowl games with scores for each game play.

Official Encyclopedia of Football, by Robert Trent. Rev. 11th ed.
  A. S. Barnes, 1973. (ISBN 0-498-01378-2)
  This does for professional football what the Encyclopedia of Football did for the collegiate game. It presents a year-by-year history of the game, listing all coaches and players who have appeared on a pro team and giving roster and team records for each year. There are charts of each major league stadium and statistical records for every facet of the game.

Pro-Football Hall of Fame, by Arthur Daley. Grosset & Dunlap,
  1971. (ISBN 0-448-02508-6)
  Biographical sketches of all players and coaches elected to the Pro-Football Hall of Fame. Gives a brief history of the game but its important function is biographical.

FOREIGN AFFAIRS

This is a very broad field, impossible to cover in a book this size, and only books answering general aspects are listed here. For information concerning TREATIES and DOCUMENTS see those headings. See also INTERNATIONAL RELATIONS.

Deadline Data on World Affairs, ed. by George E. Delury. McGraw-
  Hill, since 1956.

This is a service intended for editors of newspapers and other news services to give the immediate up-dated information on current world happenings. It is published on cards which are up-dated every two weeks. This is good for location of dates and brief facts but has very little discussion.

United Nations-Fact Book. Bookmailer, 1970. (ISBN 0-910264-28-7)
A summary of statistical and management data concerning the United Nations and its operations.

The United States in World Affairs. Council on Foreign Relations, annual since 1935.
These are annual compilations of U. S. involvement in world affairs. There is a chronology of events for each year and a long bibliography for each year's happenings. This is possibly the best summary of U. S. foreign affairs but the publication lags about two years behind the events described.

Year Book of World Affairs, ed. by George W. Keeton. Praeger, annual since 1947.
This is more of a survey of published materials in the field than original materials. As such it provides an excellent summary of world happenings supplemented by an excellent bibliography, survey articles and book reviews.

FOREIGN WORDS AND PHRASES

Most good unabridged dictionaries define commonly used foreign words and phrases, either in the body of the book or in an appendix. These sources will normally answer any question you may have, but for the occasional specific phrase not found there, the following book is recommended:

Dictionary of Foreign Words and Phrases, by Alan J. Bliss. Dutton, 1966. (ISBN 0-525-09166-1)
This supplements the general dictionary with a much wider coverage of foreign words and phrases in current usage. It gives meaning in the country of derivation if the English meaning is not a direct translation of the original.

FORESTRY

Directory of Forestry, by J. Weck. American Elsevier, 1966. (ISBN 0-444-40626-3)
A specialized dictionary limited to those words used by loggers and foresters to describe their work and their everyday activities. This defines some terms used by forest workers that do not appear in any other source.

Forestry Handbook, by Reginald Dunderdale Forbes. Ronald Press, 1955.
 This is an official publication of the Society of American Foresters and as such is a reliable guide to data needed in computing yield per acre as well as techniques and formulas for harvesting the forest. It contains tables of converting factors and basic data needed by the working forester.

World Timbers, compiled by B. J. Rendle. University of Toronto Press, 1969-1970. 3 vols.
 Vol. 1. Europe and Africa. 1967. (ISBN 0-8020-1570-0)
 Vol. 2. North and South America Including Central America...
  1969. (ISBN 0-8020-1667)
 Vol. 3. Asia, Australia and New Zealand. 1970. (ISBN 0-8020-1718-5)
 These three volumes contain descriptions of practically all the world's trees, tell where they grow and the heights and size they may reach. Especially important for estimates of present and future use.

FORMULAS, CHEMICAL

Chemical Formulary, ed. by Harry Bennett. Chemical Publishing Company. 17 vols, including cumulative index to vol. 1-16.
 Originally published in 1933, this is a timeless publication with new volumes bringing new formulas to light and old ones up to date. It is a collection of both practical and commercial formulas and recipes used for making all sorts of products in many industries. Each volume is completely indexed with a cumulative index available for volumes one through sixteen. An excellent source book for any chemical formula.

Formulas, Methods, Tips and Data For Home and Workshop, by Kenneth M. Swezey. Popular Science Publications, 1969. (ISBN 0-87468-042-5)
 Formulas used around the house for removing stains, etc. These are arranged alphabetically by broad categories but a good index is helpful in finding desired material.

Practical and Industrial Formulary, by Mitchell Freeman. Chemical Publishing Co., 1962. (ISBN 0-8206-0103-9)
 A handbook of chemical formulas used in the manufacturing of many products, both chemical and industrial. While perfectly adequate for the working chemist, it is simply enough written for the average layman to understand. There is a good index and also a buyer's guide for supplies and equipment. Less comprehensive than the Bennett book, this probably would be adequate for most libraries.

FORMULAS, MATHEMATICAL

Handbook of Mathematical Tables and Formulas, by Richard S. Burington. 5th ed. McGraw-Hill, 1973. (ISBN 0-07-009015-7)
This was compiled as an aid to students and persons engaged in mathematics, engineering, physics, chemistry and other scientific fields. As such, it is a collection of basic data and formulas for all but the most complicated mathematical problems. The first part is devoted to mathematical formulas and theorems in basic mathematics, while the latter part of the book is devoted to tables of logarithms, square roots, etc.

Handbook of Mathematical Tables, ed. by Robert C. Weast. 2nd ed. Cleveland, Ohio: Chemical Rubber Company, 1964.
This is the mathematical supplement to the CRC Handbook of Chemistry and Physics and has tables for logarithms, square roots, cube roots, reciprocals, secants, cosecants, Fourier series, etc. There are tables for practically every mathematical function.

FOSSILS

Fossil Book, by Carroll L. Fenton. Doubleday, 1959. (ISBN 0-385-06860-3)
This book records all prehistoric life other than human. It lists and illustrates many fossils from earliest time to the very near past. There are fossils of early plants, animals, birds and fishes. Only man has been neglected.

Fossils in America: Their Nature, Origin, Identification and Classification, by Jay E. Ranson. Harper & Row, 1964. (ISBN 0-06-71560-X)
While quite elementary in its approach, this will answer most background questions concerning fossils and their identification. One interesting facet of the book is a range guide to collecting sites in which possible hunting grounds are listed by state, county and neighborhood. For each site, the type of possible find is identified and described. This is intended for the beginning paleontologist or fossil collector and is easily understood. An appendix lists libraries and museums with mineral exhibits.

Index Fossils of North America, by Harvey W. Shimer. MIT Press, 1944. (ISBN 0-262-1900-X)
An index fossil is one which can be used to identify and date the other fossils found on that same strata. This book lists and illustrates fossils of all types which can act as indexes to parts of the United States and Canada.

FOUNDATIONS
see
FELLOWSHIP AND GRANTS

FRATERNITIES AND SORORITIES

Baird's Manual of American College Fraternities, ed. by John Rob-
      son. 18th ed. Menasha, Wisconsin: George Banta, 1968.
      This was first published in 1879 and has had periodic revi-
sions since that time. It is an excellent source for fraternity histories. For each fraternity, there is a descriptive analysis, a history and an account of national activities. It includes not only
social organizations for men and women but also professional and
honorary fraternities. There is a directory by school and by fraternity, giving the location of each chapter in the United States and
Canada.

FREE MATERIALS

      There is no better source of free materials than the publica-
tions of the Educators Progress Service of Randolph, Wisconsin.
These guides list free materials in a variety of fields and give addresses of Chambers of Commerce, Tourist Bureaus and other
sources of free information. This material can be bought singly or
in a group. They are revised annually for delivery at the beginning
of each school year. Their publications are:

      Educator's Guide to Free Films. 32nd ed. 1973.
      Educator's Guide to Free Filmstrips. 24th ed. 1973.
      Educator's Guide to Free Tapes, Scripts and Transcriptions.
          19th ed. 1973.
      Educator's Guide to Free Guidance Materials. 12th ed. 1973.
      Educator's Guide to Free Social Studies Materials. 12th ed. 1973.
      Educator's Guide to Free Science Materials. 13th ed. 1973.
      Educator's Guide to Free Health, Physical Education and Recre-
          ation Materials. 5th ed. 1973.
      Elementary Teacher's Guide to Free Curriculum Material.
          29th ed. 1973.

      Another excellent source of free pamphlet material is the
following:

Vertical File Index. H. W. Wilson Company. Monthly.
      Although not exclusively a listing of free materials, this does
list things which can be received for the asking. It is a subject and
title index to pamphlet materials which are considered to be of general interest to libraries. Each issue contains a listing of recent

pamphlets and for each one gives usual bibliographic information
along with its source and price.

FROGS
see also
AMPHIBIANS AND REPTILES

Handbook of Frogs and Toads of the United States and Canada, by
Albert H. Wright. 3rd ed. Comstock Press, 1949. (ISBN
0-8014-0462-2)
This is actually Volume one of the Handbook of American
Natural History series but it can stand alone. It is a handbook for
identification and study of the frogs and toads of North America and
for each one of more than 100 species there is a complete description, often accompanied by a color photograph. It gives all pertinent data concerning each type in tabular form.

FURNITURE
see also
ANTIQUES

Complete Guide to Furniture Styles, by Louis A. Boger. Rev. ed.
Scribner's, 1969. (ISBN 0-684-10029-0)
This book discusses European, American and Chinese styles
of furniture arranged chronologically by period of development. It
has many illustrations and a good bibliography. An appendix lists
artists and craftsmen.

New Encyclopedia of Furniture, by Joseph Aronson. Rev. ed. Crown
Publ., 1967.
An exhaustive work on the use of furniture, this is encyclopedic in nature; that is, it gives brief bits of information on a multitude of subjects, illustrated with pictures and photographs. There
is a glossary of terms for the furniture maker and buyer as well as
an index to designers and craftsmen. There is an especially good
section on the use of color for decoration.

Furniture Treasury, by Wallace Nutting. Macmillan, 1954. 3 vols.
in 2.
The book details all periods of American furniture with some
examples of foreign furniture in America. It also contains sections
on American hardware and household utensils. It has over 5000
plates with descriptions and often measurements and names of owners. Volume three is a listing of clocks and clockmakers of America.

GAMES

In this section, parlor games and card games will be discussed. For specific games such as BRIDGE and CHESS see those headings. For athletic events see the heading SPORTS or the name of the individual sport.

Foster's Complete Hoyle: an Encyclopedia of Indoor Games, by
Robert F. Foster, Rev. ed. Lippincott, 1963. (ISBN 0-397-00321-8)
This is a rewriting of the famous Hoyle's which has for many years been the Bible for all indoor games. For each game it gives the latest rules and regulations along with suggestions of proper play and strategy. Almost 300 games are analyzed and discussed.

Hoyle Up-To-Date: Official Rules for All Important Games, by
Albert H. Moorehead. Grosset and Dunlap, 1970. (ISBN 0-448-01984-1)
This is another version of Hoyle and is really neither better nor worse than the Foster book. One but not necessarily both should be in every library.

Fun Encyclopedia, by Elvin O. Harbin. Abingdon, 1940. (ISBN 0-687-13714-4)
This is intended as an all-purpose guidebook for entertainment in the home, church, school or club. There are stories, games, stunts, quizzes and suggestions for almost any type of gathering.

Fun In Bed, by Alice Scully. Simon & Schuster, 1969. (ISBN 0-671-20398-3
Intended for the temporarily ill, confined to the home or bed, this presents many different types of games and amusements to help pass the time and kill the boredom.

GARDENING

This section is devoted to vegetable gardening and general gardening techniques. For flower gardening, see FLOWERS.

American Home Gardening Book and Plant Encyclopedia. Editors of
American Home. M. Evans, 1964. (ISBN 0-87131-035-X)
This gives practical and easily understood instructions on the planting and care of trees, shrubs, fruits and vegetables. It is limited to those gardens which can be grown in the United States.

Vegetable Gardening, by James V. Crockett. Silver Burdett, 1972.
This volume in the Time-Life Encyclopedia of Gardening is devoted to the raising of vegetables. For each vegetable discussed,

details are given for time to plant, type of soils needed, fertilizer desirable and other needed information.   Quite comprehensive for American vegetables.

Ten Thousand Garden Questions Answered by Twenty Experts, ed.
    by Frederick Rockwell,   Doubleday, 1959.   (ISBN 0-385-06846-8)
    The editor has tried to anticipate any gardening problem which might arise and give an answer to it.   Dealing with both vegetables and flowers, this is a most complete coverage.

GEMS

    Any good encyclopedia has information concerning gems and jewelry and most, especially the Britannica, have plates of various gem stones and examples of the largest of each type.   Webster's Third International Dictionary has an excellent plate showing various types of gem stones under GEMS.

Dictionary of Gems and Gemology, by Robert M. Shipley.   6th ed.
    Gemological Institute of America, 1971.
    This is a glossary of over 4000 English and foreign words and phrases which will be encountered in writings dealing with ornaments, curios, jewelry stones and the art trades.   It includes historical matter and pronunciation of names and terms.   It also has a section on abbreviations used in the gem and jewelry trade.   While prime emphasis is given to natural stones and their mineralogical makeup, there is a section devoted to the making of synthetic stones. Famous stones are described and histories and legends concerning them are told.

Famous Diamonds of the World, by Robert M. Shipley.   6th rev. ed.
    Gemological Institute of America, 1955.
    A listing of the famous diamonds of the world along with photographs and a brief history of the finding, owners and any legends or beliefs attached to the stone.

Gems: Their Sources, Descriptions and Identification, by Robert A.
    Webster.   Rev. ed.   Shoe String Press, 1970.   (ISBN 0-208-
    00973-6)
    Color illustrations of various stones aid immensely in making this an excellent source of gem identification.   In addition to serving as a guide to identification, this book also describes the materials and equipment needed to fully study precious stones.   It is a technical book which deals with methods and ways of testing and identifying stones but it is simply enough written to be useful to the average layman.   There is a bibliography of other books on the subject.

Jeweler's Manual, by Richard T. Liddicoat.   2nd ed. Gemological
    Institute of America, 1967.

This is a manual on all aspects of the jeweler's art. It describes the various types of jewelry and the materials needed to make them as well as the type of manufacturing involved. It also gives hints on the organization and management of a jewelry store. It includes tables showing specific weights of various precious stones and metals as well as melting points, specific gravity and other important data.

Jewelry Repair Manual, by R. Allen Hardy. 2nd ed. Van Nostrand Reinhold, 1967. (ISBN 0-442-03130-0)
Although most books in this section are not devoted to the hobby side of the jewelry picture, this book was prepared as a hobby guide and is a good source for information concerning jewelry repairs and methods. It is well illustrated with pictures and diagrams and is easily understood.

Jewelry Through the Ages, by Guido Gregorietti. McGraw-Hill, 1969. (ISBN 0-07-024647-5)
A history of the use of precious stones and metals as decoration through the ages. Well illustrated and fully authentic, this was a publication of the American Heritage Magazine.

GENEALOGY
see also
HERALDRY

Very few libraries will have enough materials available to make possible any detailed research into genealogical backgrounds. Therefore, the materials listed under this section will be books on how to do such research and directories to general genealogy sources. One of the best sources of genealogical information is in Salt Lake City, Utah (the Genealogical Society Library).

American Origins, by Leslie G. Pine. Baltimore, Maryland: Genealogical Publishing Company, 1971. (ISBN 0-8063-0277-1)
Intended for the person who has determined that his family came from a specific country and who wants to make inquiries in Europe for his ancestors. For each country, there is information on types of records kept and various sources available, as well on ways to go about obtaining this information.

Researcher's Guide to American Genealogy, by Val D. Greenwood. Baltimore, Md.: Genealogical Publishing Co., 1974. (ISBN 0-8063-0560-6)
Intended as a textbook for a course in American genealogical research, this book is an excellent simple explanation of the steps necessary for genealogical research. The book is in two parts. Part I deals with basic principles of such research as applied to American ancestry; Part II discusses the records which will be helpful to the genealogist. Each type of source is discussed, evaluated

and its use explained. This is possibly the best current source of information on how to do genealogical research.

Search and Research. by Noel C. Stevenson. Rev. ed. Salt Lake City, Utah: Deseret Book Co., 1964. (ISBN 0-87747-236-X)
   This is one of the very best instructional sources on where and how to look for genealogical materials. The listing of sources is followed by lists (by state) of libraries, historical associations, archives, census records and other sources which would be helpful to you in your search. It also lists possible sources in all English speaking nations.

Searching for Your Ancestors, by Gilbert H. Doane. 3rd ed. Univ. of Minnesota Press, 1960. (ISBN 0-8166-0213-1)
   Subtitled "The How and Why of Genealogy," this is a manual for the amateur genealogist. It has chapters on every phase of the search from government records down to family papers. It is good also for its bibliography which lists many other guides which would be helpful in preparing for your search.

GENETICS

Dictionary of Genetics, by Robert C. King. Rev. 2nd ed. Oxford University Press, 1972. (ISBN 0-19-501504-5)
   This book gives good short definitions in every area of genetic research--plant, animal or human.

GEOGRAPHY

This is another subject which has many facets, and in this section only the more general geographical questions will be discussed. For questions dealing with maps and map information see MAPS. For detailed guide books on the geography of the United States see AMERICAN GUIDE SERIES. For detailed guide books to foreign countries, I can think of no better series than the U. S. Army Area Handbooks, available from the U. S. Government Printing Office. For each country on which they issue a handbook, there is detailed information concerning the government, the geography of the land, the ethnic and religious make-up of the people and chapters on manufacturing, commerce, military preparedness, etc. Each book is a veritable treasure-trove of information about the country described. At present, the following countries are available but new ones are being added regularly:

Albania   Argentina
Algeria   Brazil
Angola   Burundi

Cambodia	Malaysia
Ceylon	Mongolia
Peoples Republic of China	Morocco
Republic of China	Mozambique
Colombia	Nicaragua
Costa Rica	North Korea
Cyprus	North Vietnam
Ecuador	Oceania
Ethiopia	Pakistan
Germany	Panama
Guatamala	Philippines
Guyana	Rwanda
India	Saudi Arabia
Indonesia	Senegal
Iran	Somalia
Iraq	South Africa
Israel	South Vietnam
Japan	Soviet Union
Jordan	Syria
Kenya	Thailand
Korea	Uganda
Laos	United Arab Republic
Lebanon	Uruguay
Liberia	Venezuela
Libya	Zambia

One of the most common geographical questions is for locations of places, pronunciation of names, capital cities, heights of
mountains, etc. The easiest place to find those answers is in a
good gazetteer.

Columbia-Lippincott Gazetteer of the World, ed. by Leon E. Seltzer.
    Columbia University Press, 1952. (ISBN 0-231-01559-3)
    The names of all of the political sub-divisions of the world,
the rivers, the deserts, the mountains, and other geographical features are arranged in alphabetical order. Over 130,000 names are
listed; for each is given its location, elevation and in some cases
industry or agriculture found there.

Webster's New Geographical Dictionary, by Merriam-Webster Edi-
    torial Staff. Rev. ed. Merriam-Webster, 1972. (ISBN 0-
    87779-146-5)
    Not quite as complete as the Lippincott, this is smaller and
easier to use. 40,000 geographical names are arranged alphabetically, including both current places and historical names. For
each place location, area, population, elevation, etc. are given.
Some small maps are included. There is an introductory section
which defines common geographical terms.

Standard Encyclopedia of the World's Mountains, ed. by Anthony
    Huxley. Putnam, 1969. (ISBN 0-399-10245-0)
Standard Encyclopedia of the World's Oceans and Islands, ed. by
    Anthony Huxley. Putnam, 1969. (ISBN 0-399-10246-9)

Standard Encyclopedia of the World's Rivers and Lakes, ed. by
    Anthony Huxley.   Putnam, 1966.   (ISBN 0-399-10247-7)
    Together these three books from a comprehensive guide to
most of the world's natural formations.   They give locations and
dimensions of each mountain or body of water as well as a brief
history and description.   It is more than a gazetteer and less than
a guide book.

GEOLOGY

Dictionary of Geological Terms, ed. by American Geological Insti-
    tute.   Doubleday, 1962.   (ISBN 0-385-01491-0)
    This contains definitions of 7500 words and geological terms
for the use of the student or teacher in the study of rocks, fossils
and minerals.

Field Guide to Rocks and Minerals, by Frederick H. Pough.   Hough-
    ton-Mifflin, 1953.   (ISBN 0-395-08106-8)
    This is another of the Roger Peterson guide series and is
excellent for identifying various rocks and minerals.   There are
photographs of rocks and minerals and in cases where crystal formations are important for identification, there are diagrams of the
crystal shape.   For each rock or mineral, there is a discussion of
its use and properties and various testing methods that can be used
in identification.

GOLF

    As in the other sections dealing with sports, this section does
not list items on how to play golf, since these can easily be found
in your card catalog.   Here will be found books on the history and
great players of the game.

Golf Magazine's Encyclopedia of Golf, ed. by Robert Scharff.   Har-
    per & Row, 1973.   (ISBN 0-06-011574-2)
    An encyclopedia of golf facts, history, rules, etc.   The entire
official rules of the game are given here as well as a discussion of
golf history, club and ball development, great personalities, etc.

The Masters: Profile of a Tournament, by Dawson Taylor.   A. S.
    Barnes, 1973.   (ISBN 0-498-01251-4)
    The definitive listing of the most prestigious golf tourney of
them all.   There are photographs of the course, the players and historic spots on the course.   Each tournament is fully described and
important players identified and written about.

The Story of American Golf, by Herbert Wind.   Greenwood Press,

1972.   (ISBN 0-8371-5991-1)
The history of the game of golf as it is played in America, with a brief account of its earlier history. The growth of the popularity of the game is discussed and the various tournaments listed with winners and important events. There are biographical sketches of the great names of golf.

Golfer's Miscellany, ed. by Percy Huggins. Harper & Row, 1971.
(ISBN 0-06-011979-9)
Interesting facts, feats, funny stories and extraordinary occurrences in the game of golf.

GOVERNMENT
see also
CONGRESS; CONSTITUTIONS; ELECTIONS

The section will deal with governmental organizations on all levels. In addition, several general books such as dictionaries and handbooks are mentioned.

American Political Dictionary, by Jack Charles Plano.   3rd ed.
Holt, Rinehart and Winston, 1972.   (ISBN 0-03-091281-4)
A dictionary of political terms divided into 18 large groups dealing with American policies. It provides a reliable glossary of terms used at all levels of American government.

Political Handbook and Atlas of the World, ed. by Richard Stebbins.
Simon & Schuster. Annual since 1927.
Although announced as an annual, its publication schedule is flexible and it does not always appear each year. Each independent government is listed giving important officials, parties, newspapers and important political events. Good for very brief answers but not comparable to the Statesman's Yearbook in coverage.

Statesman's Yearbook: Statistical and Historical Annual of All the
States of the World. St. Martin's Press. Annual since 1864.
This is a basic tool for world-wide governmental information. It presents both written and tabular information of all sorts dealing with the governments of the world. For the United States, there is a section for the national government and for each of the states. For each governmental unit discussed, the following information is given: the ruler, the constitution and government, area, population, religious statistics, programs of social welfare, justice, education, finances, defense and all other phases of government. It gives a list of major diplomatic representatives to and from each country. There are also bibliographies on each country and a section on the United Nations. This is a must book for any library.

NATIONAL GOVERNMENT

U. S. Government Manual. U. S. Govt. Printing Office, annual since
1935.
Formerly called the U. S. Governmental Organizational Manual, the name has recently been shortened to emphasize its new
approach of making information available to everyone and not just
to the governmental specialist. This handbook describes each government agency, its creation and authority, its function and officers.
It covers all three branches of the national government--executive,
legislative and judicial. In addition, there are brief descriptions of
even quasi-official organizations and a few international organizations. It contains many charts and diagrams showing the organization of every branch of government and major independent agencies.
In other words, anything you need to know about your government
in Washington. This is another book which should be in every library.

STATE GOVERNMENT

Almost every state publishes a volume similar to the U. S.
Government Manual. This is usually available from the Clerk of
the Senate of the State Legislature and will bear a title similar to
"Legislative Manual of the State of _____." For a general publication dealing with every aspect of state government from the
governor's office on down, see the following:

The Book of the States. Published by the Council of State Governments. Biennial since 1935.
This is a comprehensive guide to state governments. For
each state there is a directory of officials, general information and
statistics, and many articles dealing with the problems and recent
developments of state governments in the past biennium.

MUNICIPAL GOVERNMENT

Many cities publish an annual report of the city government;
the title may vary from Handbook to Annual Report to some descriptive title, but it can be obtained from the City Council or other
governing body.
For a comprehensive overview of municipal governmental
activities for each year, the following is important.

Municipal Yearbook. International City Managers. Annual since
1934.
This is an authoritative resumé of activities and statistical
data about all American cities. The information is presented in two
ways: signed articles dealing with local developments in each field
of municipal concern, i. e., taxes, fire, police, etc., followed by
statistical tables giving information on individual cities. There is
a directory of all major municipal employees for each city and a
good bibliography on municipal problems.

GOVERNMENT PUBLICATIONS

The world's most prolific publisher is the U. S. Government but the problem is finding and utilizing the materials being published.

Monthly Catalog of United States Publications.   U. S. Government
   Printing Office, 1895-
   This is a comprehensive listing of all publications issued by various agencies of the United States Government.   It lists not only all materials available from the Superintendent of Documents but also materials published for committee use only.   This is a must for any library needing a full coverage of government publications.

Selected United States Government Publication.   U. S. Government
   Printing Office, bi-weekly since 1942.
   This free publication, sent to any library requesting it, lists those items which the Office of the Superintendent of Documents feels will be of most interest to the general public.   Good as a documents selection tool, and the price is right.   Recommended for every library.

Price Lists of Government Publications.   U. S. Government Printing
   Office.   Revised as needed.
   This might be called a subject guide to government publications in that there are 46 pamphlets each dealing with a different subject, listing pertinent government publications and order information for related materials.   It is a good selection tool, often helpful in finding just the right publication.   Again the price is right: free to any library requesting them.

Annotated List of Selected Government Publications, by Sylvia
   Mechanic.   H. W. Wilson, 1971.   (ISBN 0-8242-0405-0)
   This is a selective annotated list of government publications. It is arranged by Superintendent of Documents number but materials are easily found by use of the series and title index.   For each document or series of documents listed, there is a facsimile Library of Congress card giving full catalog entry information and then, where needed, a brief annotation giving the purpose and type of publication.

Subject Guide to Government Reference Books, by Sally Wynkoop.
   Littleton, Colo.: Libraries Unlimited, 1972.   (ISBN 0-87287-
   025-1)
   A subject guide to government publications arranged in two sections.   The first lists various bibliographic aids, the second is an alphabetical listing by broad subject fields.   Each publication listed is fully annotated and full order information is given.   Necessary for any library having a large documents collection, it would be less valuable to the smaller library.

GRANTS IN AID
see
FELLOWSHIPS; COLLEGES AND UNIVERSITIES; FOUNDATIONS

GRASSES

Grass (Yearbook of Agriculture-1948). U. S. Department of Agriculture. U. S. Government Printing Office (A 1. 10/year).
   This yearbook is devoted entirely to the various types of
grass in the United States, both cultivated and wild. For each type
is given its geographical distribution and if it is a hybrid, its historical background. It covers all types of grasses including cereals
such as rye and wheat as well as forage crops. Excellent bibliographies are combined with a good index.

Manual of Grasses of the United States, by A. S. Hitchcock. 2nd
   rev. ed. U. S. Government Printing Office, 1951. (A 1. 38:
   200/2) (Also a reprint: Peter Smith, ISBN 0-8446-0309-0)
   All grasses of the United States are described and illustrated
by drawings and identified by special identification keys. For each
variety, both the common and scientific names are given, plus
geographic range, uses and possible commercial value.

GUIDED MISSILES

Jane's Weapons Systems, ed. by R. T. Pretty. Franklin Watts.
   Annual since 1970.
   This is a definitive work on the sophisticated weapons systems currently ready for use by the nations of the world. A weapons system, as contrasted to a weapon, is considered to be self-
contained, with its own sensors and control. This is the seventh of
the series of yearbooks edited by Jane's and while it does not yet
reach the heights of All The World's Aircraft or Fighting Ships it
gives good coverage of the field, including full specifications, range
and method of use for each system. Naturally, many weapons systems fall in the category of guided missiles.

Spacecraft and Missiles of the World, by William E. Howard. Rev.
   ed. Harcourt Brace Jovanovich, 1966. (ISBN 0-15-184700-2)
   Before the advent of Jane's Weapons Systems, this was the
most comprehensive work on the subject of guided missiles. It is
now fairly dated but it does give good technical data and specifications for all missiles up to 1966.

GUNS
see
ARMAMENTS; FIREARMS

HALL OF FAME

There are Halls of Fame for almost every organized activity in this country. Particularly prevalent are those for each sports activity; for these see the individual sport; e.g., for the Baseball Hall of Fame in Cooperstown, N.Y., see BASEBALL.

For the Hall of Fame of Great Americans located in New York City, the following almanancs have a full listing of persons elected. These almanacs also have lists of each of the sports Halls of Fame; see Hall of Fame in their indexes.

Information Please Almanac, ed. by Dan Golenpaul. Dan Golenpaul Associates. Annual since 1946.

World Almanac and Book of Facts, ed. by George Delury. Newspaper Enterprise Association. Annual since 1868.

HALLMARKS

Strictly speaking, hallmarks are only used as identifying marks on gold and silverware to indicate that the mateials meet the established standards of production but it has taken on two additional meanings, the first as a mark of excellence and more commonly as an identifying mark of the manufacturer. It also has been extended to include pewter, china, pottery, porcelain as well. The following books index the various hallmarks and identify them by date and artisan. Both are well illustrated. The first title covers gold, silver and pewter; the second, pottery and porcelain.

Dictionary of Marks, by Margaret McDonald-Taylor. Hawthorn, 1962.

Collector's Handbook of Marks and Monograms on Pottery and Porcelain, by William Chaffers. Dover Press, 1968. (ISBN 0-486-22387-6)

HANDICRAFTS

There are literally thousands of books dealing with arts and crafts and on each individual hobby. Only the most helpful general books are listed here.

Creative Crafts for Everyone, by G. Alan Turner.   Viking Press,
     1959.   (ISBN 0-670-24633-6)
          This book was written by the editor of Design Magazine and
is filled with ideas that cost little but present a great challenge. It
tells how to make decorations, home furnishings, clothing and
accessories.   The instructions, though concise, are quite easily
followed but leave room for the creative talent of the worker.

Practical Encyclopedia of Crafts, by Louis DiValentin.   Sterling
     Press, 1971.   (ISBN 0-8069-5151-6)
          A true encyclopedia of the crafts, this has articles about
almost any craft imaginable.   For each, it outlines its virtues and
its drawbacks as well as tools and equipment needed and a bibliography of other books which will be helpful.   Although not really
helpful for the individual craft it is an excellent introduction to each
one.

Formulas, Methods and Tips for Home and Workshop, by Kenneth
     M. Swezey.   Popular Science Publications, 1969.   (ISBN 0-
     87468-042-5)
          Formulas for use around the home, i. e., removing stains,
etc.   These are arranged alphabetically by broad categories but a
good index is helpful in finding desired materials.

                    HARBORS AND PORTS

Ports Due, Charges and Accommodations; the Blue Book of Shipping.
     International Publications Service, annual since 1940.
          This is the shipowner's, agent's and charterer's guide to the
ports of the world.   It gives the longitude and latitude of each port
along with its major imports and exports and charges for the use of
the port and its facilities.   For each port listed, there are statistics concerning total tonnage, population, equipment available and
the authority under which the port operates.   It is arranged first by
continents and then alphabetically by city.

Ports of the World, ed. by V. A. J. Wakely, London.   Benn
     Brothers, annual since 1946.
          For each port listed, the exact geographical location is listed
along with full statistics concerning population, major imports, exports, number and size of vessels that it can accommodate, as well
as the authority under which the port operates.   It also lists the
rules of traffic and pilotage as well as the fees and charges for the
use of the port and facilities.   There is a full listing of equipment
available.   The book is arranged by continent first and then alphabetically by city.

World Port Index, by U. S. Naval Oceanographic Office.   U. S. Gov-
     ernment Printing Office, Irregular since 1957.   (TC 1. 34:year)
          This is primarily a collection of the sailing directions pub-

lished by the Naval Oceanographic Office. Each port is assigned an index number and each entry gives the exact location and sailing directions for entering and leaving the port. Since ports have different names in different languages, there is an index to the various ports by variant names and spellings.

HEATING

Heating Handbook, by Robert H. Emerick. McGraw-Hill, 1964.
    (ISBN 0-07-019300-2)
        A collection of faults and problems involved in a home heating plant with possible solutions and ways of effecting them.

Handy Man's Plumbing and Heating Guide, by Larry Eisinger. Arco,
    1952. (ISBN 0-668-00372-3)
        Excellent for its type, this is a fairly complete handbook of home heating and plumbing problems. It contains a glossary of heating and plumbing terms and directions for making home repairs on the heating plant. It has good pictures to accompany the instructions.

Home Guide to Plumbing, Heating and Air Conditioning, by George
    Daniels. Harper & Row, 1967. (ISBN 0-06-010941-6)
        This has much the same information as the other books listed but it is slightly newer and therefore a little better for newer homes or furnaces.

HELICOPTERS

Jane's All The World's Aircraft, ed. by John W. Taylor. Franklin
    Watts. Annual since 1909.
        There is no better source for information concerning individual aircraft. For each aircraft, including helicopters, there is given full and detailed specifications concerning the size, the load carrying capacity and special features dealing with engines and construction. There are photographs of each aircraft along with line drawings. This is an annual publication which adds new planes each year and deletes obsolete models, so that it is a good policy to keep back issues of the book. The book is arranged by country and then alphabetically by company manufacturing planes. A good index both to company and to model of plane facilites finding individual planes or helicopters.

Helicopters and Other Rotorcraft Since 1907, by Kenneth Munson.
    Macmillan, 1969. (ISBN 0-02-58803)
        This is a brief but interesting history of the rotorcraft of the world. There are 72 pages of color plates followed by a discussion

of each craft pictured. For each is given the armament if military, the type of engine, the diameter of the rotor, the maximum pay load, maximum speed and range. This is not a comprehensive collection but rather an analysis of the important planes in helicopter history. There is an index by name of the plane as well as the manufacturer.

Vertical Flight Aircraft of the World, by F. G. Swanborough. Aero Publ., 1964.

This is a listing of current models of the vertical flight aircraft of the world as of 1965. Not as up to date as the Jane's book, but since it is devoted entirely to VTOL aircraft, it is somewhat easier to use. The book is arranged by manufacturer and then by model number of the various planes. For each plane the usual technical data are given, along with a photograph of the plane in flight.

HERALDRY

A Glossary of Terms Used in Heraldry, by Henry Gough. Gale, 1966 (reprint of 1894 ed.).

This one is listed first because, among all the reference questions you may have, one of the most specialized vocabularies will be in the field of heraldry where such terms are bar sinister, gule, etc. are in common usage but obscure to the person not used to heraldric terms. This is actually more than a glossary, though; it gives illustrations of many symbols used and illustrations of coats of arms.

Crozier's General Armory: A Registry of American Families Entitled to Coat of Armor, by William A. Crozier. Genealogical Publications, 1972 (reprint of 1904 ed.).

This is a listing of authorized coats of arms for use by Americans (not everyone who wants a coat of arms is actually entitled to use one). This book is arranged by family name and for each family there is a discussion of the crest and the motto. Not too well illustrated except for a few line drawings. Used to illustrate the meanings of terms.

Burke's Peerage: Genealogical and Heraldic History of the Peerage, Baronetage and Knightage. International Publications Service. Biennial since 1824.

This is the Bible of English peerage. For each member entitled to listing as landed gentry there is a tracing of the name and the family from the earliest order of knighthood to the present day. There is a brief biographical sketch of the present head of the family and names of his family. A copy of his coat of arms precedes the name of the family.

Despite our previous warning, many persons who have no

official right to a coat of arms want one and many will want to design their own despite the fact that it will have no official or reliable usage. For these persons, the following books are recommended in that they point out what the various symbols and colors are meant to represent on a coat of arms. The coats of arms designed with their use will still be unofficial but at least they will be genealogically correct.

Encyclopedic Dictionary of Heraldry, by Julian Franklyn. Pergamon
  Press, 1970. (ISBN 0-08-013297-9)
Heraldry for the Designer, by William Metzig. Van Nostrand Rein-
  hold, 1970. (ISBN 0-442-11354-4)

HEREDITY
see also
GENETICS

Almost every good text book on biology has a chapter on genetic theory and any adult encyclopedia will have a good article on the subject. However, for a more detailed and specific article on the subject the following encyclopedia is recommended.

Encyclopedia of Biological Sciences, ed. by Peter Gray. 2nd ed.
  Van Nostrand Reinhold, 1970. (ISBN 0-442-15629-4)
  This is a one-volume encyclopedia entirely devoted to the biological sciences. There are 800 subject areas about which specialists have written signed articles. These long articles are detailed in their definitions, explanations and descriptions. There is an excellent section on genetics with a good bibliography. This reference book is simply enough written to be of use to the high school student as well as to the biological specialist.

HISTORIANS

American Men and Women of Science, ed. by Jaques Cattell Press.
  12th ed. Bowker, 1971-1973. 8 vols.
  This eight-volume set comes in two parts. Part I is Physical and Biological Sciences. Part II is Social and Behavioral Sciences and includes biographies of historians. For each person, the Who's Who type of information is given, i.e., date and place of birth, parents, education, publications, associations, present position, etc.

Directory of American Scholars, ed. by Jaques Cattell Press. 5th
  ed. R. R. Bowker, 1969. 4 vols including index.
  This biographical dictionary to American scholars was published with the support of the American Council of Learned Societies

and includes over 33,000 biographical sketches of the scholars of America. Each volume is devoted to persons of a specific discipline, chosen on the basis of their training, their publications and their importance in the field. There is an index to names so that a person can be located even if you are unaware of his specialty. Volume I is devoted to historians and in it you will find the normal Who's Who type of entry.

Famous Historians, by Frank Hill. Dodd, Mead, 1966. (ISBN 0-396-05286-X)
   Although written on a very elementary level (it is intended for junior high school students), this does give a good background of the life and times of the classic historians.

HISTORY

Many facets of history are covered by specific sections in this book, e.g., BATTLES, CHRONOLOGY, DOCUMENTS, DATES, KINGS AND RULERS etc. This section is devoted primarily to encyclopedic type coverage of the broad field rather than material on specific events or persons.

BIBLIOGRAPHIES

Guide to Historical Literature, ed. by George Frederick Howe. Macmillan, 1961. (ISBN 0-02-55516)
   This is more than a good bibliography. Its critical comments and notes evaluate the books listed as well as giving sources of other reviews. There is a classified listing of books in all fields of history. It is quite good for general use and particularly for out of print items.

Guide to the Study of the United States of America, ed. by General Reference and Bibliography Section, U.S. Library of Congress. U.S. Government Printing Office, 1960.
   There are 32 chapters dealing with every aspect of American life and history: literature, geography, military history, local history, general history; in other words, every facet of American culture. There are over 6000 entries, many of them annotated and many containing references to other works. The big handicap is that coverage is limited to the period prior to 1958.

Harvard Guide to American History, ed. by Oscar Handlin. Harvard University Press, 1954. (ISBN 0-674-37550-5)
   Despite its date of publication, this remains one of the prime bibliographical sources of American historical writings.

INDEXES

America: History and Life, A Guide to Periodical Literature.

American Bibliographic Center, since 1964.

Historical Abstracts, A Bibliography of the World's Periodical Literature. American Bibliographic Center, since 1955.

These two publications are abstract journals. The Historical Abstracts deals with periodical articles on world history and America:History and Life deals with periodical articles about American history. Both indexes while including articles from all parts of the world, are heavily American in nature. Both the United States and Canada are included in America: History and Life.

GENERAL HISTORIES

Cambridge Ancient History. Cambridge University Press. 12 vols.
Cambridge Medieval History. Cambridge University Press. 8 vols.
Cambridge Modern History. Cambridge University Press. 12 vols.

These three sets are the basic general histories for the periods covered. They are useful not only because of their highly readable presentation of facts but also because of the bibliographies and supplement tables. For example, Modern History has genealogical tables and lists of ruling houses; Ancient History has lists of Kings of Ancient History, etc. Each of the three sets is written by specialists and each offers full bibliographies at the end of each volume. These three sets are almost a must for even the smallest library.

AMERICAN HISTORY

For histories of individual states see AMERICAN GUIDE SERIES in this volume. For general history of the U. S. A. see:

Dictionary of American History, ed. by James Truslow Adams.
Scribner's, 1940-1963. 6 vols and index. (available only by direct order from publisher; not available through book trade)

Brief articles, each signed by a noted authority, dealing with every facet of American history. It does not give biographies of historical figures, only mentions them in connection with specific events, since it is a companion to the Dictionary of American Biography. This book lists in alphabetical order political, social, military and cultural events. Important laws, battles or social events are listed by their popular name.

Oxford History of the American People, by Samuel E. Morison.
Oxford University Press, 1965. (ISBN 0-19-50030-7)

Some may object to Professor Morison's approach to history since he tells it from a personal viewpoint. You may disagree with his interpretations but the facts are there and you can enjoy them even while disagreeing. This is a history not so much of the United States as a nation of America as a people.

Pageant of America: A Pictorial History of the United States, ed. by Ralph Henry Gabriel. Yale University Press, 1925-1929. 15 vols.

This is a pictorial account of America divided into 15 large subject subdivisions. Although there is a readable text the import-

ant aspect of this work is its pictures and it would be a prime
source of pictorial information on all subjects dealing with American
history.

ATLASES, HISTORICAL

Shepherd's Historical Atlas, by William R. Shepherd. 9th ed. rev.
and updated. Harper & Row, 1973. (ISBN 0-06-013846-7)
Possibly the classic in the field of historical atlases, for
many years this was out of print. For a while it seemed that the
book would never be revised due to the destruction of the original
plates during the bombings of Germany but this new edition has been
done by offset lithography and preserves the excellent maps and
texts complete. It has been augmented by an additional segment
prepared by C. S. Hammond and Company which brings the historical
atlas right down to 1973. For each historical period and for each
country there are historical maps showing battle fields, changing
boundaries and political subdivisions. There is a good index by
which any city or country can be located on any of several maps.
It contains 232 maps and 80 insets all in full color.

Atlas of American History, ed. by James Truslow Adams. Scribner's, 1943. (available only on direct order from publisher;
not sold through book trade)
This is a companion volume to the above mentioned Dictionary of American History. It includes 147 black and white maps with
an index to cities, counties, battlefields and other locations found on
those maps. The maps are arranged in sequence to show growth,
expansion, military conquest, etc. The index refers to both current
and historical names of places.

HOCKEY

Famous Hockey Players, by Trent Frayne. Dodd, Mead, 1973.
(ISBN 0-396-06848-0)
A biographical listing of the greats of ice hockey. Although
hero-worshiping in tone, it gives a readable short life of the men
who have made hockey exciting over the years.

The Pocket Hockey Encyclopedia, by the National Hockey League Research Statisticians. Scribner's, 1972. (ISBN 0-684-13070-X)
Gives latest rules as well as hockey records by player and
by team. This is the statistical handbook of the sport.

The Thinking Man's Guide to Pro Hockey, by Gerald Eskenazi. Dutton, 1972. (ISBN 0-525-21731-2)
An excellent introduction to hockey as a spectator sport. It
lists latest rules, tells you what to look for in play and how to anticipate actions.

Who's Who in Hockey, by Harry C. Kariher. Arlington House, 1973.
(ISBN 0-87000-221-X)
This provides brief biographical sketches of all current major
league hockey players as well as outstanding players of the past.

HOLIDAYS
see also
FESTIVALS
and names of individual holidays, e.g., CHRISTMAS

American Book of Days, by George William Douglas. 2nd ed.
H. W. Wilson Co., 1948. (ISBN 0-8242-0002-0)
"A compendium of information about holidays, festivals, notable anniversaries and holy days both Christian and Jewish with
notes concerning other American anniversaries worth remembering"
--subtitle. This is a day-by-day arrangement of the important holidays of the American year with a good index.

Anniversaries and Holidays, by Mary Emogene Hazeltine. 2nd ed.
American Library Association, 1944. (ISBN 0-8389-0009-7)
"A calendar of days and how to observe them"--subtitle.
This is a chronological arrangement, first, month by month, and
then daily, of all the anniversaries and celebrations, primarily in
America but world-wide in scope. Not only does it list holidays
but also gives some indication of means of celebrating them. Ex-
cellent bibliography of related works.

Book of Days: A Miscellany of Popular Antiquities in Connection
With The Calendar..., ed. by Robert Chambers. 2 vols. Gale
Research, 1967 (reprint of 1886 ed.).
Although very dated, this is probably the very best of the
books dealing with dates and holidays. It is also arranged by month
and day and then giving things that happened on those days in history. It is more than a directory of holidays since it gives information for every day of the year.

HONORARY SOCIETIES
see
FRATERNITIES AND SORORITIES; ASSOCIATIONS

HORSE RACING
see
RACING

HORSES

America's Horses and Ponies, by Irene Brady.   Houghton Mifflin,
     1969.   (ISBN 0-395-06659-X)
     This gives the history, appearance and conformation and per-
formance of 50 different breeds of American horses ranging from
the Arabian down to types of Zebras.   There is a section which describes the various gaits and means of teaching them.

Horses in America, by Francis Haines.   Crowell, 1971.   (ISBN 0-
     690-40395-X)
     This is a study of the importance of the horse in the history
of American development.   There are maps and charts showing the
types and distribution of equine animals from pre-history to the present day.

Horses, Their Breeding, Care and Handling, by Heather S. Thomas.
     A. S. Barnes, 1973.   (ISBN 0-498-01072-4)
     The subtitle of this book outlines its coverage.   It deals with
descriptions of various types of horses and the necessary steps for
proper care and handling.

Horseman's Encyclopedia, by Margaret C. Self.   Arco, 1973.   (ISBN
     0-668-02777-0)
     This is a typical encyclopedic type publication with short
articles, alphabetically arranged, dealing with almost every aspect
of horses.   This includes their breeding, their care and the use of
horses for all purposes both utilitarian and sport.   Good for historical background as well as current information.

HOSPITALS

Hospital Literature Index.   American Hospital Association, Quart-
     erly with annual cumulation since 1945.
     An index to literature dealing with hospitals and hospital man-
agement.

Hospital Statistics.   American Hospital Association, annual.
     All types of statistics concerning hospital admissions, costs,
doctors in service, nurses, etc.

Hospitals Magazine, ed. by James E. Hague.   American Hospital
     Association, semi-monthly since 1936.
     This is the official publication of the American Hospital As-
sociation and the June issue each year, the "Administrator's Guide
Issue, " acts as a directory to hospitals and hospital administrators
around the country.

HOTELS AND MOTELS

Hotel and Motel Red Book. American Hotel Association Directory
Corporation, annual since 1886.
This is the official directory of American Hotels and Motels
Association members and includes hotels not only in the United
States but in major cities and resort areas around the world. Ar-
ranged by state or by country; for each hotel it gives number of
rooms, rates, address, etc.

In addition, there are two series of annual publications which
are excellent guides to hotels of the world.

The Michelin Red Travel Guides, distributed annually by the French
and European Publications Incorporated.
The most authoritative, comprehensive and trustworthy of
hotel guides for the countries covered. At present there are guides
to France, Italy, the Benelux countries, Germany, Spain and Por-
tugal and guides to the cities of Paris and New York. This provides
information concerning location, prices and special features.

The Fodor Travel Guides, published annually by Donald McKay Co.
In addition to normal travel information, gives lists of suggested hotels in each price range; however, it does not give exact
prices. There are 23 countries at present. For the full list see
the publisher's list in the Publisher's Trade List Annual.

HUNTING
see also
FIREARMS

Hunter's Handbook, by Jerome Knap. Scribner's, 1973. (ISBN
0-684-13569-8)
An illustrated guide to hunting and firearms, with data concerning every type of hunting done in the United States. Various
weapons, short guns, etc. are described and their use discussed.

New Hunter's Encyclopedia, ed. by Leonard Miracle. Stackpole
Press, 1965. (ISBN 0-8117-0860-8)
A quick reference book for a multitude of questions concerning waterfowl, game birds and animals in North America. It gives
hints on hunting methods and equipment, and where to find each type
of game, as well as the keeping of game records and a summary of
national laws concerning hunting.

Pocket Guide to Animal Tracks. Stackpole Press, 1968. (ISBN 0-
8117-1290-7)
A well illustrated guide to the tracks of the birds and animals
of the woods and how to recognize them.

HYMNS

Dictionary of Hymnology, by John Julian. 2nd ed. Dover Press,
1907. 2 vols.
This contains almost all the Christian hymns from all nations
that will be found in the ordinary church hymnal, for the most part
limited to English language hymnals. There are articles dealing with
writers of hymns, individual hymns and the various aspects of hymnology. It is alphabetically arranged with important articles signed
and often carrying bibliographies.

IDIOMS

Almost any dictionary will list and define many of the idioms
in common use today and should be consulted first. For slang
idioms and the speech of the underworlds see the heading SLANG in
this book.

Concise Dictionary of English Idioms, by William Freeman. 2nd ed.
Writer, 1963. (ISBN 0-87116-023-4)
Although called a dictionary of English idioms, this lists
American idioms as well. They are arranged alphabetically by key
word and are defined, using examples in sentences as well as formal
definitions. It contains almost 4000 idioms in common use in Britain and America and should be an excellent source for the new
learner of English. Also helpful to the average person who runs
across an idiom in his everyday reading which he does not recognize.

INCOME TAX

Here there is an embarrassment of riches since there are so
many sources of information available for the user that no library
can possibly stock them all. The following are a selection which
the editor believes to be among the most useful in the completion of
income tax forms. For just a simple listing of general provisions
and for tables of deductions and payments as well as statistics on
income tax collections, my favorite books of reference are useful
sources:

World Almanac and Book of Facts. Newspaper Enterprise Associ-
ates. Annual since 1868.
Information Please Almanac, ed. by Dan Golenpaul, Dan Golenpaul
Associates, Annual since 1946.

For more detailed information concerning filing of taxes see:

Your Federal Income Tax for the year.   Internal Revenue Service,
   U. S. Dept. of the Treasury.   U. S. Government Printing Office.
   Annual.
      This is designed by the Commissioner of Internal Revenue to
help you with the preparation of your income tax.   It is written in
plain language and uses completed income tax forms and schedules
to indicate the proper way to make reports and to take legal deductions.   It is quite comprehensive and should be adequate for most
questions.

J. K. Lasser's Your Income Tax, prepared by the Lasser Tax Institute.   Simon & Schuster.   Annual.
      This is probably the most popular of all the income tax
guides and is quite simply written and easily understood.   The important feature is an excellent index which makes it easy to find
and understand information concerning deductions, income reporting,
income averaging and all the rest of the complicated features of the
whole operation.   It can be used not only at tax time for figuring
the tax but also throughout the year to figure future tax strategy.

How to Save Time and Money on Filing Your Personal Tax Return.
   Prentice Hall.   Annual.
      This is a portion of the Federal Tax Bulletin series published
by Prentice Hall which covers every aspect of federal taxation in the
United States.   This pamphlet, number 51, is published annually and
deals with the filing of the income tax forms.   It can be purchased
separately.   It explains in simple terms the procedures to be used
in determining the proper forms to use and the proper methods of
filing the report.   There are completely filled out forms to illustrate every contingency.   Once again, an excellent index helps tre-
mendously.

INDIANS

      Every major encyclopedia has excellent articles dealing with
the American Indian and these probably will answer many of your
general questions.   The one best source for information concerning
Indians of America is the following:

Handbook of American Indians North of Mexico, by Frederick W.
   Hodge.   Rowman & Littlefield.   (reprint of 1912 ed.).   (ISBN
   0-87471-004-9)
      This is a publication of the Bureau of American Ethnology
and is an excellent scholarly work dealing with every facet of the
history, culture, and life of the American Indian in the area that is
now the United States and Canada.   It has sections on Indian languages, tribes, and possibly most importantly, biographical information
on important Indian leaders, often with a black and white picture.
There is an excellent index.

Indians of the United States: Four Centuries of Their History and
   Culture by Clark Wissler. Doubleday, 1966. (ISBN 0-385-
   00757-4)
       This is a popularized introduction to the anthropology of the
United States and unlike the Hodge book is quite up to date. Each
chapter is devoted to a different facet of Indian culture and life.
One interesting aspect of the book is an appendix in which there are
questions and answers concerning the Indian.

The American Indian, by Clark Wissler. 3rd ed. Peter Smith, 1957.
   (ISBN 0-8446-1482-3)
       Unlike the previously mentioned book, this one is not entirely
devoted to Indians of North America but mentions Indians in both the
continents of the New World. It has a general treatment of such
subjects as food, religion, agriculture, social customs and mythology.
There are specific treatments of such things as physical appearance
of the various tribes, languages and artifacts and archeology. There
is a large two-part map which identifies the home locations of each
of the many tribes of the Indians of America.

INSECTS

       The United States Government, and particularly the Depart-
ment of Agriculture, has some of the best materials concerning insects; especially insects as they affect the agriculture of this country.
For a complete listing of the publications available from the government on the subject see:

Price List #41. Superintendent of Documents. U. S. Government
   Printing Office. Irregular since 1898.
       The complete list of price lists of the Superintendent of Docu-
ments Office arranged by broad subject areas is available free of
charge from the U. S. Government Printing Office.

Yearbook of Agriculture, 1952. U. S. Department of Agriculture.
   U. S. Government Printing Office. Annual since 1895.
       The 1952 Yearbook is devoted entirely to insects, especially
insect pests and their control. It is well indexed and has several
excellent bibliographies. It also has 72 color plates of insects for
identification, with descriptions and data concerning ways of control-
ling them.

Field Book of Insects of the United States and Canada, by Frank E.
   Lutz. Rev. ed. Putnam, 1948. (ISBN 0-399-10289-2)
       A well illustrated guide book for the identification of the
many insects of the United States. For each one there is a description as well as sizes, colors, likely geographical distribution
and all factors needed for true identification.

INSURANCE AND INSURANCE COMPANIES

Dictionary of Insurance, by Lewis E. Davids. 2nd ed. Rowman,
   1970.
   This is a dictionary of terms used in the insurance field and
the words commonly associated with that field.

Best's Insurance Reports, Life-Health. Best, annual since 1906.
Best's Key Rating Guide: Property-Liability. Best, annual since
   1906.
   These two reports cover the whole insurance field, both personal and property insurance. They supply, in a quick way, the
most up-to-date information concerning the various insurance companies, showing their financial conditions, general standing, and
types of insurance offered.

Moody's Bank and Financial Manual, ed. by Roy H. Krause. Moody's
   Investors Service, annual.
   The final two sections of the Bank and Finance Manual deal
with insurance companies. For each company is given the offices,
the number of employees, subsidiaries or parent organizations, Board
of Trustee members, a full financial statement and credit rating.
The Moody services are excellent source material for all financial
information but must be used with an index because the arrangement
is poorly organized.

INTERNAL REVENUE
see
INCOME TAX

INTERNATIONAL RELATIONS

   This is another broad field in which only the more general
reference items are given here. For information concerning
TREATIES or DOCUMENTS of international importance, see those
headings in this book. See also FOREIGN AFFAIRS.

Deadline Data on Foreign Affairs. Deadline Data, Inc. Bi-weekly
   since 1956.
   This is a basic chronology of important events in the field of
international relations. It is published on 5" x 8" cards which are
updated every other week. There are cards for each country, commercial or military alliance (SEATO, NATO, COMMON MARKET,
etc.), and for each entry the updated cards give the latest political
or military events. Excellent for an overall view of recent events
leading up to current situations. This pinpoints the actual date of
any happening and can be used more or less as an index to the local
newspaper.

Foreign Affairs Bibliography. Various editors. R. R. Bowker.
This vast bibliography has been published since 1932 in ten-
year volumes: 1932-1942, edited by Robert G. Woolbert, 1969
(ISBN 0-8352-0211-9); 1942-1952, edited by Henry L. Roberts, 1969
(ISBN 0-8352-0212-7); 1952-1962, edited by Henry L. Roberts, 1964
(ISBN 0-8352-0046-9). The 1962-1972 volume has been announced
but was not yet published at time of the compilation of this work.
(There is a reprint of the earlier 3-volume set, 1919-1932, available from Russell). This is an annotated guide to the most signifi-
cant books published in the field of foreign relations for the periods
covered. It is a joint project of the Foreign Affairs Magazine and
the Council on International Relations. It lists not only English
language publications but books printed in all parts of the world. It
is the most comprehensive bibliography in the field.

Foreign Affairs: Fifty Years Index, 1922-1972. Council on Foreign
Relations. R. R. Bowker, 1973. (ISBN 0-8352-0584-3)
The Foreign Affairs Magazine is the outstanding periodical
publication in the field. It is published quarterly and contains articles by world leaders and political analysts dealing with every aspect of foreign affairs. This volume, which was published as a
joint effort of the Committee on Foreign Relations and the magazine,
is an alphabetical index to author, title and subject areas of materials which have appeared in that periodical in the fifty-year period.
For each article cited there is full bibliographical information given.

International Relations Dictionary, ed. by Jack C. Plano. Holt,
Rinehart & Winston, 1969. (ISBN 0-03-074675-2)
An excellent discussion of the current language of the foreign
relations field. It is divided into twelve main topical headings but
there is a good index which enables one to find specific information
readily.

INVENTIONS

Questions on inventions are often for information concerning
the safeguarding and patenting of a person's own invention. For information concerning that aspect, see PATENTS in this book.
Specific inventions are often discussed in the major encyclopedias and if one is looking for background on a specific invention
that would be the first place to look.

Famous First Facts, by Joseph N. Kane. 3rd ed. H. W. Wilson
Company, 1964. (ISBN 0-8242-0015-2)
This is a combination of the earlier Famous First Facts and
More First Facts and contains the first happenings in almost every
field in America. This includes the listing of the first patents
granted on various obscure inventions. It will give you information
concerning the date, inventor and use. For detailed information you
will have to look elsewhere.

Official Gazette of the United States Patent Office.   U. S. Patent
    Office, U. S. Government Printing Office.   Weekly since 1872.
    For the person wanting to know everything about a specific
patent, there is no better source than the Official Gazette.   For
each patent, there is a drawing and a full description, not only of
the patent but also of the things that the item will accomplish. This
publication also gives the latest court decisions concerning patents
and trademarks.

INVESTMENTS

    The library cannot be the brokerage business and cannot
safely offer advice on the investment of monies or materials but they
should supply information concerning the various companies in which
persons may wish to invest.   There are many services available for
this type of information and the ones suggested are a purely personal
choice of the writer.

Value Line Investment Survey.   Published by Arnold Bernhard and
    Company, 55 East 44th Street, New York, N. Y. 10017.
    This is a subscriber service to information and advice on
future stock market activities.   It gives advice on the selection of
stocks for the portfolio and how to determine which stocks will best
suit your investment goals.   Each week there are evaluations of
several companies giving full financial analysis of their position and
an estimate of the way that they will perform in the coming months.
Each week's publication gives suggestions of stocks for purchase and
for selling.

Standard and Poor's New York Stock Exchange Stock Reports.   New
    York: Standard and Poors Corporation.
    This subscriber publication provides weekly updated sheets
analyzing various companies as to future and present investment
opportunities.   It gives both short- and long-term prospects and recent dividend data.   The new entry starts out with a recommendation
concerning action to either buy or sell at the time of publication.

Investment Companies, Mutual Funds and Other Types.   Weisen-
    berger Services, annual since 1940.
    This provides information about mutual funds and other invest-
ment companies, with a complete explanation of their functions and
the ways they meet the needs of the individual investor.   There are
data on the investment policy, the management, the historical background and finances of all open and closed investment companies of
the country, including income and dividend records, price ranges
and comparative operating data.   Different aspects of the mutual
fund industry are featured each year, and there are good discussions
of such things as the Keogh plan, tax hints, etc.   A quarterly up-
date of all information is sent to subscribers.

Standard and Poor's Industry Surveys. New York: Standard and
  Poors, quarterly.
      This is basically an industry survey, i. e. how well industries
in specific areas of manufacturing or services are doing and how
well they can be expected to do.   Less useful for specific recommendations but good background information for the serious investor.

IRON

Commodity Yearbook, ed. by Harry Jiler.   Commodity Research
  Bureau, Inc.   Annual since 1939.
      This publication gives prices and production statistics for
each of the various commodities needed for our national welfare.
Under IRON one finds statistics on world iron production as well as
salient statistics of the iron ore industry of the United States. There
are summary statistics for each iron producing state as well as an
estimate of iron ore reserves and probable future value.

Iron Ore.   American Iron Ore Association, 600 Bulkley Bldg. Cleveland, Ohio.   Annual.
      The American Iron Ore Association publishes yearly a com-
pilation of data concerning the production of iron ore in the United
States and Canada, with some mention of world-wide production.   It
gives maps of principal iron producing regions and a review of each
year's activity and future projections.   There are statistical tables
covering every aspect of iron ore production as well as grade names
and analysis, a directory of iron producing companies of the United
States and Canada, and an excellent index.

Minerals Yearbook.   Bureau of Mines.   U. S. Government Printing
  Office.   Annual since 1932.   (I 28. 37)
      A summary of iron ore production by state and region as
well as an analysis of iron ore reserves can be found under the
heading IRON.

Natural Resources for U. S. Growth, by Hans S. Landsberg.   Peter
  Smith, 1963.   (ISBN 0-8446-2423-3)
Trends in Natural Resource Commodities, by Neal Potter.   Johns
  Hopkins Press, 1962.   (ISBN 0-8018-0536-8)
      These two books complement each other.   Trends in Natural
Resource Commodities gives statistics of prices, output, consump-
tion and employment in the industries including iron ore which deal
with our natural resources from 1870-1957.   Natural Resources for
U. S. Growth was originally published by Johns Hopkins Press as a
companion volume and was entitled Resources in America's Future.
It gives patterns and availability of various resources including iron
ore for the years 1960-2000.

IRRIGATION

World Geography of Irrigation, by Leonard M. Cantor, 2nd ed.
Longmans, 1970. (ISBN 0-05-001566-4)
This is a basic introduction. In addition to a fine historical
introduction to irrigation from primitive times to the modern day,
it gives a regional survey of irrigation throughout the world. There
are many photographs of irrigation projects and 50 maps showing
irrigation needs. It has a good bibliography and index.

U. S. Census of Agriculture. U. S. Census Bureau. U. S. Government Printing Office. Published in years ending in 9. (C 3. 31/9)
In the years ending with the number 9, the Five-Year Census
of Agriculture is supplemented with information concerning the irrigation of farm lands and range land of the United States. These
reports cover every county and state in the country and give full
data for type of irrigation used and for what purposes.

ISLAM

Shorter Encyclopedia of Islam, ed. by H. A. Gibbs. Cornell University Press, 1953. (ISBN 0-8014-0150-X)
This is a condensation, with the addition of some new materials, of the British work, An Encyclopedia of Islam, edited by H.
A. Gibbs. The shorter work is usually sufficient for smaller libraries but the longer work is available from Brill Press in London.
This highly authoritative work, with signed articles, is the most
complete now in print in English. It covers every aspect of Islamic
life--biography, history, geography, religious beliefs, manners and
customs, tribes, industries as well as artistic and scientific contributions.

Dictionary of Islam, ed. by Thomas P. Hughes. Kelley Publishers,
1965 (Reprint of 1895 ed.). (ISBN 0-678-09953-7)
A dictionary of terms relating to the Muslim faith and to the
political and religious aspects of Islam.

JAZZ

Encyclopedia of Jazz, by Leonard Feather. New ed. Horizon Press,
1960. (ISBN 0-8180-1203-X)
Encyclopedia of Jazz in the Sixties, by Leonard Feather. Horizon
Press, 1966. (ISBN 0-8180-1205-6)
These two books, usually boxed and sold as a set, together
form a comprehensive encyclopedia of jazz music in America. Together, they have 3000 biographical sketches and almost 500 photo-

graphs of leaders in the field.   In addition to discussion of jazz
music, there are such additional features as lists of musicians by
date of birth and place of birth, and lists of jazz organizations, recording companies and booking agents.

JEWELRY

For information concerning gem stones and the jewelry trade
see GEMS.   For information on amateur jewelry making see
HANDICRAFTS.

JEWISH PEOPLE

Jewish Encyclopedia, ed. by Isidor Singer.   New York: KTAV Publishing House, 1964 (Reprint of 1904 ed.).   12 vols.   (ISBN 0-
87068-104-4)
Although dated this is an outstanding work, absolutely necessary for the history of the Jewish people and their religion.   It is
often the only source of biographical material on little known persons and is excellent for its articles on various tenets of the Jewish
faith.   For those items which are timeless and not in need of con-
stant revision and updating, this is an excellent source.   It is particularly good for manners, customs and literature.

American Jewish Yearbook.   Jewish Publishing House, annual since
1899.
This is an up-to-date survey of the international Jewish situation and covers all aspects of Judaism.   It includes population statistics, directories of organizations, listings of Jewish publications,
a Jewish calendar, and a necrology of prominent Jews who have died
during the past year.

A Social and Religious History of the Jews, by Salo W. Baron. 2nd
ed.   rev. and enl.   Columbia University Press, 1952-69. 14
vols.
This is a continuing history of the Jews which at present goes
up to the time of the Late Middle Ages, 1650.   It is the definitive
history of the Jewish people and their accomplishments and it is
hoped that Mr. Baron lives long enough to bring it up to the present
day.   Each volume is filled with notes, descriptions and references
which verify and bolster the historical presentation.   There is an
index volume available for the first eight volumes.

Encyclopedia of Zionism and Israel, ed. by Raphael Patai.   McGraw-
Hill, 1971.   2 vols.   (ISBN 0-07-048735-9)
Recognizing that the scope of this encyclopedia is quite limit-
ed, i.e., the study of the Zionist movement and its history, it succeeds

very well indeed. It should be useful in any school or library in which there is a good deal of interest in Israel.

Who's Who in World Jewry, ed. by I. Carmen Karpman. 3rd ed. Pitman, 1972.
The usual who's who type of information concerning the important leaders of Jewish background. For each person it gives the date of birth, place of birth and residence, activities and all pertinent data in tabular form.

Traveler's Guide to Jewish Landmarks of Europe, ed. by Bernard Postal. New York: Fleet Press, 1971. (ISBN 0-8303-0112-7)
This is a travel guide to 32 countries including the Soviet Union. For each it gives a rundown of the percentage of Jewish population, some aspects of Jewish life in that country, listing of cemeteries, synagogues and landmarks of interest to Jewish travelers.

JOKES
see
QUOTATIONS

JOURNALISM

American Journalism, by Frank L. Mott. 3rd ed. Macmillan, 1962. (ISBN 0-02-38423)
This is the best history of journalism in the United States, covering the period from the establishment of the first newspaper in the country, in 1690, down to 1960. It surveys the whole journalistic picture, lists and describes the famous newspapers and gives biographical information concerning the editors and journalists who made them great.

Informing the People, by Charles H. Brown. Holt, Rinehart and Winston, 1957. (ISBN 0-03-004955-5)
Intended as a textbook in journalism, this is an excellent exposition of the way to write news stories and press releases.

Newsmen Speak, ed. by Edmond E. Coblentz. Books for Libraries, 1954. (ISBN 0-8369-0318-8)
A facsimile reprint of a standard work on journalism in which famous newspaper men write about their profession and give the beginning newspaper man ideas on how to pursue his trade.

JUDO AND JUJITSU

The Hand Is My Sword: A Karate Handbook, by Tobert A. Trias.
    Charles E. Tuttle, 1973. (ISBN 0-8048-1077-X)
        Karate means "empty handed" but the use of karate makes
that hand into a sword. This book teaches the basic katas and techniques. Each movement is illustrated by either photos or sketches,
more than 600 in all. This book is useful to the beginner but will
be of help to any degree through the Black Belt.

Judo and Karate Belt Degrees, by Bruce Tegner. Thor Publishers,
    1963. (ISBN 0-87407-011-2)
        This is a listing of all the requirements along with the rules
and regulations of the various degrees in judo.

Natural Weapons: A Manual of Karate, Judo and Jujitsu Techniques,
    by Karl Freudenberg. A. S. Barnes, 1962. (ISBN 0-498-04086-
    0)
        This is a basic introduction to the various forms of judo in-
cluding karate and covers each phase, i. e. , grappling, throwing and
footwork. It is illustrated with good demonstration of the various
holds and moves.

KARATE
see
JUDO AND JUJITSU

        So far as I can determine, KUNG FU is merely a refinement
of other forms of judo, mainly karate.

KINGS AND RULERS

        Once again, for a complete listing of the rulers of the vari-
ous nations of the world there are few better sources than the two
almanacs, each of which includes listings of the rulers of each
country from the earliest days to the present time.

Information Please Almanac, ed. by Dan Golenpaul. Dan Golenpaul
    Associates. Annual since 1946.
World Almanac and Book of Facts, ed. by George De Leury. News-
    paper Enterprise Association. Annual since 1868.

        Another good source for historical rulers:

An Encyclopedia of World History, by W. L. Langer. 5th ed.
    Houghton-Mifflin, 1972. (ISBN 0-395-07886-5)

A chronological arrangement of history which contains appendixes listing the Roman Emperors, Byzantine Emperors, the Caliphs, Popes, Holy Roman Emperors, British rulers and ministers, French rulers and ministers and French presidents.

For a listing of current rulers of the various countries:

Statesman's Yearbook, ed. by John Paxton. St. Martin's Press, annual since 1864.
A statistical and historical annual of the various countries of the world giving descriptive information for all the governments of the world. For each country, there is a listing of the current ruler, king or president along with a listing of the important cabinet members.

KNOTS AND SPLICES

Encyclopedia of Knots and Fancy Rope Work, by Raoul Graumont. 4th ed. Cornell Maritime Press, 1953. (ISBN 0-87033-021-7)
This is an encyclopedia on the making of knots and other fancy arrangements of rope and twine. It gives detailed instructions for many different types of knots, telling how each is used and something of the history if known. There is a glossary of words used by sailors and others using knots.

Scout Handbook, ed. by Frederick L. Hines. 8th ed. Boy Scouts of America, 1972. (ISBN 0-8395-6500-3)
The official handbook of the Boy Scouts of America gives data on all types of scouting activities, including a very good section on the tying of various knots.

KORAN
see also
ISLAM

For a direct translation of the Koran:

The Koran, ed. by J. M. Rodwell. Dutton. (ISBN 0-460-00380-1)
An easily understood and simple translation of the text.

For commentary of the inner meaning of the Koran:

Meaning of the Glorious Qur'an, Arabic and English, by Mohammed Marmaduke Pickthall. Orientalia, Inc., 1970. (ISBN 0-87902-282-9)
This translation of a book originally meant for Mohammedans has been done in such a way as to make the basic tenets understandable to other than true believers.

LABOR AND LABOR UNIONS

American Labor Unions, by Florence Peterson. 2nd ed. Harper & Row, 1963. (ISBN 0-06-034830-5)
The subtitle, "What they are and how they work, " explains the thrust of this book. It contains the history of the general labor movement, the government of the normal labor union, the relationships between labor and management, and the beneficial activities of the labor unions in other than professional ways.

Annual Digest of State and Federal Labor Legislation. U. S. Bureau of Labor Standards. U. S. Government Printing Office, annual since 1935. (L 16. 3)
This is an annual digest of labor legislation within the United States.

Monthly Labor Review. U. S. Bureau of Labor Statistics. U. S. Government Printing Office. Monthly since 1915.
This is a monthly compilation of statistics dealing with various aspects of labor relations and salaries. There is a regular reporting of such things as employment, hours worked, earnings, turnover, labor force, consumer price indices, etc.

Price List #33, Labor. U. S. Government Printing Office. Irregularly revised.
A listing of printed materials from the U. S. Government dealing with the subject of labor.

Representative Bibliography of American Labor History, by Maurice F. Neufeld. New York School of Industrial Research, 1964. (ISBN 0-87546-021-6)
This is a representative collection of writings dealing with the labor movement in the United States from the radical left to the ultra-right. It is a good cross-section of writings both pro and con on the labor movement.

Sourcebook on Labor, by Neil W. Chamberlain. Abridged and revised edition. McGraw-Hill, 1964. (ISBN 0-07-010438-7)
This collection of documents includes such things as constitutions of labor unions, collective agreements, court decisions affecting labor and labor unions, and speeches made by labor leaders. Although this is an abridgement of the earlier 1958 edition, it contains many new items. The usefulness of the work is lessened by the absence of an index.

LAW

Always keeping in mind that the librarian is not a lawyer and therefore should not answer questions concerning legal problems in other than a general way, this section deals with the laws which govern this country--general, federal, state and municipal.

GENERAL

Black's Law Dictionary, ed. by Henry Campbell Black. 4th ed.
    West Publishing Company, 1968.
        Probably the best known and almost certainly the most complete of the general legal dictionaries available, this defines adequately the many words, terms and phrases common in both American and British legal proceedings. These definitions range from ancient to modern usage and cover all forms of law; constitutional, commercial, medical, etc. There is also a collection of quotations concerning the law and a table of abbreviations.

Everyone's Legal Advisor, by William Capitman. Rev. ed. Simon
    & Schuster, 1961. (ISBN 0-671-23308-4)
        This book, written for the layman, deals with the common problems which face each of us in our everyday life. It answers in fair detail those legal questions which can be met without an attorney and gives samples of various legal forms and proper steps to take prior to calling in a professional lawyer. It has a good index.

Index to Legal Periodicals. H. W. Wilson Company. Monthly with
    triennial cumulations since 1909. (Available from 1952 to present.)
        This indexes 372 legal publications, including yearbooks, annual publications of institutes, and other various annual reviews. There are four parts to the index; author and title indexes, a table of cases and a book review section. This index is compiled with the advice of the American Association of Law Libraries.

Legal Aid Directory. National Association of Legal Aid Associa-
    tions. Annual.
        This lists for each state and city the branches of the Legal Aid Association.

Martindale Hubbell Law Directory. New York: Martindale Hubbell.
    Annual since 1868.
        This is a biographical directory of the lawyers of the country. In addition to the biographical section there is a section dealing with the geographical distribution of legal experts by state and then by city or county within the state. In addition to the biographical information there are also sections listing Federal Courts and their justices, firms supplying legal needs, special investigators, etc.

FEDERAL

The best source of information concerning federal statutes is the Federal Government itself. The following publications are invaluable in determining exact laws.

U. S. Code, Containing the General and Permanent Laws of the

United States.   U. S. Government Printing Office.   (Y 4. J89/1:
Un3/3/)
This contains the general and permanent laws of the United
States arranged in general legal categories.   It is prepared under
the direction and supervision of the Committee of the Judiciary of
the House of Representatives.   New editions are published every six
years, with cumulative supplements published annually.

United States Statutes at Large, Containing Laws and Concurrent Resolutions.   U. S. Government Printing Office.   Annual. (GS4.
111:)
This is a preliminary publication to the U. S. Code and as
such is simply a chronological arrangement of the laws as enacted.
No effort is made to arrange the laws by subject or to show how
they may affect earlier laws, this being taken care of in the next
revision of the U. S. Code.

Public Laws.   U. S. Government Printing Office.   (GS4. 110:)
These so-called slip laws, the first official publications of
statutes, are in pamphlet form and each law is published separately.
These precede the appearance of the statutes in the U. S. Statutes at
Large.

Code of Federal Regulations...   Division of the Federal Register.
U. S. Government Printing Office.   (GS4. 108:)
This is a codification of federal regulations which, while not
laws, carry the effect of laws.   These are the general and permanent administrative rules under which our government operates.

Federal Register.   National Archives of the U. S.   U. S. Government
Printing Office.   (GS4. 107:)
This is a listing of executive orders, presidential proclama-
tions, and announcements of important rules and regulations.   It is
published daily except Sunday and Monday and holidays, with indexes
published and cumulated monthly, quarterly and annually.   Much of
this material eventually appears in the Code of Federal Regulations.

STATE

Most state governments follow the same general pattern of the
Federal government in issuing a state code of laws and generally a
code of regulations.   To see what the various states publish, the
following book is important.

State Law Digest.   U. S. Library of Congress.   U. S. Government
Printing Office.   (LC21. 8:)
This is an index to recent state legislation compiled and
edited by the Legislative Reference Section of the Library of Congress.

For texts of laws, we give the following example which can
usually be found in each state:

Code of Laws, Annotated.   Code Commissioner of the State of South

Carolina.   Charlottesville, Va. : Michie Company.   (Every ten years).

This is a sample of the typical code of laws of the various states.   Traditionally, they are given out to commercial publishers to be printed and distributed and contain the full text of the laws of the state involved.   They are always fully indexed and usually annotated to show which laws have materially altered previous statutes.

MUNICIPAL

The pattern of city government around the nation is so varied that a listing of all types of city regulations would be impossible here.   For a copy of your own municipal laws and regulations consult the City Clerk's Office and they will give you the exact title and order procedure.   In addition, it must be remembered that no city operates without a charter from the state so that there will be laws in the Code of Laws of the State which will affect any city operation.

LEAVES
see
TREES

LIBRARIES AND LIBRARIANS

American Library Directory: A Classified List of Libraries With
      Personnel and Statistical Data, ed. by Helaine MacKeigan.
      R. R. Bowker.   Biennial since 1923.
            Each edition lists by state and then by city the libraries of the United States.   For each library is given a summary of statistical information along with the major subject departments and library administration.   It includes not only public and college but special libraries as well.   There are appendixes which list state school library agencies, state public library agencies, library schools, Armed Forces libraries overseas and USIS agencies.   There is also a full text of the National Interlibrary Loan Code.

Bowker Annual of Library and Book Trade Information.   Council of
      National Library Associations.   R. R. Bowker.   Annual since
      1956.
            This is almost a must for any library administrator.   It gives statistical data on book prices, periodical subscription prices, recent library developments, and directories for all types of information and services.   This is an administration tool which is very useful in the preparation of library budgets or proposals.

A Biographical Directory of Librarians in the United States and
      Canada, ed. by Lee Ash.   American Library Association.   Issued
      irregularly since 1933.

The first four editions of this publication were titled <u>Who's Who in Library Service</u> and were published by various publishers. The directory contains the usual biographical data found in such publications: i. e. , date of birth, place of birth, marital status, education, positions, publications, honors, etc.

LINGUISTICS

<u>Glossary of Linguistic Terminology</u>, by Mario Pei. Columbia University Press, 1966. (ISBN 0-231-03012-6)
    This is an alphabetically arranged listing of terms applied in all fields of the study of languages and linguistics. There is identification of basic language groupings and within those groups of outstanding dialects.

<u>Loom of Language</u>, by Frederick Bodmer. Norton Press, 1944. (ISBN 0-393-04168-9)
    This is a study of languages from four aspects: the natural history of language, the mixture of languages, the world language problem and the language museum. This last part is a listing of words which, while they no longer exist, survive in English as base roots for common words.

    The following all deal with the pronunciation and meaning of language as it is spoken in the United States.

<u>Linguistic Atlas of New England</u>, by Hans Kurath. AMS Press (reprint of 1939 edition). 3 vols. (ISBN 0-404-10040-6)
<u>Pronunciation of English in the Atlantic States</u>, by Hans Kurath. University of Michigan Press, 1961. (ISBN 0-472-04541-5)
<u>Word Geography of the Eastern United States</u>, by Hans Kurath. University of Michigan Press, 1966. (ISBN 0-472-08532-8)
    Together these present an excellent overview of the linguistic variations in the eastern half of our country, written by the outstanding expert in the field.

LITERARY AGENTS

<u>Literary Market Place</u>. R. R. Bowker Company. Annual since 1940.
    This book lists a variety of information concerning every aspect of publishing and it has an excellent list of literary and artistic agents. For each agent is given name, address and specialty and whether or not the agent listed is a member of the Society of Author's Representatives.

LITERARY PRIZES AND AWARDS

For a listing of the available prizes and awards:

Literary Market Place. R. R. Bowker Company. Annual since 1940.
    Under the heading in the table of contents, LITERARY
AWARDS, PRIZES AND FELLOWSHIPS, you will be directed to a
complete listing of various awards and prizes available. For each
prize or award is given the name of the award, who sponsors it,
what the conditions are for receiving it, and the value of the prize
or award. It also gives the date and frequency of the award. For
prize contests, the same information is given. For literary fellowships and grants, it gives the name of the fellowship or grant, the
conditions, who sponsors it, the amount, and closing dates for
application.

For a listing of prizes that have been awarded during the
past year:

Bowker Annual of Library and Book Trade Information. Council of
    National Library Associations. R. R. Bowker, annual since 1956.
    Look under LITERARY AND LIBRARY PRIZES AND AWARDS
in the index.

Facts on File, an Indexed Record of World Events, ed. by Lester A.
    Sobel. Facts on File, Inc. Weekly with annual cumulations
    since 1944.
    This weekly cumulation of facts picks up national awards as
presented. Look under the name of the award in the annual index.

LITERATURE

If you desire information concerning a specific author, see
AUTHORS; if you desire plot information for a specific book, see
BOOKS--PLOTS AND CHARACTERS.

AMERICAN LITERATURE

Cambridge History of American Literature, ed. by William P. Trent.
    Macmillan, 1953. 3 vols. in 1.
    Although quite dated this is still an important history of
American literature and should be in most collections. It covers
from the early Colonial period up to the beginning of the present
century and has articles dealing with literary forms, writers, subjects, trends, etc. It is particularly good for early writings not
covered elsewhere, i. e., travels of early writers, colonial publications, etc. This was originally published by Putnam and contained
bibliographies. This edition, otherwise identical, omits the bibliographies.

Literary History of the United States, ed. by Robert E. Spiller. 3rd
ed. Macmillan, 1972. 3 vols.
More up-to-date than the Cambridge History and in some
ways superior to it, this one presents a survey of American Literature from colonial times to the present day. Each chapter is written by a different expert but good editing has made them an inte-
grated whole. Although the chapters are not signed there is a listing of the authors in a special section at the end of the volumes.
There are voluminous bibliographies.

Oxford Companion to American Literature, ed. by James David Hart.
4th ed. Oxford University Press, 1965. (ISBN 0-19-500565-1)
Quite a comprehensive one-volume treatment of American
literature, with short biographies and bibliographies of major writers
and summaries of plays and fictional pieces. In addition, there are
explanations of major literary trends, societies and periodicals
through the years. It is arranged alphabetically for easy use but
also contains a chronological listing of all authors or movements
mentioned so that they can be properly placed historically.

GENERAL LITERATURE

Reader's Encyclopedia, by William Rose Benet. 2nd ed. T. Y.
Crowell, 1965. (ISBN 0-690-67128-8)
This covers world literature with brief articles on authors,
their works, and national and international trends in writing and literature. It also identifies literary characters, allusions, etc.

Encyclopedia of World Literature in the Twentieth Century, ed. by
W. B. Fleischmann. Ungar, 1967-71. 3 vols. (ISBN 0-8044-
3091-8)
This translation of a standard German work on world literature is an alphabetical arrangement of brief articles concentrating
primarily on the European countries.

Cambridge History of English Literature, ed. by W. W. Ward.
Cambridge University Press, 1903-33. 15 vols.
The most important and comprehensive general history of
English literature yet written. It covers, in a systematic way, from
the earliest time down to the beginning of this century. Each chapter
is written and signed by specialists and all major writers of English
literature are analyzed and placed in their proper perspective. It
does not give texts of poems and other works but often does include
criticisms of individual works and of an author's complete contribution. It should be in virtually every library.

Oxford History of English Literature, ed. by Bonamy Dobree. Oxford University Press, 1945- (still in process).
This mammoth work is projected to run to 12 volumes and
when completed will probably replace the Cambridge History as the
definitive history of the English literary scene. It has excellent
coverage of the areas completed and has good bibliographies.

Oxford Companion to English Literature, ed. by Paul Harvey. 4th ed.
      Oxford University Press, 1967. (ISBN 0-19-500163-X)
      This handbook, although primarily devoted to English writers,
schools, and trends in literature, includes other than English writers when their work profoundly affects English writings.

LOCOMOTIVES
see
ENGINES - RAILROAD

MAGAZINES

DIRECTORIES

The Standard Periodical Directory, ed. by Leon Garry.   Oxbridge
      Publishing Co.   Approximately every three years.
      This directory lists more than 50,000 periodical publications
in the United States and Canada.   The arrangement is topical, then
alphabetical by title within the subject.   There is a title index at the
rear of the book.   Information given for each publication includes
name and address of publisher, price by subscription and per copy,
year founded, frequency of publication, total circulation, advertising
rates, etc.

Ulrich's International Periodicals Directory, A Classified Guide to
      Current Periodicals, Foreign and Domestic.   R. R. Bowker,
      Published in alternating years.
      This is a classified listing of the world's periodical publica-
tions.   For each periodical the usual information is given: publisher,
editor, place of publication, price of subscription, total circulation,
and places that the periodical is indexed.   It contains all the information listed in the Standard Periodical Directory in a much more
pleasing format.

Magazines for Libraries, by Bill Katz.   2nd ed.   R. R. Bowker Co.,
      1972.   (ISBN 0-8352-0554-1)
      This is an annotated classified listing of periodicals recom-
mended for all types of libraries.   For each periodical listed, the
usual directory and subscription information is given along with a
critical annotation telling what the periodical is trying to achieve and
how well the editor feels it has reached this goal.   For the small
library, this might be a more useful publication than one of the more
comprehensive directories.

INDEXES

      There are multitudes of indexes to periodical literature and
it would be impossible to list them all.   The ones listed here are

those published by the H. W. Wilson Company, since they represent
the epitome of the indexing art and cover most periodicals found in
any but the largest libraries.

Applied Science and Technology Index. Monthly with annual cumula-
     tion since 1936. Prior to 1958 this was a part of the Industrial
     Arts Index.
Art Index. Quarterly with annual cumulations since 1929.
Biography Index. Quarterly with three-year cumulations since 1946.
Biological and Agricultural Index. Monthly with annual cumulations
     since 1964.
Business Periodicals Index. Monthly with annual cumulation since
     1958. Prior to 1958 this was a part of the Industrial Arts Index.
Library Literature. Bi-monthly with two-year cumulations since
     1921.

Reader's Guide to Periodical Literature. Semi-monthly with annual
     cumulations since 1900.
     This is the granddaddy of all periodical indexes. The peri-
odicals covered are general in nature and suited to the general library collection. There is an Abridged Reader's Guide for smaller
libraries.

Social Science and Humanities Index. Quarterly with annual cumula-
     tion since 1965. Prior to 1965, this was entitled International
     Index. Beginning June 1974, the index was split into two parts:
     Humanities Index and Social Science Index.

UNION LISTS

Union List of Serials in Libraries of the United States and Canada,
     ed. by Edna Brown. 3rd ed. H. W. Wilson Co., 1965.
     This publication lists 156,499 serials held by 956 libraries in
the United States and Canada. For each title there is a listing of
libraries holding the title and indicating which years they have. There
is an indication if the library will either loan or allow photocopying
from their copies. It is an invaluable set for interlibrary loan purposes. Since this only goes up to 1949, it is brought up to date by:

New Serial Titles, 1950-1970. Library of Congress. R. R. Bowker,
     1973. 4 vols.
     This is a continuation of the Union List... and contains those
periodicals which began publication after 1949. This publication
supersedes two previously issued publications, New Serial Titles,
1961-65 and ... 1966-69. It contains the same type of information
found in the Union List.

MAGIC

Two approaches to the subject of magic--serious study of the phenomenon of magic in history and the how-to-do-it type of books dealing with magic tricks as performed by stage magicians--are covered in this section.

History of Magic and Experimental Science, by Lynn Thorndike. Columbia University Press, 1923-1958. 8 vols.
This is the definitive history of magic and witchcraft from quite early times up through the eighteenth century. It is a well documented history of the effects that magic had on the history of the times. One handicap is that there is no single index to the set. Volume 4 indexes volumes 1-4; volume 6 indexes volumes 5-6; volume 8 indexes volumes 7-8.

Witchcraft, Magic and Occultism, by W. B. Crow. Borden, 1968.
This is an often fascinating history of the various aspects of the occult sciences, featuring both magic happenings and witchcraft. It covers from pre-history right up to the present day and is well indexed for reference use.

Beginner's Book of Magic, by Francis J. Rigney. Devin-Adair, 1963.
Originally written for Cub Scouts, this is still a worthwhile book for the amateur magician, and the tricks described are often baffling in the hands of a gifted person. However, since it was written for young boys it is easily understood and the tricks are easily performed.

Complete Illustrated Book of Card Magic, by Walter Gibson. Doubleday, 1969. (ISBN 0-385-06314-8)
The principles and techniques of the basic card tricks which form the core of most magic shows are fully revealed with text and photographs so that any person with average dexterity can perform them.

Houdini's Fabulous Magic, by Walter Gibson. Chilton, 1962. (ISBN 0-8019-0651-2)
A modern day master of magic exposes the great magic tricks of one of the greatest magicians of all times. This book unveils the illusions and tricks and describes how they were performed and what equipment is needed to duplicate them. It is an excellent textbook for either an amateur or professional magician.

Scarne's Magic Tricks, by John Scarne. Crown Publishers, 1951.
The master of the card table turns his hand to magic and gives illustrated instructions on the presentation and performance of 200 magic tricks. He includes instructions on hand gesticulations and word play designed to mislead the audience. Although leaning heavily on card tricks, he also presents tricks of hypnotism, mindreading and fortune telling.

MAMMALS

Field Guide to Animal Tracks, by Olaus Murie. Houghton-Mifflin, 1954. (ISBN 0-395-08037-1)
   An almost complete listing of animal tracks of North American Mammals with line drawings of the tracks and textual explanation of specific things to look for in identification.

Field Guide to the Mammals, by William H. Burt. 2nd ed. Houghton-Mifflin, 1964. (ISBN 0-395-07471-1)
   An illustrated guidebook for identifying the mammals of the United States and Canada. There are descriptions and illustrations of each animal.

Hoofed Mammals of the World, by Ugo Mochi. Scribner's, 1971. (ISBN 0-684-12382-7)
   This is the only really reliable work in handbook form dealing with the hoofed mammals of the world. It covers all living species and even some fairly recently extinct species. It is illustrated with silhouette outlines of the animal. It has an excellent index to aid in locating the individual animal desired. The text fully describes the animals as to size, coloration, typical life span and geographical distribution.

Mammals of North America, by E. Raymond Hall. Ronald Press, 1959. 2 vols.
   This manual gives the common name of mammals of the United States and Canada followed by the scientific names, a full description with line drawings and a discussion of the size, coloration and geographical distribution of each species.

Mammals of the World, by Michael Boorer. Grosset and Dunlap, 1971. (ISBN 0-448-00860-2)
   This is one of Grosset's all-color guides to wildlife and it carries on the fine tradition established by that series. There is an introductory section dealing with the place of mammals in the world scheme of things, followed by descriptions of the various mammals in an orderly arrangement and color photographs. One interesting feature is a listing of zoos of the world in which the various animals can be seen.

Paw Prints: How to Identify Rare and Common Mammals by their Tracks, by O. C. Lempfert. Exposition Press, 1972. (ISBN 0-622-47371-5)
   This book has ink impressions of the paw prints of 32 North American mammals and a full textual discussion of the various points to look for in identifying specific types. Although limited in coverage, it supplements the Murie book.

MANNERS AND CUSTOMS
see also
ETHNOLOGY

How Did It Begin, by R. Brash. McKay, 1966. (ISBN 0-679-
  50032-2)
    A small book devoted to uncovering the background of curious
customs that we still follow without knowing why. The book traces
the beginnings often back to prehistoric or very early times.

Primitive Manners and Customs, by James A. Farrar. Finch Press
  (reprint of 1879 edition).
    Provides an explanation of primitive customs and manners in
terms of the folklore attached to the group as well as its religious
and psychological significance.

Curiosities of Popular Customs, by William S. Walsh. Gale, 1966
  (Reprint of 1898 edition).
    This is probably the most reprinted volume of information
concerning curious customs of the world. It is a collection of facts
concerning the curious customs, rituals, ceremonies and ways of
doing things in all parts of the world. It points out origins of holidays and the legends and superstitions which surround each of them.

MANUFACTURERS

Thomas' Register of American Manufacturers. Thomas Publications.
  Annual since 1905.
    This multivolume annual publication is divided into four parts.
Part one is an alphabetical listing of product classification. For
each type of manufactured article there is a geographical listing
showing where each article is made; for example, under caskets
there is a full listing by states and by city of all casket manufacturers in the United States. Part two is an alphabetical listing of
manufacturers, showing what each company manufactures. Part
three is a product and trademark and brand name index; for example,
if you want to know who manufactures Brand-X, look under that
name and it will tell you who the manufacturer is. Part four is a
collection of catalogs of manufacturers, arranged in alphabetical
order.

MAPS

    It scarcely seems necessary to list the many good atlases
which contain maps of the world, the nation, the state or the region.
Every good encyclopedia has good maps and the National Geographic

Magazine is continually putting out interesting map supplements of the areas discussed in the magazine. Any library would be well advised to start a collection of these and other maps which could be arranged alphabetically in the vertical file of the library.

MARINE CORPS
see
ARMED FORCES

MARKETING

Marketing Handbook, by Albert W. Frey. 2nd ed. Ronald Press, 1965.
This is a guide for anyone interested in the marketing of goods and services. It includes statistical and mathematical calculations for determining needs and market possibilities as well as the normal information concerning sales and business.

Editor and Publisher Market Guide. Editor and Publisher Magazine. Annual since 1924.
This is a comprehensive analysis of the various metropolitan districts and markets around the country. There is an arrangement by state and then by city and for each market district the necessary data for determining market capabilities. These include such things as population, location, transportation facilities, climate, principal paydays and average payroll in selected industries and the type of industry prevalent. It also lists any schools or colleges in the area and gives for each city the principal newspapers and the person to contact for advertising.

Reference Guide to Marketing Literature, by Allen L. Pennington. D. H. Mark Publishers, 1970.
A computer-produced bibliography of more than 3000 recent articles. Small print size detracts from what otherwise would be an excellent bibliography.

MARRIAGE

Here the questions are many and the sources almost as widespread. For ease in handling the various types, this section is divided into the ETIQUETTE of the ceremony, the LAWS under which marriages are conducted, and the statistical data concerning marriages in this country.

ETIQUETTE

The major sources for information concerning etiquette are the two books by Post and Vanderbilt. These books cover every aspect of conduct and manners in all situations and can be fully relied upon to answer most of your questions concerning the proper conduct of the wedding.

Amy Vanderbilt's Etiquette, by Amy Vanderbilt. Rev. ed. Doubleday, 1972. (ISBN 0-385-03915-8)
Emily Post's Etiquette, ed. by Elizabeth L. Post. 12th ed. Funk and Wagnalls, 1969. (ISBN 0-308-10038-7)

For complete information concerning the preparations for the marriage, the ceremony, the invitations, the reception and all the many details concerning the big event, see:

Wedding Etiquette Complete, by Marguerite Bentley. Manor Books, 1972.
McCalls' Engagement and Wedding Guide, by Joan McClure. Saturday Review Press, 1972. (ISBN 0-8415-0130-0)

MARRIAGE LAW

The best source of information concerning marriage laws is the Code of Laws for your state. A small book which summarizes marriage laws for the entire country is:

Marriage, Divorce and Adoption Laws of the United States, by the Editors of Gould Press. Gould Press, 1973. (ISBN 0-87526-645-4)

STATISTICS

Vital Statistics of the United States. U. S. Bureau of the Census, Division of Vital Statistics. U. S. Government Printing Office. Annual since 1937. (HE 20.2212:)
Statistical Abstract of the United States, by the U. S. Bureau of the Census. U. S. Government Printing Office. Annual since 1878. (C3.134:)

MATHEMATICS
see also
FORMULAS, MATHEMATICAL

Handbook of Applied Mathematics, ed. by Edward E. Grazda. 4th ed. Van Nostrand Reinhold, 1966. (ISBN 0-442-02820-2)
This is an application of mathematics to the problems of industry and manufacturing. It has a good coverage of the basic principles of mathematics and then its use in such fields as plumbing, car-

pentry, etc. There is a good index.

Handbook of Business Mathematics, by William R. Minrath. 2nd ed.
    Van Nostrand Reinhold, 1967.   (ISBN 0-442-05411-4)
    This is the application of mathematical principles to the
arithmetic of the business world, with particular attention to the use
of the computer.

History of Mathematics, by David E. Smith. Peter Smith. 2 vols.
    1923-1925.   (ISBN 0-8446-2955-3)
    An excellent work on the history of mathematics with empha-
sis on the various schools of mathematicians and development. Excellent for reference purposes since it has a good index.

Mathematics Dictionary, by Glenn James. 3rd ed.   Van Nostrand
    Reinhold, 1968.   (ISBN 0-442-04088-1)
    A dictionary of mathematical concepts and terms alphabet-
ically arranged.

Men of Mathematics, by Eric T. Bell.   Simon & Schuster, 1961.
    (ISBN 0-671-46400-0)
    A biographical listing of the famous men in the field of math-
ematics giving, in addition to the usual biographical information, the
contributions that each made to the field of mathematics.

MEDALS
see
DECORATIONS AND MEDALS

MEDICINE

    Once again the warning must be sounded that the library is
not authorized to give medical advice and the information found
herein is intended for the information of the patron in answer to
specific questions and not for analysis of disease or illness.

Blakiston's Gould Medical Dictionary, by Arthur Osol. 3rd ed.
    McGraw-Hill, 1972.   (ISBN 0-07-005683-8)
    This is a standard dictionary of medical terms dealing with
all branches of medicine and health.   It covers medical applications
in related fields such as zoology and botany.   There are illustrations
and diagrams to explain definitions.

Dorland's Illustrated Medical Dictionary, ed. by William Dorland.
    24th ed.   Saunders, 1965.   (ISBN 0-7216-3146-0)
    This is a collection of the terminology of all phases of med-
ical treatment and disease.   In all, well over 100,000 terms and
words are defined.   As indicated by the title there is profuse use

of illustration to make the definition more easily understood.

Family Health Encyclopedia: An International Reference in the Health Sciences, Lippincott, 1970. 2 vols. (ISBN 0-397-55952-6)
This is based on an original Swedish publication and while some of the indexing is obscure due to the different use of words in the various countries, the overall coverage is very good. The articles are short and written for the layman, not the doctor. In addition to health and medical hints, there is a brief history of medicine along with a chart showing the chronological development of medical services and a listing of all winners of the Nobel prize for medicine.

Merck Index: An Encyclopedia of Chemicals and Drugs, ed. by Paul G. Stecher. 8th ed. Merck and Company, 1968. (ISBN 0-911910-25-5)
This is a handbook to the chemicals and drugs in common use today and more than 10,000 different items are described. For each item described, the properties affecting its use are discussed, i.e., the boiling point, the color, the specific weight, etc. For each item listed there is a suggested medical or other use indicated. Both the scientific and trade names are listed for most materials.

Merck Manual of Diagnosis and Therapy, ed. by David N. Holvey. 12th ed. Merck and Company, 1972. (ISBN 0-911910-01-8)
This is intended for the physician or the informed layman and gives information about the treatment of various diseases. This is one of the books which if used improperly could cause catastrophic results.

METALS

Commodity Yearbook, ed. by Harry Jiler. Commodity Research Bureau, Inc. Annual since 1939.
This publication gives prices and production statistics for each of various commodities. Under the name of each of the various metals, one finds statistics concerning world production as well as salient statistics of the industry in the United States. There are summary statistics for each state and for each metal, with an estimate of current production, future reserves and probable future use.

Dictionary of Metallurgy, by W. E. Clason. American Elsevier, 1967. (ISBN 0-444-40124-5)
Definitions of many terms covering all phases of the mining, manufacture and production of metal products.

Minerals Yearbook. U. S. Bureau of Mines. U. S. Government Printing Office. Annual since 1932. (I. 28. 37:)
There is a summary of each type of metal ore production by state and region as well as an analysis of metal ore reserves. The

statistics for each metal can be found under the heading of that metal.

Natural Resources for U. S. Growth, by Hans S. Landsberg. Peter Smith, 1963. (ISBN 0-8446-2423-3)
Trends in Natural Resource Commodities, by Neal Potter. Johns Hopkins Press, 1962. (ISBN 0-8018-0536-8)
These two books, complement each other. Trends in National Resource Commodities gives statistics of prices, output and consumption in the industries dealing with commodities including the metal and metal ore industries. This book covers the period from 1870-1957. Natural Resources For U. S. Growth was originally published by Johns Hopkins as a companion volume and was entitled Resources in America's Future. It gives patterns of availability of various resources for the years 1960-2000.

METEORITES

First Book of Meteors and Meteorites, by David C. Knight. F. Watts, 1969. (ISBN 0-531-00582-8)
Written for the junior high school, this discusses the various types of meteors and meteorites and their origins. It discusses meteor showers, mineralogical make-up and other factors concerning meteors. Although simply written, it is accurate and is supplemented by photographs and prints from the American Museum of History and other museums.

Meteorites and Their Origins, by G. J. McCall. Halsted Press, 1973. (ISBN 0-470-58115-8)
This is the latest good book on the origin of meteorites and their chemical and physical properties. It is well illustrated with pictures of actual meteorites and of the crystal formations within individual meteorites. There are good discussions on the physical makeup, the nature and origin of meteorites, and the relationship of the moon and the planet Mars. There is a good bibliography and an index.

METEOROLOGY
see also
CLIMATE

Handbook of Meteorology, by Frederic A. Berry. McGraw-Hill, 1945. (ISBN 0-07-005030-9)
This handbook presents a variety data on meteorological phenomena. Each article is written by an expert and there are charts and tables in which the mathematical and statistical data are given. It includes articles on thermodynamics, atmosphere, kinematics, as

well as description of equipment used and the plotting of weather data.

Standard Dictionary of Meteorological Sciences, by Gerard Proulx. McGill University, 1971. (ISBN 0-7735-0066-9)
This is a bilingual dictionary (French-English, English-French) of meteorological terms--the most comprehensive such dictionary available. It provides easily understood definitions of all major words and phrases.

METRIC SYSTEM

Metrics: Measurement for Tomorrow, by Helmer Ronnigen. Macmillan, 1969.
This little book is an excellent start towards understanding the eventual change from the current systems of weights and measurements in this country to the metric system. It provides equivalent tables which allow for easy transfer from the U. S. system to the metric system and back again. There are chapters dealing with weights and measures, area, heat, power, lengths, temperature, clothing sizes, etc.

MICROFORMS

Guide to Microforms in Print, ed. by A. J. Diaz. Washington, D. C.: Microcard Editions. Annual since 1959.
Originally called Microcard, Microfiche Catalog, this annual listing now has been enlarged to take in all types of microforms and includes books, periodicals, annual publications and other materials which may appear on microfilm, microfiche or other microforms. There is a listing of publishers provided in each volume. Not listed are theses and dissertations.

Subject Guide to Microforms in Print. Washington, D. C.: Microcard Editions. Biennial.
This is a listing by subject categories of the materials which are available on various types of microform from United States publishers. Theses and dissertations are not listed.

Microform Source Book, ed. by Mitchell Badler. New Rochelle, N. Y.: Microfilm Publishing Co., 1972.
This is a directory intended to identify all types of equipment needed by users of microforms. Products are listed by manufacturers and type of equipment, with price at time of publication. There is a directory of trade names, a directory of associations dealing with microforms and, possibly most importantly, a glossary of terms used in libraries and other institutions using microforms.

Guide to Microforms and Microform Retrieval Equipment, by Mark
  McKay. Washington, D. C. : Applied Library Resources, 1972.
    This is a very brief presentation of various types of micro-
forms and the equipment needed in their use. It outlines the general
considerations for purchase of the various types of equipment and
has descriptions of each type of microform reader or printer. The
information is largely tabular in format so that one can easily compare brands and equipment.

MILEAGES
see
DISTANCES

MILITARY FORCES
see
ARMED FORCES

MINERALOGY

Dictionary of the Names of the Minerals, Including Their History
  and Etymology, by Albert H. Chester. Finch Press (reprint of
  1896 ed).
    This is an alphabetical listing of the names of the various
minerals which gives the background for the name, whether for a
person or a quality, and the circumstances under which it got its
name. There is a brief description of each mineral.

Field Guide to Rocks and Minerals, by Frederick H. Pough. 3rd ed.
  Houghton Mifflin, 1953. (ISBN 0-395-08106-8)
    An excellent identification guide for rocks and minerals. This
book has photographs of various rocks and minerals accompanied by
diagrams of the crystal formations of the minerals described. For
each mineral described, there is given the physical properties, the
composition, a suggested test for identification and other distinguishing characteristics.

Mineral Facts and Problems. U. S. Bureau of Mines. U. S. Government Printing Office, 1971. (I 28. 3:)
    This is one of a series of irregularly published scholarly re-
ports of the Bureau of Mines and belongs in the numbered sequences
of its Bulletin. This is number 650. It is in reality an encyclopedia of current information on various metals, minerals and fossil
fuels. It is easy to read and understand and the arrangement makes
it an excellent reference source. It takes up 93 different commodities and for each one gives the background, the outlook up to the
year 2000, the problems involved, and a bibliography of information.

Minerals Yearbook. U. S. Bureau of Mines. U. S. Government
   Printing Office. Annual since 1932. (I 28. 37:)
   This annual publication is published in four parts. Part one
deals with metals and minerals, part two with fuels, part three with
domestic area reports and part four with international reports.
There are separate chapters for each mineral giving such data as
production, shipments, principal mines, prices, consumption, etc.

MINING
see
MINERALOGY; METALS
or names of specific materials mined--COAL, IRON, etc.

MISCELLANY

       This section is devoted to those items for which libraries
are always getting calls but which can not be easily categorized
under a specific subject heading. The books mentioned here cover
a variety of subjects which may be helpful to the reference librarian.

Curious Questions In History, Literature, Art and Social Life, by
   Sarah Killikelly. Gale Research, 1969 (Reprint of 1900 ed.).
   3 vols.
       This collection has a very interesting arrangement. The first
section is a presentation of 750 numbered questions on a variety of
subjects covering all fields of life, and the second section is devoted
to answering these curious questions. There is a good index to
make the whole thing intelligible.

Dunlop Illustrated Encyclopedia of Facts, by Norris McWhirter.
   Doubleday, 1969. (ISBN 0-385-01119-9)
       This is a collection of miscellaneous facts arranged by broad
subject headings. Excellent for browsing but useless unless index
is used.

Handy Book of Curious Information, Comprising Strange Happenings
   in the Life of Men and Animals, Odd Statistics, Extraordinary
   Phenomena, and Out of the Way Facts Concerning the Wonder-
   lands of the Earth, by William S. Walsh. Gale Research, 1970
   (Reprint of the 1913 ed.).
       The title tells the whole story. It is a conglomeration of
facts of all types which provide many answers otherwise almost impossible to find. Good indexes make the book usable.

Handy Book of Literary Curiosities, by William S. Walsh. Gale Research, 1966 (Reprint of 1892 ed.).
       A companion volume of the Handy Book of Curious Informa-
tion... This one presents little known facts concerning books of literature.

Popular Fallacies, a Book of Common Errors: Explained and Cor-
    rected with Copious Reference to Authorities, by A. S. Acker-
    man. 4th ed. Gale Research, 1970.
        This book is topically arranged by subject. Popular in ap-
proach, it quotes frequently from recognized authorities in the refu-
tation of popular fallacies. The table of contents is arranged alphabetically and there is a good index.

Treasury of the Familiar, by R. L. Woods. Macmillan, 1942, 2
    vols. (ISBN 0-02-63149)
Third Treasury of the Familiar, by R. L. Woods. Macmillan, 1970.
    (ISBN 0-02-63142)
        These books are an excellent source of fugitive facts of prose
and poetry. They answer quickly those questions which sound as if
you could find the answer immediately but sometimes have a hard
time locating--such questions as the full text of Casey at the Bat or
The Face on the Barroom Floor. These books are filled with such
familiar pieces. There is no logical arrangement, so use of the
index is essential.

MOHAMMEDANISM
see
ISLAM

MONASTIC ORDERS

The Catholic Almanac, ed. by Filician A. Foy, O. R. M. Doubleday,
    annual since 1904.
        This is a comprehensive almanac of information dealing with
the Roman Catholic Church and contains statistical and historical
data on all phases of the religion. Under the heading of "Orders"
will be found a complete listing of religious orders giving correct
name, date of founding, motherhouse, membership, and religious
dedication.

New Catholic Encyclopedia, ed. by Catholic University of America.
    McGraw-Hill, 1967. 15 vols. (ISBN 0-07-010235-X)
        This is a comprehensive encyclopedia dealing with the beliefs,
teachings, history, organization and activities of the Roman Catholic
Church and of all events which have affected the history of that
church from the time of Christ to the present day. Volume 9 includes an excellent article dealing with the history of the monastic
movement, and in various volumes under the names of specific orders there are histories and discussions of those orders.

MONEY

Probably the most frequently asked question concerning money has to do with foreign exchange, e.g., how many lira do I get for my dollar? At one time this was a relatively easy matter but the rate of exchange now varies so greatly from day to day, that the best advice today is to contact the foreign exchange department of the local bank and ask for the latest exchange figures. The Wall Street Journal carries a daily listing of foreign exchange quotations.

America's Money, the Story of Our Coins and Currency, by J. Earl Massey. T. Y. Crowell, 1968. (ISBN 0-690-08656-3)
This is an excellent history of American money from the time of barter to the present day. There is a discussion of the use of Spanish and other foreign coins as legal tender in the United States, a history of colonial and continental coins and currency and of the development of modern coins and currency. There is a listing of each type of money issued along with some background information as to why such a piece of money was necessary.

Current Coins of the World, by Richard S. Yeoman. 5th ed. Racine, Wis.: Western Publishing Company, 1972.
This is primarily meant for the coin collector and as such is a detailed description of the various coins of the world. It has a millimeter scale for measurements, a conversion table for dates of the various world calendars, a translation of foreign language numbers and a general index. Not basically good for currency history, this compares favorably to stamp catalogs.

Documentary History of Banking and Currency, ed. by H. E. Kroos. McGraw Hill, 1969. 4 vols. (ISBN 0-07-079785-4)
This is the definitive history of the use of currency in the United States, with documents showing the history of that use. More than 300 documents are included, beginning with the one published in 1637 making the use of wampum legal tender in Massachusetts, and ending with the 1968 document which deals with the abandonment of gold as a basis for American currency.

Encyclopedia of U.S. Coins, by Mort Reed. Rev. ed. Regnery, 1972.
This is an excellent encyclopedic coverage of all aspects of U.S. coinage. It covers die preparation, coinage methods, and for each coin provides a detailed discussion of the various types and series. There is a section on the identification of counterfeit coins and a good index.

Paper Money of the United States: A Complete Illustrated Guide with Valuations, by Robert Friedberg. New York: Coin and Currency Institute, 1972. (ISBN 0-87184-507-5)
This is probably the best reference source to the types of paper currency that have been used in our country. It covers all official United States currency including the Civil War currency and the fractional currency no longer in use. There is also a complete

listing of national bank notes issued by the individual states. This
is an absolute must for any library wanting good numismatic coverage.

Pick's Currency Yearbook, by Franz Pick, New York: Pick Publish-
    Corporation, annual since 1955.
        This is an annual publication giving the description of 94 cur-
rencies of the world and an evaluation of the monetary conditions of
the countries covered. There is also a currency exchange table but
this is of limited use in these times of rapidly changing exchange
rates.

World's Money, How It Works, by William M. Clarke. Praeger,
    1971.
        This is a readable account of the world's monetary system.
It tells of the basis for world-wide monetary control and how it
works, covering the use of gold as a base, the balance of payments
concept, exchange rates and all the other factors that go into determining the value of money around the world. It gives a brief
history of the use of money but its main thrust is current application.

MOTELS
see
HOTELS AND MOTELS

MOTION PICTURE DIRECTORS
see
ACTORS AND ACTRESSES

MOTION PICTURES
see also
ACTORS AND ACTRESSES

Actor Guide to the Talkies, by Richard Bertrand Dimmitt. Scare-
    crow Press, 1967. 2 vols. (ISBN 0-8108-0000-4)
Title Guide to the Talkies, by Richard Bertrand Dimmitt. Scare-
    crow Press, 1965. 2 vols. (ISBN 0-8108-0171-X)
        These two sets should be considered together since they are
intended to supplement one another. The Title Guide to the Talkies
is the more comprehensive, covering 16,000 feature-length films
made between October 1927 and December 1963. Basically this book
is intended to locate the original source of the plots of movies and
ideally will answer the question, "I have seen the movie and now I
would like to read the book, where can I find it?" Each movie is
entered under title, gives the date of issue, the producer and com-

pany and the author and title of the original work on which it was based. There is also a cross reference to different movies made from the same source, so that it is easy to determine how many versions of the same story have been made.

Actor Guide to the Talkies is a comprehensive listing of 8,000 feature-length films made between 1949 and 1964. Volume 1 is a list of movies by title; for each is given the date of release, the company making the film, and then a listing of the actors who took part in that film. Volume two is a listing by actors' names, referring to every film in which they have appeared. It is excellent for answering such questions as: "Did Lon Chaney appear in Gone With The Wind?" or a listing of Clark Gable's movies for that period.

The American Movies Reference Book: The Sound Era, ed. by Paul Michael. Prentice Hall, 1969. (ISBN 0-13-028134-4)
While not as comprehensive as the first two mentioned books this is more literary in style. There is a brief history of the making of the motion picture, particularly the sound picture, and it provides bibliographic information concerning about 1,000 films. For each film listed there are dates and full credits but the important thing about this book is the Who's Who section titled "The Players" in which almost every film actor is listed; his original name, his dates, place of birth and a complete listing of all the films in which he took part are given.

Dictionary of One Thousand Best Films, by R. A. E. Pickard. Association Press, 1971. (ISBN 0-8096-1805-2)
This is a listing of film plays giving the date of production, the company producing, a list of principle actors and a brief synopsis of the film play.

Forty Years of Screen Credits, 1929-1969, by John T. Weaver. Scarecrow Press, 1970. 2 vols. (ISBN 0-8108-0299-6)
Twenty Years of Silents, 1908-1928, by John T. Weaver. Scarecrow Press, 1971. (ISBN 0-8108-0401-8)
Once again, the two books supplement one another to provide a comprehensive history of the film art. It lists every person who has appeared in the movies, and for each gives a listing of his or her film credits.

The International Encyclopedia of Film, ed. by Roger Manvell. Crown Publishers, 1972. (ISBN 0-517-50146-5)
This is a well made and beautifully illustrated book dealing with every aspect of the film industry both American and foreign. There is a history of the making of film and the various developments such as sound and color films. There is also an index to films, an index to names of actors and producers, and a very good bibliography of the film art.

International Motion Picture Almanac, ed. by Richard Gertner. Quigley Publishing Company. Annual since 1929.
This annual publication might be considered to update and

supplement the Dimmitt books since it is published annually and lists
the same type of information available in those books. In addition,
it is filled with up-to-date data concerning film making and cinema
history.

MOTTOES

A Handbook of Mottoes: Borne By The Nobility, Gentry, Cities,
Public Companies, Etc., by C. N. Elvin. Genealogical Press,
1971. (ISBN 0-8063-0481-2)
This is a reprint of an 1860 work and like wine it gets better
with age. As originally published, it gave the mottoes and told by
whom they were borne but did not give the reverse answer--what the
mottoes or crests of particular individuals or cities were. When
the Genealogical Press reissued it, an index of 5000 names was
added, and it is now a much more useful book.

State Names, Flags, Seals, Songs, Birds, Flowers and Other Symbols, by George E. Shankle. Greenwood Press (Reprint of 1938
ed.). (ISBN 0-8371-4333-0)
In addition to the other miscellaneous information concerning
each state of the United States, this book gives the state motto.

MUSEUMS

Official Museum Directory, United States and Canada. American
Association of Museums. Crowell-Collier, annually.
This is the official directory of the American Association of
Museums and gives a geographical listing of every museum in the
United States and Canada, first by state or province and then by
city. It also has a directory for finding individual museums by
memorial name and by type of museum. There is also a directory
of museum directors and department heads.

MUSIC AND MUSICIANS
see also
BALLADS; BALLET; CONDUCTORS; COMPOSERS;
DANCES; OPERA; SONGS

Dictionary of Music and Musicians, by Sir George Grove. 5th ed.
St. Martin's Press, 1954. 10 vols.
This is the standard encyclopedia dealing with music and
musicians and covers the entire field of music from 1450 to the
present day, but with primary emphasis on the English-speaking

world. Later revisions do not always maintain the high standards set by the 1860 edition, but for musical history and biography there is no better source. Most of the articles are signed by experts and they deal with several thousand different subject headings in one alphabet. These subjects will vary from simple definitions of musical terms to long dissertations on forms, theory and development. It is an excellent source for musical bibliography.

Encyclopedia of Popular Music and Rock, by Irwin Stabler. St.
 Martin's Press, 1973.
 Dealing entirely with the field of popular music this is a good collection of information on composers, performers, titles of songs, and terminology used in the popular music field. There is a section devoted to the winners of the various musical awards each year.

Harvard Dictionary of Music, by William Apel. 2nd rev. ed. Harvard University Press, 1969. (ISBN 0-674-37501-7)
 Although this omits all biographical materials, it is a very good source of information for historical approaches to various aspects of music. It contains all types of definitions and has good bibliographies of books and periodicals dealing with music.

International Cyclopedia of Music and Musicians, ed. by Robert Sabin. 9th ed. Dodd, Mead, 1964. (ISBN 0-396-01840-8)
 This naturally cannot compete with the mammoth Grove's Dictionary but for a one-volume work it does quite an adequate job of covering much of the same materials. For the library that has few musical questions or a very small budget, it could be considered an alternative to Grove's.

Popular Titles and Subtitles of Musical Compositions, compiled by Freda P. Berkowitz. Scarecrow Press, 1962. (ISBN 0-8108-0116-7)
 This is a listing of over 500 titles and subtitles associated with works of serious music from 1600 A.D. to the present day. The names are listed alphabetically. There is a list of composers as well as an excellent bibliography. Although well known foreign names are identified, emphasis is given to English names. An expanded and updated edition will be published in 1975.

MYTHOLOGY

Bulfinch's Mythology: The Age of Fable, The Age of Chivalry: Legends of Charlemagne, ed. by Thomas Bulfinch. 2nd rev. ed. T. Y. Crowell, 1970. (ISBN 0-690-57260-3)
 This has long been the standard popular work on mythology and it gives, in addition to the usual Greek and Roman coverage, a good introduction to Eastern mythology as well. This edition also has coverage of the legends of chivalry and of Charlemagne.

Crowell's Handbook of Classical Mythology, ed. by Edward Tripp.
    T. Y. Crowell, 1970. (ISBN 0-690-22608-X)
        This handbook contains discussions of prevailing motifs and
ideas of classical mythology. Particularly good for analysis of the
works of classical writers. There is a good index and bibliography.

Encyclopedia of Religion and Ethics, ed. by James Hastings. Scrib-
    ner's, 1908-1927. 13 vols. (Available only from publisher; not
    available through book trade.)
        This is the most comprehensive encyclopedic work in the field
of religion and ethics, and includes quite a good coverage of the
myths of the world. All articles are signed and all are by noted
authorities.

Funk and Wagnall's Standard Dictionary of Folklore, Mythology, and
    Legend, ed. by Maria Leach, 1972. Funk and Wagnalls, 1949-
    50. 2 vols. (ISBN 0-308-40090-9)
        This is an encyclopedia in dictionary form in which all the
major gods, goddesses, heroes, customs, folktales, songs, etc. of
the various civilizations of the world are discussed in brief but
authoritative articles; however, there are lengthy articles on national mythologies. Each article is written and signed by an expert.

The Golden Bough, ed. by James G. Frazer. 3rd ed. St. Mar-
    tin's Press. 13 vols. (Also available in one-volume edition.)
        This goes into the evolution of religious beliefs and the myth-
ology surrounding those beliefs. It is particularly good for the
Greek and Roman myths, the Egyptian myths and the mythology of
Northern Europe. There is a detailed index to myths, names, beliefs and an excellent bibliography. The one-volume edition should
suffice for most librarians.

NAMES

        For geographic place names see GEOGRAPHY. For nick-
names, pseudonyms and sobriquets see NICKNAMES. This section
deals with personal, literary and family names.

FAMILY NAMES

American Surnames, by Elsdon C. Smith. Chilton Press, 1969.
    (ISBN 0-8019-5263-8)
        This book examines the background of American surnames,
their origins, their meanings and distribution. There is a good bibliography and index.

New Dictionary of American Family Names, by Elsdon C. Smith.
    Harper & Row, 1973. (ISBN 0-06-013933-1)
        This is possibly the most complete study made of the origins
of the American family names. There are more than 10,000 entries

giving both the predominant and the variant spellings of almost every name in the United States. For each name, there is given the country of origin, the basic meaning of the name and some history if available.

GENERAL

Webster's Dictionary of Proper Names, ed. by Geoffrey Payton. G. C. Merriam Company, 1971. (ISBN 0-87779-083-3)
    This contains about 12,000 proper names: mythological heroes, place names, villains, titles of books, biblical personages, fictional characters, etc. Good for identification but for little else.

PERSONAL NAMES

Dictionary of Given Names, by Flora H. Loughead. Glendale, Calif.: Arthur H. Clark Company, 1966. (ISBN 0-87062-048-7)
History of Christian Names, by Charlotte M. Yonge. Gordon Press, 1966.
The Name For Your Baby, by Jane Wells. Westover Press, 1972. (ISBN 0-87858-020-4)
    These three books will be widely used for that universal question, "What should I name my baby?" The first two are more scholarly and give much more historical detail concerning each name but all three give the meaning of the name, the country of its origin and suggested names for twins or other combinations.

PETS

Pet Names, by Jean E. Taggart. Scarecrow Press, 1962. (ISBN 0-8108-0111-6)
    This book is arranged by type of pet--dogs, horses, cats, and even provides small sections for less common pets such as insects and birds. For each type there is given a suggested list of names. In the case of pets such as dogs, where there are many breeds from various parts of the world, there are specific sections for each breed.

NATIONAL PARKS AND MONUMENTS

    Once again the national government is the best possible source for information on the national parks and monuments. For a complete listing of the publications of the National Government see Price List # 35 - National Parks. (The complete list of Price Lists of Government Publications is available free of charge from the Superintendent of Documents, Washington, D. C., 20202.)

    The American Guide Series will have a description of any national parks or monuments for each state; for a complete listing, see AMERICAN GUIDE SERIES.

Exploring Our National Parks and Monuments, by Devereux Butcher.
6th ed. Houghton-Mifflin, 1969. (ISBN 0-395-07473-8)
This is a well illustrated description of our national parks
and monuments with many of the pictures in full color. For each
of the national parks there is a full description and history of the
park and some ideas of how it is used. There is a full bibliography
and a good index.

World Wildlife Guide: A Complete Handbook Covering All the World's
Outstanding National Parks, Reserves and Sanctuaries, ed. by
Malcolm Ross-McDonald. Viking Press, 1972. (ISBN 0-670-
79018-4)
This was published for the World Wildlife Fund and while it
is particularly good for the coverage of the wildlife of the world, it
is also excellent for information on the famous national parks of the
world. There are excellent illustrations.

NATURAL RESOURCES
see also
CONSERVATION
and names of specific resources, e.g., COAL, etc.

Natural Resources for U.S. Growth, by Hans S. Landsberg. Peter
Smith, 1963. (ISBN 0-8446-2423-3)
Trends in Natural Resource Commodities, by Neal Potter. Johns
Hopkins Press, 1962. (ISBN 0-8018-0536-8)
These two books complement each other. Trends in National
Resource Commodities gives the statistical background of all commod-
ities for the years 1870-1957. Natural Resources for U.S. Growth
was originally published by Johns Hopkins as a companion entitled
Resources in America's Future. It gives patterns of production and
availability of various natural resources for the years 1960-2000.

NATURALIZATION

How to Become a Citizen of the United States, by Libby F. Jessup.
3rd. ed. rev. Oceana Publications, 1972. (ISBN 0-379-11065-2)
This is a volume in the Oceana Publications Legal Almanac
Series, which deals with common legal problems. It gives in simple
and easily understood terms the steps one must take to gain citizenship in the United States.

NATURE STUDY

Handbook of Nature Study, by Anna B. Comstock. 24th ed. Comstock (order from Cornell University Press), 1939. (ISBN 0-8014-0081-3)
   This is a comprehensive guide covering, in addition to wildlife and wildflowers, a study of geology, astronomy and other aspects of natural life. It is well illustrated and has been a standard in the field for many years.

Nature Atlas of America, ed. by Roland Clement. Rev. ed. Hammond, 1973. (ISBN 0-8437-3511-2)
   This is a well illustrated nature study atlas covering rocks, trees, wildlife, birds, fish, insects, etc. found in each region of the United States. There are maps showing the geographic distribution of each variety of species as well as maps locating the national parks of the United States and Canada. In addition to the geographical materials there is a good glossary of nature study terminology.

Nature Study for Conservation, by John W. Brainerd. Macmillan, 1971. (ISBN 0-02-31347)
   This handbook for environmental education was sponsored by the American Nature Study Society and was written by an authority on conservation and nature study. It covers both the concepts and techniques involved in nature study, with detailed instructions on reporting data of observed resources and proper collection and experimentation. It also emphasizes the necessity of protecting our natural resources. Although not written for the junior high school student, its approach is simple enough to be of use to all levels of students above the elementary grades.

New Field Book of Nature Activities and Hobbies, by William Hillcourt. Putnam, 1970. (ISBN 0-399-10290-6)
   This is an excellent source book for adult leaders of young people, such as scout leaders or Sunday School teachers who are looking for a handbook on all areas of nature study. This covers birds, animals, insects, plant life, snakes, etc. and is filled with ideas for nature study projects or nature-related activities.

NAVIGATION

The Air Almanac. U.S. Naval Observatory. U.S. Government Printing Office. 3 times per year. (D 213.7:)
   Each issue gives the necessary astronomical data for air navigation during the coming year. It includes a star index and time charts for all areas of the world.

Air Navigation. Hydrographic Office. U.S. Government Printing

Office, 1963.   (D 203. 22:216)
This is intended both as a textbook for the U. S. Navy and as a general reference book on air navigation in general.

American Ephemeris and Nautical Almanac.   U. S. Naval Observatory. U. S. Government Printing Office.   Annual since 1855. (D 213. 8:)
This is prepared jointly by the U. S. Naval Observatory and the British Nautical Almanac Office and gives the tables of apparent locations and movements of the sun, moon, planets, and stars.   Information concerning eclipses, daily rising and setting of sun and moon in various parts of the world, and other such data are given.

American Practical Navigator.   U. S. Hydrographic Office.   U. S. Government Printing Office.   Published since 1802. (D 203. 22:9)
This is the book commonly referred to as Bowditch as it was originally written by Nathaniel Bowditch.   Now the Bible for sea navigation in this country, it has been a government publication since 1868.   It gives the latest possible information on every aspect of navigation for sea-going vessels.

NAVY
see
ARMED FORCES

NEGROES
see
BLACKS

NEUROLOGY

Medical Neurology, by John Gilroy.   Macmillan, 1969.   (ISBN 0-02-34366)
This is a handbook on the diseases of the nervous system and the muscles.   Although designed primarily for neurologists, it is clearly enough written to act as a ready reference source for all users.   There are bibliographies at the end of each section giving references to other pertinent materials.

The Nervous System: Introduction and Review, by Charles R. Noback.   McGraw-Hill, 1972.   (ISBN 0-07-046846-X)
An elementary introduction to the subject of neurology, illustrated with excellent drawings.   In addition to the strictly technical presentation, a good glossary of terms used in the field is not included.   It is a book not only for the potential practitioner but for the general public as well.

NEWSPAPERS

For a history of journalism or for the writing of newspapers see JOURNALISM.

Ayer's Directory of Publications, ed. by Leonard Bray. Ayer Press. Annual since 1869.

This is the most comprehensive and longest lasting of all the directories to newspapers. It is intended as a guide to publications printed in the United States and its territories as well as the provinces of Canada. Currently, it covers almost 23,000 publications, both periodicals and newspapers, and is arranged by state and then by city. For each publication reviewed is given the name of the paper, its frequency, the editor, the publisher, political affiliation, price, size, circulation figures, and some information concerning each city, village or hamlet in which a newspaper is published.

New York Times Index. New York Times. Semimonthly with annual cumulation since 1913.

Although a specific index to the New York Times this can be used as a general index to the coverage of most any newspaper in the country due to the mammoth coverage of the Times. For strictly local events, it will not be adequate but for general national or international events, this can be used for any newspaper to locate the date and approximate time of publication.

NICKNAMES

American Nicknames, by George E. Shankle. 2nd ed. H. W. Wilson Company, 1955. (ISBN 0-8242-0004-7)

This gives the origin and meaning of the nicknames of American History and is not limited to nicknames of persons but includes those applied to various places, institutions, ships, objects, etc. It is arranged alphabetically with cross references from nickname to real name and vice versa.

Handbook of Pseudonyms and Personal Nicknames, compiled by Harold S. Sharp. Scarecrow Press, 1972. 2 vols. (ISBN 0-8108-0460-3)

This is an excellent source book on the alternate names by which real people both living and dead have been known. Approximately 15,000 real name entries are made with reference to and from 25,000 nicknames or pseudonyms. There is an alphabetical arrangement with a thorough cross reference from the real to the pseudonym and vice versa. For each person listed there is a brief identification, dates and a listing of all known variant names. A large supplement is to be published in 1975.

Hawthorn Dictionary of Pseudonyms, compiled by Andrew Bauer.

Hawthorn Press, 1971.
This is an alphabetical listing of legal names and pseudonyms covering primarily people in the fields of literature and the arts. For each person there is a listing of known pseudonyms and from each pseudonym there is a reference to the person using it.

Nicknames and Sobriquets of U. S. Cities and States, by Joseph Kane. 2nd ed. Scarecrow Press, 1970. (ISBN 0-8108-0325-9)
This is an excellent geographical work in which one can find the answers to such questions as "Which city is the Rose Capital?" There are more than 10, 000 entries divided into four sections. The first section is geographical by cities with their nicknames; the second section is from nicknames to cities; the third section is from state to nicknames, and the fourth from nickname to state.

For nicknames of college and other athletic teams see:

Information Please Almanac, ed. by Dan Golenpaul. Dan Golenpaul Associates. Annual since 1946.
See index under nicknames.
World Almanac and Book of Facts, ed. by George Delury. Newspaper Enterprise Associations. Annual since 1868.
See index under nicknames.

NOBEL PRIZES

For a cumulative listing of winners by year and prize:

Information Please Almanac, ed. by Dan Golenpaul. Dan Golenpaul Associates. Annual since 1946.
See Nobel Prizes in index.
World Almanac and Book of Facts, ed. by George E. Delury. Newspaper Enterprise Associations. Annual since 1868.
See Nobel Prizes in index.

For announcement of annual awards:

Facts on File, an Indexed Record of World Events, ed. by Lester A. Sobel. Facts on File, Inc. Weekly with annual cumulations since 1940.
This is the premier source of current event information. It is a reference service which publishes a 20-page weekly digest of the news with regular cumulative subject indexes that greatly aid in finding needed information. To find recent awards of Nobel Prizes see that heading in the latest cumulative index.

NOBILITY
see
HERALDRY

NUMBERS

From Zero to Infinity: What Makes Numbers Interesting, by Con-
    stance Reid. 3rd ed. enlarged. T. Y. Crowell, 1965. (ISBN
    0-690-32053-1)
        This is a popularly written account of the development of the
number system. It gives the history and some of the folklore, legends and stories concerning each number and its configuration.

Number Words and Number Symbols, by Karl Menninger. MIT
    Press, 1969. (ISBN 0-262-13040-8)
        This is a much more scholarly presentation of the history of
numbers than the Reid book. It recounts the development of numbers as they are spoken and written, and the numerical symbols
which symbolize each. This is more than a history; it is a cultural
and ethnological presentation as well.

NUMISMATICS
see
COINS; MONEY

NURSERY RHYMES

Children and Books, by May Hill Arbuthnot. 4th ed. Scott, Forse-
    man, 1972.
        Intended as a textbook for the study of children's literature,
this has an excellent section dealing with the history and background
of the nursery rhyme and its use in dealing with children.

A Critical History of Children's Literature, by Cornelia Meigs.
    Macmillan, 1969. (ISBN 0-02-58390)
        Another textbook of children's literature with an excellent
chapter on the history and development of the nursery rhyme.

The Annotated Mother Goose, by William Baring-Gould. Potter, 1970.
        This is the complete text with illustrations by such illustra-
tors as Caldecott, Crane, Greenaway and Rackham and historical
woodcuts. In addition to the complete text of the rhyme there are
accompanying historical comments. In addition to a title index there
is also a first line index.

Oxford Dictionary of Nursery Rhymes, by Iona Opie.   Oxford University Press, 1951.   (ISBN 0-19-869111-4)
This is the most complete and scholarly study ever made of
nursery rhymes as a part of our literary heritage.   It gives accounts of their earliest appearance and then the text of the accepted
version of the nursery rhyme along with the many variations.   In
several cases, more than a dozen different versions are cited.
There are many illustrations from early editions and by famous
illustrators.

NUTRITION
see also
FOODS

Handbook of Diet Therapy, by Dorothea Turner.   5th ed.   University
of Chicago Press, 1970.   (ISBN 0-226-81718-0)
This handbook is excellent for determining the optimal nutri-
tional benefits of various diets.   The latest data available on the
composition of various foods and the latest recommended dietary allowances are included, plus a good glossary of dietetic terms.   There
are sample diets and some hints on food preparation for best nutrition.   There is a good index and bibliography.

Dictionary of Nutrition and Food Technology, by Arnold E. Bender.
3rd ed.   Shoestring Press, 1968.   (ISBN 0-208-00759-8)
An excellent collection of terms commonly used in the field
of nutrition and food preparation with full definitions.   In addition,
there is a bibliography to longer materials on the same subjects.

Recommended Dietary Allowances, by The Food and Nutrition Board.
7th ed.   National Academy of Science, 1968.   (ISBN 0-309-
01694-0)
An official publication of the Food and Nutrition Board of the
National Academy of Sciences, this gives the latest tables of recommended allowances with discussions of various foods.

Calories and Carbohydrates, by Barbara Kraus.   Grosset and Dunlap, 1970.   (ISBN 0-448-01982-5)
Over 7000 various brand names of foods are analyzed and
listed in alphabetical order, with the caloric content and carbohy-
drate count for each.

Composition of Foods, by Bernice K. Watts.   United States Printing
Office, 1963.   (Agriculture Handbook # 8, U.S. Department of
Agriculture.)
This is a handbook which gives the approximate nutritive
value of various types of foods.

OBITUARIES

New York Times Obituaries Index, 1858-1968. Arno Press, 1970.
    This is an index to 350,000 obituaries which appeared in the
New York Times from 1858-1968, giving the date, page and column
in which each appeared.

New York Times Index. Arno Press. Bi-weekly with annual cumu-
    lations since 1913.
    The New York Times has the largest obituary coverage of any
paper in the United States and through the use of its index one can
usually find the obituary of any person who achieved any degree of
prominence.

    In addition to these sources, both the major almanacs have
necrologies for persons who died during the year.

Information Please Almanac, ed. by Dan Golenpaul. Dan Golenpaul
    Associates. Annual since 1946.
World Almanac and Book of Facts, ed. by George Delury. News-
    paper Enterprise Association. Annual since 1868.

OCCUPATIONS
see
CAREERS

OPERA
see also
MUSIC

Annals of Opera, 1597-1940, by Alfred Loewenberg. 2nd ed.
    Scholarly Press, 1972. (ISBN 0-403-01376-3)
    This history of the opera covers in detail almost 3,600
operas in all languages. For each one it gives the date of the first
performance and the persons performing, as well as information on
important later presentations. There is an index to composer, li-
brettist and title. It has a limited dictionary of operatic terms (by
no means a complete operatic dictionary) but it is probably the most
important book for a library to have on the subject.

New Encyclopedia of the Opera, by Davis Ewen. Hill and Wang,
    1971. (ISBN 0-8090-7262-9)
    This is not quite as complete for operatic history as the
Loewenberg book but it is written in a popular vein and is a comprehensive reference book on the opera. It gives plots of opera,
history of each opera, a list of important characters and other basic
information. One interesting aspect is the pronunciation guide for

composers and titles.

New Milton Cross' Complete Stories of the Great Operas, by Milton
   Cross. Doubleday, 1955. (ISBN 0-385-04324-4)
More Stories of the Great Operas, by Milton Cross. Doubleday,
   1971. (ISBN 0-385-08546-X)
   These two present the best collection of opera plots yet available. There are detailed plots of over 100 major operas contained
in the two books and they are written in an easily understood but
still enjoyable style. There are also sections on the enjoyment of
the opera, a comparison of opera and ballet and a bibliography of
other operatic materials.

ORGANIZATIONS
see
ASSOCIATIONS

OSCAR WINNERS
see also
MOTION PICTURES

   The books on the motion pictures will be the best sources
for discussions of the various winners but if one wants only a listing of who won what award in what year, the two almanacs will provide this information.

Information Please Almanac, ed. by Dan Golenpaul. Dan Golenpaul
   Associates. Annual since 1946.
   In index under Academy Awards or Oscar (Awards).
World Almanac and Book of Facts, ed. by George Delury. News-
   paper Enterprise Association. Annual since 1868.
   In index under Academy Awards.

PAINTERS
see also
ARTS AND ARTISTS - BIOGRAPHY

Bryan's Dictionary of Painters and Engravers, by George Williamson. Kennikat Press, 1971 (Reprint of 1905 ed.). 5 vols.
   (ISBN 0-8046-0052-X)
   This is the most comprehensive biographical dictionary of
painters and engravers. It lists not only the major works of each
artist but in many cases gives the location as well. Volume 5 gives
monograms and marks used by painters and engravers.

Cyclopedia of Painters and Painting, ed. by John D. Champlin.

Gordon Press. 4 vols.

Although this originally appeared in 1892 and has not been updated, it is still the best source of information on older artists. It contains much factual and critical data about painters from all schools and parts of the world. There is one alphabetical arrangement which lists both names of great painters and of great paintings.

Dictionary of Art and Artists, by Peter Murray. Penguin Books, 1972. (ISBN 0-14-051014-1)

This presents over 1000 short biographies of painters, sculptors and engravers as well as definitions of terms, schools, trends and artistic movements.

Encyclopedia of Painting, ed. by Bernard S. Meyers. 3rd ed. Crown Publishers, 1970.

This provides a good overall coverage of outstanding painters, movements, styles and techniques from the cave man to the modern painter. The main emphasis is on European painters but some Eastern countries are represented.

PALEONTOLOGY
see
FOSSILS; GEOLOGY

PARLIAMENTARY PROCEDURES

Roberts' Rules of Order, by Henry Martyn Robert. 75th Anniversary edition, Morrow, 1971. (ISBN 0-668-31374-4)

This is the book for deciding any parliamentary procedural question. For seventy five years it has been the best place to locate information for parliamentary law, for explaining the organization of clubs and associations and for conducting of business of organizations. It contains many charts and diagrams of activities.

Although to most people Roberts is the Bible for parliamentary procedures, the following books can also be highly recommended as being reliable and easily understood.

Handbook of Parliamentary Procedure, by Henry A. Davidson. 2nd ed. Ronald Press, 1968.

Sturgis Standard Code of Parliamentary Procedure, by Alice F. Sturgis. 2nd ed. McGraw-Hill, 1966. (ISBN 0-07-062272-8)

PASSPORTS

Since the United States Government issues passports, it is

logical to turn to that source for the latest official information on ways to apply for a passport, and the rules and regulations concerning the passport and its use. The following two publications are basic in answering these questions.

Information for Passport Applicants. U. S. Department of State, Passport Office. U. S. Government Printing Office. Revised as needed.
This gives all the necessary information for obtaining your passport and the basic laws which govern its use.

You and Your Passport. U. S. Department of State, Passport Office. U. S. Government Printing Office. Revised as needed.
This gives much the same information as the former title but also gives some hints as to passport renewals, vaccinations, visas, conduct abroad and what you can expect from your American Consul in foreign lands.

PATENTS

Official Gazette of the Patent Office. U. S. Patent Office. U. S. Government Printing Office. Weekly with annual index since 1872. (C 21. 5:)
This is the official listing of all patents granted in the United States and contains descriptions and simple drawings of all items for which patents have been issued. It also contains the official decisions of the Commissioner of Patents and the United States courts in all patent cases.

How to Protect and Patent Your Invention, by Irving Mandell. Oceana Publications, 1951. (ISBN 0-379-11028-8)
This volume in the Oceana Legal Almanac Series deals with the steps one takes to insure the proper patenting of an invention and ways to protect that invention until such time as the patent has been approved.

Rules of Practice of the United States Patent Office in Patent Cases. U. S. Patent Office. U. S. Government Printing Office. (C 21. 14:)
Trademark Rules of Practice of the U. S. Patent Office with Forms and Statutes. U. S. Patent Office. U. S. Government Printing Office. (C 21. 14:)
These two publications present the official rules as published by the U. S. Patent Office concerning the ways to secure and protect a patent or trademark. They include forms and statutes which can be applied in each case.

Roster of Attorneys and Agents Registered to Practice Before the U. S. Patent Office. U. S. Patent Office. U. S. Govt. Printing Office. (C 21. 9:)
This is a listing of attorneys who are registered and present cases before the patent courts. It is arranged first by state, then by

city, and finally alphabetically by patent lawyer.

PENOLOGY

American Correctional Association Directory. The Association.
Annual since 1955.
This is a directory of correctional institutions, federal and state, in the United States, Canada, England and Scotland.

The Prison and the Prisoner, ed. by Dorothy Campbell Tompkins. University of California Press, 1972. (ISBN 0-87772-140-8)
This is a bibliography of material related to prisons and correctional institutions in the five-year period between 1967 and 1972. It is divided into six major parts: The Prison (this is general materials dealing with the overall question); State Prisons; Federal Prisons; Prison Administration; the Prisoner; and finally, proposals for prison reform.

PERSONAL FINANCE

J. K. Lasser's Managing Your Family Finances, by the J. K. Lasser Tax Institute. Rev. ed. Doubleday, 1973. (ISBN 0-385-03582-9)
This is a guide to all phases of personal and family finance. It lists in easily understood form: ways to set up a budget, ways to implement that budget, and how to cope with the inevitable problems which threaten to destroy the budget. In addition, it gives hints on the times when it is better to borrow rather than use your money, suggestions for investments, insurance and retirement planning as well as ways to plan for lower income tax.

New York Times Guide to Personal Finances, by Sal Nuccio. Harper & Row, 1968. (ISBN 0-06-034731-7)
The premise of this book is that the person most in need of financial advice is the very one who receives it the least; that is, the person in the middle or upper middle income bracket. This book attempts to remedy that situation with advice on every aspect of family finances from income tax to mortgages. Although aimed at the middle income level, the material is presented in such a manner that it can be of help to persons on all financial levels.

PERSONAL NAMES
see
NAMES

PETROLEUM

Commodity Year Book, ed. by Harry Jiler.   Commodity Research
    Bureau, Inc.   Annual since 1939.
        This publication gives prices and production statistics for
each of the commodities necessary to the national welfare.   Under
PETROLEUM, one finds statistics on the world production of petroleum as well as salient statistics on the petroleum industry of the
United States.   There' are summary statistics for each oil producing
region of the United States with statistics for oil reserves and
probable future uses.

Minerals Year Book.   U. S. Bureau of Mines.   U. S. Government
    Printing Office.   Annual since 1932.   (I 28. 37:)
        There is a summary of petroleum production as well as an
analysis of petroleum reserves in each state and region under the
heading of PETROLEUM.

Natural Resources for U. S. Growth, by Hans S. Landsberg.   Peter
    Smith, 1963.   (ISBN 0-8446-2423-3)
Trends In Natural Resource Commodities, by Neal Potter.   Johns
    Hopkins Press, 1962.   (ISBN 0-8018-0536-8)
        These two books complement each other.   Trends In Natural
Resource Commodities gives statistics of prices, output, consumption and employment in industries, including the petroleum industry,
from 1870-1957.   Natural Resources for U. S. Growth was originally
published by Johns Hopkins Press as a companion volume titled Resources in America's Future.   It gives patterns and availability of
various resources including petroleum for the years 1960-2000.

Petroleum Facts and Figures.   Committee of Public Affairs.   Amer-
    ican Petroleum Institute.   Annual since 1928.
        This is an official annual publication of the American Petro-
leum Institute and is intended to present as much relevant and valid
data as possible concerning the petroleum industry.   This book presents, in tabular statistical form, information concerning production
by state and region, refining by state and region as well as by type
of product, transportation, marketing, prices and taxation, as well
as such general information as finances, labor problems, fires and
safety problems, and data for world production and use.   There is
an index for finding pertinent data.

PETS

        Much of the information on pets will be found under the
names of the individual type of pet, e. g., DOGS, CATS, TROPICAL
FISH.   This section lists books covering the general field of pet
care and handling.

ASPCA Guide To Pet Care, by Diana Henley. Taplinger, 1970.
(ISBN 0-8008-0453-8)
Intended to increase the humane treatment of our animal pets, this gives instructions as to the proper treatment of each type of pet kept by humans.

Book of Wild Pets, by Clifford B. Moore. T. Branford Co., 1954.
(ISBN 0-8231-2001-5)
This book gives information on the care and feeding of all sorts of wild animals which are kept as pets, and on their natural life habits and identification. There are many illustrations.

How to Keep Your Pet Healthy, by Elizabeth Charles. Sterling Press, 1972. (ISBN 0-8069-3716-5)
A book devoted to possible diseases that may attack various breeds of pets and the ways to combat those diseases.

Pet Names, by Jean E. Taggart. Scarecrow Press, 1962. (ISBN 0-8108-0111-6)
This book is arranged by type of pet, giving a suggested list of names for each. In the case of pets such as dogs which have many breeds, there are specific suggestions for each breed.

Pets, by Leon Whitney. McKay, 1971. (ISBN 0-679-50219-X)
This is a comprehensive book dealing with practically every type of pet kept by humans, giving hints on their care, feeding and training.

PHILATELY
see
STAMPS

PHILOLOGY
see
LINGUISTICS

PHILOSOPHY AND PHILOSOPHERS

Dictionary of Philosophy, ed. by Dagobert Runes. Littlefield Adams, 1971 (Reprint of 1960 edition).
Good for the elementary student or the average layman but too limited in scope or coverage to be of help to the college or advanced student.

Encyclopedia of Philosophy, ed. by Paul Edwards. Macmillan, 1967. 8 vols.

This is scholarly work but easily understood by the average high school or college student. It covers aspects of both Western and Oriental philosophies and introduces most philosophers and their schools of philosophy. The articles are all signed by outstanding persons and the coverage is international in scope. There is a good index and there are usually bibliographies for the more important articles.

Masterpieces of World Philosophy in Summary Form, ed. by Frank N. Magill. Harper & Row, 1961. (ISBN 0-06-003840-3)
One can scarcely be philosophical in summary form but this book achieves that goal as well as any book could do. It is a part of the Magill Library of Masterplots and is reminiscent of others in the same group. It is good for synopses of the basic philosophical thoughts and schools from the most ancient to fairly modern times. It is also good in its definition of philosophical terms.

New Encyclopedia of Philosophy, by Johan Grooten. Philosophical Library, 1972. (ISBN 0-8022-1634-X)
This is a one-volume encyclopedia translated from the Dutch. While it does not compare in coverage to the Encyclopedia of Philosophy, it is very good for the definition of philosophical ideas and terminology. A more accurate name of this work would be "A Dictionary...."

PHOTOGRAPHY

Focal Encyclopedia of Photography. Focal Press. Rev. ed. McGraw-Hill, 1969. (ISBN 0-07-0121410-7)
This is a combination of photographic history, definitions of terms and a how-to-do-it guide to photography. It is well illustrated and the articles are written by experts in the field. There are more than 2000 articles dealing with all phases of photography, with bibliographic references attached to major articles.

Manual of Photography, ed. by Alan Horder. 6th ed. Amphoto, 1971. (ISBN 0-8019-5655-2)
This is the direct successor to a standard work on photographic work which was published in various editions from 1891 to quite recently. This has revised the Ilford Manual of Photography and presents a fully up-to-date guide to modern methods, techniques and developments.

Picture History of Photography: from the Earliest Beginnings to the Present Day, by Peter Pollack. Abrams, 1970. (ISBN 0-8109-0404-7)
Although the textual history of photography is excellent, the photographic presentations are even better. There are examples of the works of photographers from the very beginning to the present day. There are special chapters devoted to color photography and

microphotography and an excellent bibliography which not only refers to other texts on photography but also to books and periodicals giving the lives of photographers.

In addition to the examples cited there are numerous books dealing with photographic techniques but usually they stay in print for a very short time due to changing technology which renders them obsolete quite quickly. In addition, there are guides for each type of camera and equipment.

PLACE NAMES
see
GEOGRAPHY

PLANTS

Dictionary of Plant Names, by H. L. Gerth van Wigk. Stechert-
    Hafner, 1971.   2 vols.
    This is a polylingual dictionary of plant names arranged al-
phabetically by the Latin name of each plant and then giving for each
the popular name in English, Dutch, French and German.   It includes
all names of both cultivated and wild plants and indicates major
varieties and subvarieties.   It is quite accurate and is really the
only reference book giving the information.

Diseases and Pests of Ornamental Plants, by Pascal Pirone.   4th ed.
    Ronald Press, 1970.
    This is an official publication of the New York Botanical
Gardens and as such is fully authoritative and factual.   It is arranged in two sections: a general approach to diseases and pests of
ornamental plants and shrubs, and a specific section dealing with
the diseases of specific plants and shrubs.   There are excellent illustrations and diagrams which aid in not only recognizing the disease but also treating it.   Since the plants are arranged by botanical name, the excellent index from common to scientific names is
an important feature.

Manual of Botany, by Asa Gray.   8th ed.   Van Nostrand Reinhold,
    1950.   (ISBN 0-442-22250-5)
    This handbook of the flowering plants and ferns of the United
States and Canada has been the standard textbook in the field of
botany for more than 100 years.   It systematically catalogs and indexes plants and is encyclopedic in coverage.

Manual of Cultivated Plants, by Liberty H. Bailey.   Rev. ed. Mac-
    millan, 1949.   (ISBN 0-02-50552)
    This is a manual for recognizing the plants of North America
both indoor and outdoor.   It is arranged by scientific name but has

a good index, a glossary of terms and a list of plant families.

Plant Disease Handbook, by Cynthia Westcott. 3rd ed. Van Nostrand Reinhold, 1971. (ISBN 0-442-09353-5)
This gives detailed information on all diseases which might attack plants. There is a brief history of plant diseases and a discussion of the various chemicals which have been developed to combat them. There is a classification of various diseases and the main body of the book is devoted to ways to combat each type. For each plant, there is also a list of possible diseases which might attack that plant. Special features which add greatly to the value of the book include a list of county agricultural agents and their addresses, a glossary of terms and a bibliography.

World of Plant Life, by Clarence J. Hylander. 2nd ed. Macmillan, 1956. (ISBN 0-02-55805)
This is a well illustrated guide to the various families of plants in the world. It is arranged first by family of the plant then by groups within the family. There is a good index as well as bibliography.

PLASTICS

Dictionary of Plastics, by A. J. Wordingham. Littlefield, 1964.
A brief dictionary of terms dealing with the plastics industry and manufacturing.

Modern Plastics Encyclopedia. McGraw-Hill, annual since 1941.
Actually a supplement to Modern Plastics Magazine, this is more a dictionary of manufacturers of plastics and of machinery used in the production of plastics than an encyclopedia on the plastics industry. It is an excellent source for directory-type information.

Practical Guide to Plastics Application, by Edward G. Crosby. Cahners, 1972. (ISBN 0-8436-1205-3)
This guide attempts to gather together from many sources information on ways in which plastics can be used, and to offer it in such a manner that the designer or manufacturer can easily find the material desired. It covers the whole realm of plastics application, i. e., types of plastics available, the things they can and cannot be used for, and their various chemical or conductive properties.

PLAYS - PLOTS

Best Plays of the Year. Dodd, Mead. Annual since 1899.
The series was originally edited by Burns Mantle but there

have been several editors; the current one is Otis L. Guernsey, Jr. Each year the ten most representative plays which appeared on the American stage are excerpted and condensed for publication in this series. In addition to the plot summaries, there are complete listings of all plays produced on Broadway, giving full cast, length of the run and dates of opening and closing. There is also a Who's Who type section in which dates of birth and death are given for prominent actors as well as a necrology of actors who have died in the past year.

McGraw-Hill Encyclopedia of World Drama: An International Reference Work in Four Volumes. McGraw-Hill, 1972. (ISBN 0-07-79567-3)
 This is intended primarily as a biographical directory of dramatists of the world, but in giving the biographies of the dramatists, the major plays of the dramatist are summarized and discussed.

Plot Outline of One Hundred Famous Plays, by Van Henry Cartmell. Peter Smith, (Reprint of 1952 ed.).
 Good plot summaries but limited to early plays primarily of the classical tradition.

Plot Summary Index, compiled by Carol L. Koehmstedt. Scarecrow Press, 1973. (ISBN 0-8108-0584-7)
 This is an index to summaries of the major plays, poems, novels, and well known non-fictional works and is intended to help the harried reference librarian to quickly locate such summaries. For each plot indexed, it gives a listing of works in which the summary appears as well as the exact pages in which the plot is summarized. The arrangement is by title and also by author.

Reader's Encyclopedia of World Drama, ed. by John Gassner. T. Y. Crowell, 1969. (ISBN 0-690-67483-X)
 Although not primarily a book of plot summaries, this book does give very brief summaries of almost every play written. Primarily meant as a handbook and companion for the playgoer, it is an alphabetical arrangement of all terms dealing with the theater, including writers, plays, types of plays, etc.

Thesaurus of Book Digests, by Hiram Haydn. Crown Publishers, 1949.
 This is a book of digested plays, novels and other writings from earliest times up until 1949. It contains 2000 digests and for each play digested gives a brief plot summary as well as the date of writing and first performance.

POETRY

 This is too large a subject to be covered adequately in a book of this size. This section lists only poetry indexes, a few comprehensive collections and two major histories.

INDEXES

Granger's Index to Poetry, ed. by William J. Smith. 6th ed. Columbia University Press, 1973. (ISBN 0-231-03641-8)
  First edited in 1904 by Edith Granger, this work has remained a faithful reference tool through six editions. It is an index
to collections of poetry in collections, arranged in three parts: an
author index, a title and first line index and a subject index. Anthologies including poems listed are indicated by symbols, and there
is an identification chart of symbols in the front of each edition.
The coverage of anthologies changes with each edition, some being
added and others dropped. Thus many libraries keep all six editions. For most medium sized libraries, the latest edition will be
adequate.

Index to Children's Poetry, compiled by John E. Brewton. H. W.
 Wilson, 1942. (ISBN 0-8242-0021-7)
 First supplement, 1954. (ISBN 0-8242-0022-5)
 Second supplement, 1965. (ISBN 0-8242-0023-3)
  This is an author, title, subject and first line index to more
than 30,000 poems in more than 200 anthologies of children's poetry.
Each book of poetry listed is graded for suitability by grade level
and interest.

Index to Poetry for Children and Young People: 1964-1969, by John
 W. Brewton. H. W. Wilson Company, 1972. (ISBN 0-8242-
 0435-2)
  Although there has been a title change, this is actually an
extension of the earlier three books.

Subject Index to Poetry for Children and Young People, ed. by Violet
 Sell. American Library Association, 1957. (ISBN 0-8389-
 0059-3)
  This is an older and less comprehensive subject index than
the Wilson publications.

COLLECTIONS

Home Book of Verse, American and English with an Appendix Con-
 taining a Few Well Known Poems in Other Languages, ed. by
 Burton E. Stevenson. 9th ed. Holt, Rinehart and Winston, 1953.
 (ISBN 0-03-028035-4)
Home Book of Modern Verse: an Extension of the Home Book of
 Verse..., ed. by Burton E. Stevenson. 2nd ed. rev. Holt,
 Rinehart and Winston. 1953. (ISBN 0-03-028030-3)
  These two books together provide the most comprehensive an-
thology of verse in the English language now available. They are
arranged by subject but have excellent indexes to author, title and
first line.

  Another set of invaluable collections of various types of poetry is the Oxford Books of Verse published by the Oxford University Press. These titles combined with the Stevenson books will contain most of the poems that you will be asked for and both sets are completely indexed in Granger's.

New Oxford Book of English Verse, 1250-1950, chosen and edited by Helen Gardner. Oxford University Press, 1972. (ISBN 0-19-812136-9)

Oxford Book of American Verse, ed. by F. O. Matthiessen. Oxford University Press, 1950. (ISBN 0-19-500049-8)

Oxford Book of Light Verse, ed. by W. H. Auden. Oxford University Press, 1938. (ISBN 0-19-812118-0)

Oxford Book of Modern Verse, 1892-1935, ed. by W. B. Yeats. Oxford University Press, 1936. (ISBN 0-19-500177-X)

Oxford Book of Twentieth-Century English Verse, comp. by Philip Larkin. Oxford University Press, 1973. (ISBN 0-19-812137-7)

HISTORY AND CRITICISM

Cambridge History of English Literature, ed. by A. W. Ward. Cambridge University Press, 1907-1933. 15 vols.

Oxford History of English Literature, ed. by Bonamy Dobree. Oxford University Press, 1945- 12 vols. (still in preparation)

The Cambridge History has for many years been the outstanding history of the English Literature and has signed articles written by experts on each era and genre. For each poet mentioned there is an analysis of his age, his life and the works, often with commentary on individual poems. As fine as the Cambridge History is, the Oxford History when completed will be a more comprehensive and more up-to-date publication. Both are excellent and both can be highly recommended for any questions dealing with the history of English Literature and the persons who wrote it.

POLICE
see also
CRIME AND CRIMINALS

Book of the States. Lexington, Ky.: Council of State Governments. Biennial since 1935.

This publication covers every aspect of state government in the United States, including information on police administration and activity on the state level. In its index, look under Law Enforcement and under Public Safety Officials. Also there are chapters dealing with Law Enforcement and Public Protection and Highway Safety.

Municipal Yearbook. Chicago, Ill.: International City Managers Association. Annual since 1934.

This is the official publication of the International City Managers Association and is an authoritative resume of urban data and developments. For a summary of recent and current activities of city police departments see the chapter on Public Safety and the headings Police and Law Enforcement in its index.

Police Administration: A Bibliography, by Dorothy Ramm.   Rev. ed. Traffic Institute of Northwestern University, 1971.
This is an up-to-date bibliography of articles and books deal-ing with police administration.   The books are listed by subject with many annotations and a good index.

POLITICAL LEADERS

Congressional Staff Directory, ed. by Charles B. Brownson.   Wash-ington, D. C. : Congressional Staff Directory.   Annual since 1959.
This is an unofficial supplement to the Official Congressional Directory.   It gives lists of the important unelected officials in Washington, the staffs of various congressmen, committees, sub-committees.   There is a personal and geographical index.

International Yearbook and Statesmen's Who's Who.   London, Eng-land: Burke's Peerage.   Annual since 1953.
This book is intended to provide rapid information concerning international organizations and political and statistical information concerning each country of the world.   The Who's Who section gives sketches of the political leaders of every country of the world.

Official Congressional Directory.   U. S. Congress.   U. S. Govern-ment Printing Office.   Irregular since 1865.
This is the best source of information concerning members of Congress.   It presents short biographies of members of both the House and Senate and lists of each member's committee appoint-ments, his terms of service, his room and telephone number and the name of his special assistants or secretary.   The Official Direc-tory is not limited to Congressional members; it also lists members of the Federal courts, ranking military leaders, governors, diplo-matic representatives, etc.   There is also a diagram and description of the Capitol and its grounds, and a series of maps showing con-gressional districts for each state.

Who's Who in American Politics: A Biographical Directory of United States Political Leaders, ed. by Paul A. Theis.   4th ed.   R. R. Bowker, 1973.   (ISBN 0-8352-0617-3)
Almost 20, 000 American political leaders are listed in this publication which covers leaders on all levels of government from the local to the national level.   The information can usually be con-sidered accurate since it is provided by questionnaires answered by the persons listed, but there may be some "halo" effect which should be taken into consideration.   This is one of the few places that some local or municipal leaders can be found.   There is a geographical directory which locates politicians by area.   It is highly recom-mended for any library.

POLITICAL PARTIES

American Party System: An Introduction to the Study of Political
    Parties in the United States, by Charles E. Merriam.   4th ed.
    Johnson Reprint Corp., 1969 (Reprint of 1949 edition).
        This is the standard work on the history of the various de-
velopments which led to the formation or dissolution of the various
parties in our country.

American Party Systems: Stages of Political Development, by Wil-
    liam N. Chambers.   Oxford University Press, 1967.   (ISBN 0-
    19-500849-9)
        This book resulted from a conference on the development of
the American Political Party held at Washington University in St.
Louis, Missouri in 1966 and presents the views of ten outstanding
political historians on that development.   The arrangement is chronological, with each historic period covered by separate articles.

        Although not actually books on political parties per se, the
following two books are excellent for study of party development
since they give the entire texts of the major and minor party platforms for each election.

National Conventions and Platforms of all Political Parties, 1879-
    1900, ed. by Thomas Hudson McKee.   Scholarly Press, 1971
    (Reprint of 1900 ed.).   (ISBN 0-403-00356-3)
National Party Platforms, 1840-1968, ed. by Kirk H. Porter. 4th
    ed.   University of Illinois Press, 1970.   (ISBN 0-252-00137-0)

POPES

        Once again, for just a simple listing of the Popes and their
dates of service, the quickest place to look is in one of the major
almanacs.

Information Please Almanac, ed. by Dan Golenpaul.   Dan Golenpaul
    Associates.   Annual since 1946.
World Almanac and Book of Facts, ed. by George Delury.   News-
    paper Enterprise Association.   Annual since 1868.

        For a more comprehensive account of the lives and careers
of the various Popes see:

History of the Popes, by Leopold Von Ranke.   Ungar, 1966.   3 vols.
    (ISBN 0-8044-1766-0)
        There are more comprehensive histories of the Papacy, in-
cluding one published in England which is still incomplete but which
already has reached forty volumes; however, for most libraries,
this three-volume set will give adequate biographical information

concerning papal actions.

Every encyclopedia has articles dealing with the individual Popes but the best encyclopedia for this type of article is:

The New Catholic Encyclopedia, ed. by the Catholic University of
America. McGraw-Hill, 1967. 15 vols. (ISBN 0-07-010235-X)

POPULATION

For U. S. population statistics there is no better source of information than the publications of the Census Bureau. For a complete listing of Census publications see:

Price List # 70-Census Publications. Superintendent of Documents
U. S. Government Printing Office. Revised as needed. (The whole collection of price lists are available free of charge from the U. S. Govt. Printing Office.)

For statistical data concerning population:

Statistical Abstract of the United States. U. S. Bureau of the Census. U. S. Government Printing Office. Annual since 1878.
(C 3. 134:)
This one-volume condensation of the materials found in the voluminous census publications is the standard summary of information concerning all phases of American life. It has statistics concerning population and the distribution of that population by age, race, education, geography or any other desired statistic. This book should be in every library. Of course, this is not as comprehensive as the decennial Census of Population but it will contain most of the information needed by the average library.

Demographic Yearbook. United Nations. International Publications
Services. Annual since 1949.
This United Nations publication gives vital statistics of the nations of the world, including birth rate, deaths, and population and population movements. There are historical articles as well as current statistics.

For a simple listing of populations of cities, states and nations, the following publications will be helpful:

Statesman's Yearbook, ed. by John Paxton. Macmillan. Annual since
1864.
Information Please Almanac, ed. by Dan Golenpaul. Dan Golenpaul
Associates. Annual since 1946.
World Almanac and Book Of Facts, ed. by George Delury. News-
paper Enterprise Association. Annual since 1868.

<u>PORTRAITS</u>

Pictures of individuals are often asked for, and they are sometimes harder to locate than one would think. However, the following sources may be of help. For many persons who are mentioned in encyclopedias, there is an accompanying portrait, so that it is often the best place to start.

<u>Author Series.</u> H. W. Wilson Company. (see AUTHORS in this book for complete listing.)
Most of the authors written about in this series have photographs accompanying their biographies.

<u>Biography Index.</u> H. W. Wilson Company. Quarterly with 3 year cumulations since 1946.
Although an index to biographical materials, there is a notation in each biographical reference indicating whether or not it is accompanied by a photograph.

<u>Current Biography.</u> H. W. Wilson Company. Monthly with annual cumulations since 1940.
Current biographies of recently important persons; each sketch is usually accompanied by a photography.

<u>If Elected... Unsuccessful Candidates for the Presidency, 1796-1968.</u> U. S. National Portrait Gallery. U. S. Government Printing Office, 1972. (SI 11. 2 P 92/)
There never is any difficulty in finding pictures of presidents of the United States, but what about the persons who ran and were not elected? This book solves that problem. Primarily, it is a biographical directory of unsuccessful candidates but for each one there is a portrait.

<u>National Cyclopedia of American Biography.</u> Clifton, N. J.: James T. White Company, 1898-1966, 50 vols.
This is the most comprehensive of the American biographical directories but not always reliable, since most of the biographical data is supplied by members of the biographee's family and is often unchecked by the editors for factual accuracy. There are no bibliographies but the main strength of the set is the fact that biographies are often accompanied by portraits of the person written about.

<u>National Portrait Gallery of Eminent Americans,</u> by Evert A. Duyckinck. Finch Press (Reprint of 1874 edition).
Although this book is also a biographical directory, including the biographies of 150 famous early Americans, it is not for factual purposes that it is best used. Other biographical sources are much better for factual materials but this one has a good steel engraving for each person written about.

PORTS
see
HARBORS AND PORTS

PRECIOUS STONES
see
GEMS

PREPARATORY SCHOOLS
see
PRIVATE SCHOOLS

PRESIDENTS - U. S.

There is no difficulty in finding information about the presidents of the United States.   The items listed here are ready reference materials useful in answering specific factual questions.

Facts About the Presidents, by Joseph N. Kane.   2nd ed.   H. W.
    Wilson Co., 1968.   (ISBN 0-8242-0014-4)
    A massive cumulation of data and facts concerning the men
who have served as president of the United States.   It has information not only about their lives but their families, their wives, the
elections in which they came to office, the men who served in their
cabinets, and their main accomplishments or problems while in
office.   Each president is pictured and a facsimile of his signature
is given.

The Book of Presidents, by Tim Taylor.   Arno Press, 1972.   (ISBN
    0-405-00226-2)
    This is a factual book concerning the men who have served
as president and for each one gives the usual biographical information.   Each biographical sketch is divided into four sections: the
first deals with his non-political career such as schooling, military
service, family life or civic career: the second with his political
career prior to becoming president; the third outlines the presidential years which make up the major portion of the biography, and
here one finds a list of important appointments either to the Supreme
Court or the Cabinet, a list of important legislation introduced or
enacted and any events of national importance; the final section deals
with his post-presidential years and outlines his activities after leaving the office.

Wives of the Presidents, by Arden Davis Melick.   Hammond, 1972.
    (ISBN 0-8437-3813-8)
    This is a collection of very brief biographical sketches of

wives of the presidents. The longer sketches may run four or five pages but most are much shorter. For each one there is a photograph or portrait often in full color. Most of these articles originally appeared in the American Heritage Magazine.

For very brief biographical sketches of presidents and their wives see:

World Almanac and Book of Facts, ed. by George Delury. Newspaper Enterprise Association. Annual since 1868.

PRICES

Economic Indicators. U. S. Council of Economic Advisors. U. S. Government Printing Office. Monthly since 1948.
This publication presents basic statistics on the total output, income, spending, employment and unemployment, wages, production, business activities, currency, credit, markets, Federal finances and prices. For prices there are charts concerning both consumer and wholesale prices by date, broken down for services, food, and other commodities and giving an overall figure for each item. There is also a chart showing prices paid by farmers.

Economic Theory of Cost of Living Index Numbers, by Melville J. Ulmer. AMS Press, 1972 (Reprint of 1949 ed.). (ISBN 0-404-51550-9)
Although the publication is dated now, the theory behind the use of the Cost of Living Index numbers is still valid, and although the base has been changed several times since 1949, the same principles can be applied.

Monthly Labor Review. U. S. Bureau of Labor Statistics. U. S. Government Printing Office. Monthly since 1915.
This monthly periodical carries articles on various aspects of industrial relations and reports regularly statistics on employment, hours, earnings, labor turnover and all information dealing with the labor picture in this country. A part of this is a monthly report of the Cost of Living Index. Under prices is given the Consumer and Wholesale price indexes by general summary, by groups of expenditures, by selected cities, and by items for sale arranged by date. There is also a price index for selected industries.

PRISONS AND PRISONERS
see
PENOLOGY

PRIVATE SCHOOLS

Handbook of Private Schools. An Annual Descriptive Study of Independent Education. Boston, Mass.: Porter Sargent. Annual
  since 1915.
  This is the best source of authoritative information concerning the 2,000 boarding and day schools in this country. For each
school the following information is given: name, address, presiding
officer and names of outstanding administrators of the school, cost,
size of student body, faculty-student ratio, physical facilities and
age spans covered. In addition to the strictly informational section,
there is a section of paid advertisements called "Private Schools
Illustrated" which presents frankly promotional materials in an at-
tractive way.

PRIZES
see
LITERARY AWARDS or the names of individual awards
  such as NOBEL PRIZES or OSCAR WINNERS

PRONUNCIATION

Every good dictionary will give pronunciation of the words
defined, and often will give variant pronunciations in descending
order of acceptability. But in dictionaries, pronunciation is a
secondary factor. The following books deal specifically with pronunciation.

English Pronouncing Dictionary, by Daniel Jones. 13th ed. E. P.
  Dutton, 1968. (ISBN 0-525-09863-1)
  This lists the most commonly mispronounced words in the
English language and indicates their proper pronunciation by use of
the International Phonetic Alphabet.

N. B. C. Handbook of Pronunciation, ed. by James F. Bender. 3rd
  ed. T. Y. Crowell, 1964. (ISBN 0-690-57472-X)
  Since American speech is affected and in many ways determined by the use of speech on television, this is a very important
book. It was compiled as a determinant in the use of pronunciation
by announcers and newsmen for the National Broadcasting Company.
It gives pronunciation of more than 15,000 words which commonly
cause trouble, with emphasis on geographical and foreign words.
The pronunciation is given in simplified spelling and also by the
standard phonetic alphabet.

Pronouncing Dictionary of American English, ed. by John S. Kenyon.
  2nd ed. G. C. Merriam Co., 1953. (ISBN 0-87779-047-7)

Compiled by the publishers of Webster's Third New International Dictionary, this is an authoritative dictionary of pronunciation, although it is devoted more to regional differences than to standardization of the tongue.

PROOFREADING

Guide for Authors: Manuscript, Proof and Illustration, by Payne E. Thomas. 2nd ed. C. C. Thomas, 1972. (ISBN 0-398-01916-9)
This handbook for prospective authors in the preparation of their manuscript for presentation includes a section on the proofreading and printing of the book.

Proofreading and Copy Preparation, by Joseph Lasky. Agathon Press, 1971. (ISBN 0-87586-023-0)
This handbook gives not only information on preparation of the manuscript but also detailed information concerning the proper way to proofread the manuscript. It gives rules of capitalization, punctuation, abbreviations, etc.

Words Into Type, by Marjorie E. Skillin. Rev. ed. Appleton-Century-Crofts, 1964. (ISBN 0-390-81130-0)
A handbook for preparation of manuscripts for writers, editors, proofreaders and printers. Gives hints on grammar, punctuation style, and use of words.

PROVERBS

Dictionary of American Proverbs and Proverbial Phrases, 1820-1880, by Archer Taylor. Harvard University Press, 1958. (ISBN 0-674-20500-6)
This is a listing of those proverbial sayings which had their origin in the new world and in its development. It covers those in use during the major part of the 19th Century and gives for each one its source, meaning and first recorded use.

Oxford Dictionary of English Proverbs, by F. P. Wilson. 3rd ed. Oxford University Press, 1970. (ISBN 0-19-869118-1)
This is an alphabetical arrangement of proverbs in current usage in the English-speaking world but with primary emphasis on proverbs which originated in the British Isles. For each saying listed there is a date of the first known or recorded use, the source and variant wordings if in common usage.

Proverbs: A Comparative Book of English, French, German, Italian, Spanish and Russian Proverbs with a Latin Appendix, ed. by

Jerzy Gluski.   American Elsevier, 1971.   (ISBN 0-444-40949-1)
     This is a collection of the major proverbs from each of the
seven languages mentioned and for each language approximately a
thousand proverbs are listed.   The arrangement is topical and is
divided into 48 general sections.   When there are duplicate or near
duplicate proverbs in several languages, the nearest variant in each
language is given.

Racial Proverbs: A Selection of the World's Proverbs Arranged
     Linguistically, ed. by Selwyn G. Champion.   Barnes and Noble,
     1966.   (ISBN 0-7100-1169-5)
     This is a world-wide collection of proverbs arranged by lan-
guage of origin.   There are four indexes; geographical, subject,
race, and chief word.   Each country or racial section is introduced
by an article by an expert in that field.

PSEUDONYMS
see
NICKNAMES

PSYCHIATRY

Guide to the Literature in Psychiatry, ed. by Bernice Ennis.   Los
     Angeles, Calif.: Partridge Press, 1971.   (ISBN 0-913306-01-0)
     This is more than a periodical or literature index.   It has
organized the materials dealing with psychiatry into various source
centers, i. e. , periodical literature, index or reference materials,
books dealing with psychiatry, non-book materials in the field, government publications, translations, libraries specializing in psychiatry, and finally a list of publishers in the field.

Handbook of Psychiatry, by Philip Solomon.   2nd ed.   Los Altos,
     Calif.: Lange Medical Publications, 1971.   (ISBN 0-87041-161-6)
     This is a handbook primarily intended for the practitioner in
the field of psychiatry or medicine and not really of much use to
the untrained person, although it is a good presentation of the major
issues in psychiatric treatment and of possible future directions.
Probably most important for the average user are the bibliographies
at the end of each section.

Psychiatric Dictionary, by Leland E. Hinsie.   4th ed.   Oxford Uni-
     versity Press, 1970.   (ISBN 0-19-501132-5)
     The standard dictionary of psychiatric terms.   It defines al-
most 10, 000 words and terms in common usage in the profession
and covers all fields of psychiatric care from community and social
psychiatry to clinical psychiatry.   The new edition conforms fully
with the latest International Classification of Diseases in nomenclature.

PSYCHOLOGY

Annual Review of Psychology, ed. by Paul Mussen. Palo Alto,
Calif.: Annual Reviews. Annual since 1949.
Outstanding writers and practitioners in the field of psychology have combined each year to write an annual review of the events
of the year and to point to directions for the future.

Dictionary of Psychology, by James Drever. Rev. ed. Penguin
Books, 1964. (ISBN 0-14-051005-2)
Although British-oriented, this is an excellent collection of
psychological terms and their definitions.

Dictionary of Psychology, by Phillip L. Harriman. Citadel Press,
1971 (Reprint of 1960 ed.). (ISBN 0-8065-0252-5)
This gives fairly brief but generally adequate and accurate
definitions of many specialized terms and ideas used in psychology
and psychiatry.

Harvard List of Books in Psychology. 4th ed. Harvard University
Press, 1971. (ISBN 0-674-37601-3)
This has long been the definitive bibliography in the field of
psychology. Each edition has added some titles and deleted others,
and this new edition represents a 40% change from the third. The
books listed are carefully annotated and give an overall view of the
field from classical works on the subject down to contemporary
topics.

Psychological Abstracts. American Psychological Association. Annual since 1927.
This is a collection of abstracted materials from new books
and periodical articles dealing with all phases of psychology. It is
published monthly and cumulated with author and subject indexes
each year.

School Psychologist's Handbook, by Arthur Atwell. Los Angeles,
Calif.: Western Psychological Services, 1972. (ISBN 0-87424-
122-7)
This is a very brief introduction to the profession of school
psychologist. It contains a glossary of terms, a list of tests available, and publishers of materials on psychology as applied to the
school situation.

PUBLIC ADMINISTRATION
see
GOVERNMENT

PUBLIC HEALTH

Directory of Local Health Units.   U. S. Public Health Service. U. S.
Government Printing Office.   Annual since 1942.
   This lists the local health units and state health officers by
state and then by locale.   It gives for each unit the name of the re-
sponsible officer and the address.

Health and Development: An Indexed Annotated Bibliography, compiled by Kathleen N. Williams.   Department of International
Health, Johns Hopkins University, 1972.
   A good bibliography of articles from books and periodicals
dealing with every aspect of public health.

Health Manpower.   U. S. Public Health Service.   National Center for
Health Statistics.   U. S. Government Printing Office, 1971.
(HE 20. 1500:T23)
   Statistical data on the personnel involved in health maintenance in the United States.   There are tables showing the distribution of doctors, dentists, pharmacists, nurses and other medical
personnel.   The book is arranged by state, standard metropolitan
district, by county and by city.

Health Service Reports.   Health Service and Mental Health Administration.   U. S. Government Printing Office.   Monthly since 1971.
(HE 20. 2010/2)
   These are monthly publications of a scientific, technical or
administrative nature, of interest to persons interested in public
health.   Formerly called Public Health Reports, 1952-1971.

A History of Public Health, by George Rosen.   New York: M. D.
Publications, 1958.   (ISBN 0-910922-06-3)
   This is a comprehensive history of public health from the
earliest recorded account up to the middle 1950's.   It has a list of
important persons in the field of public health and for each gives a
brief biographical sketch.   There are also lists of public health
periodicals arranged by country of publication and a listing of societies and associations devoted to public health services.

PUNCTUATION

Dictionary of Usage and Style: The Reference Guide for Professional
Writers, Reporters, Editors, Teachers and Students, by Roy
Copperud.   Hawthorn Press, 1964.
   This comprehensive guide to writing term papers, articles
and other materials gives hints on the proper use of words and
phrases.   It also has articles dealing with particular subjects of interest such as punctuation.

A Manual For Writers of Term Papers, Theses and Dissertations, by Kate Turabian. 4th ed. University of Chicago Press, 1973. (ISBN 0-226-81620-6)

This manual for preparation of term papers has been adopted as the official policy for many colleges and universities and has a good section on accepted punctuation.

Proofreading and Copy Preparation, by Joseph Lasky. Agathon Press, 1971. (ISBN 0-87586-023-0)

Although intended primarily as a manual for the preparation and proofreading of manuscripts, this has a good section dealing with normal punctuation.

Words Into Type, by Marjorie J. Skillin. Rev. ed. Appleton-Century-Crofts, 1964. (ISBN 0-390-81130-0)

This gives the rules for punctuation as used by writers and editors.

PUNS

Perhaps there is no place for a book of puns in a reference book but one does get questions about puns, or speakers who want to use a pun in place of a more conventional quotation.

Bennett Cerf's Treasury of Atrocious Puns, by Bennett Cerf. Harper & Row, 1968. (ISBN 0-06-010691-3)

While not actually a reference book this is the most useful book of puns available.

QUOTATIONS

One of the most frequent questions, especially in an academic or school library, is for quotations by some specific person or about some specific topic. Speakers and writers are always wanting to sprinkle other people's wisdom in their own efforts and one of the easiest ways to do this is to use direct quotations.

The two most common methods of arranging books of quotations are by the persons being cited or by the subject of the quotation. Since most questions are for quotations about a specific subject, this seems to be the more logical arrangement, but whatever arrangement is used, the book is never better than its index, which must be complete and accurate if the necessary information is to be easily found. There should be an index to subject, to speaker, and to the main words of the quotation.

AUTHOR ARRANGEMENT

Although this is the less desirable of the two arrangements,

surprisingly the most famous of all quotation books is arranged by
author.

Bartlett's Familiar Quotations, by John Bartlett. 14th ed. Little,
    Brown, 1968. (ISBN 0-316-08273-2)
        This is arranged by the person quoted and those persons are
arranged not alphabetically but chronologically. This necessitates
use of the index for virtually any question. Despite this handicap
this is a very useful book. It cites almost 200,000 quotations and
for many has footnotes explaining the circumstances under which the
quotation was made. It has an excellent index for authors, subjects,
key words and often sources.

Oxford Dictionary of Quotations. 2nd ed. Oxford University Press,
    1953. (ISBN 0-19-211523-5)
        This one is also arranged by author but at least it is ar-
ranged alphabetically rather than chronologically. In its introduction,
it states its scope as a dictionary of familiar quotations, not a
comprehensive dictionary of all quotations. There is an excellent
index to all key words of the quotation making any desired quotation
easy to find.

SUBJECT ARRANGEMENT

Dictionary of Quotations, ed. by Bergen Evans. Delacorte Press,
    1968.
        This one is arranged by large subject headings and, being
newer than the other two, can be used to supplement the Bartlett
and Stevenson books. It is particularly well indexed with three
separate indexes: a topical index, an author index, and a key word
index. The quotation citations give author and book but generally do
not give date of quotation.

Home Book of American Quotations, ed. by Bruce Bohle. Dodd,
    Mead, 1967. (ISBN 0-396-05508-7)
        This book is frankly patterned on the format and arrangement
of the Stevenson's Home Book of Quotations and follows it very well.
Quotations are arranged by subject heading and for each quotation
cited it gives the author, the work and, most of the time, the date
of the quotation. There is an excellent index to subjects and key
words; however, there is no separate index to persons cited, which
may prove a handicap in some questions. The quotations cited are
all by Americans or deal with America.

Home Book of Quotations, by Burton Stevenson. Rev. ed. Dodd,
    Mead, 1967. (ISBN 0-396-02533-1)
        This book is the ultimate in collections of quotations and can
be recommended for first purchase by libraries of any size. The
quotations are arranged by subject with an excellent index to key
words in the quotation as well as a listing, by author, of quotations
from that author. The author and source as well as pagination within the source are given for each quotation cited.

Speaker's Encyclopedia of Stories, Quotations and Anecdotes, ed. by

Jacob Braude. Prentice Hall, 1971. (ISBN 0-13-824151)
Although not devoted entirely to quotations, this book of speaker's helps contains many quotations, citing the person quoted but not the original source. The stories are arranged by subject, with index to subject and author.

RACES
see
ANTHROPOLOGY

RACING

The subject of racing falls into several different categories, e.g., automobile, aircraft, horse, and boats. For general information concerning recent racing events, and the outcome of specific races, see the following:

Facts on File, an Indexed Record of World Events, ed. by Lester A. Sobel. Facts on File, Inc. Weekly with annual cumulations since 1941.
The index will give you the winners of various types of races during the period in which they occur.

Information Please Almanac, ed. by Dan Golenpaul. Dan Golenpaul Associates. Annual since 1946.
See name of sport in index for listing of winner for the past year.

World Almanac and Book of Facts, ed. by George Delury. Newspaper Enterprise Association. Annual since 1968.
See name of sport in index for listing of recent winners of various races.

AIRPLANE RACING

Racing Planes and Air Races, ed. by Reed Kinert. Aero Press, 1967-1972. 8 vols.
This is the complete history of air races in the U.S. and the world. Volume one covers the years 1901-1923 and each volume covers an additional period until volume eight which covers the activity of 1971. Hopefully, this will now be continued indefinitely. This gives a good history of each type of sports flying and the various awards that have been offered and won over the years, plus short sketches of the men who flew the planes.

Sky Racers: Speed Kings of Aviation's Golden Age, by Joseph F. Hood. Grosset and Dunlap, n.d. (ISBN 0-448-02152-8)
This is a biographical directory of the men who made air

racing history and the races in which they competed.

AUTOMOBILE RACING

Encyclopedia of Auto Racing Greats, by Robert Gutter. Prentice
Hall, 1973. (ISBN 0-13-275206-9)
This is a biographical directory of the men who have made
car racing history. For each person listed there is a fairly long
biographical sketch, many accompanied by pictures, in which normal
biographical data is given along with his contributions to the field
and any races or honors that he has won. This is often the only
place that such biographical information can be found.

Encyclopedia of Motor Sports, ed. by G. N. Georgano. Viking
Press, 1971. (ISBN 0-670-29405-5)
This is a well illustrated book with 62 excellent color plates
of racing cars, drivers, and organizations. This lists types of
cars, famous drivers, and organizations which sponsor racing events.

BOAT RACING

American Power Boat Association Year Book and Racing Rules.
Detroit, Mich.: American Power Boat Association, annual.
This annual publication of the American Power Boat Association gives the latest rules for races along with a compilation of
racing records, winners of championship events and a directory of
members of the association.

HORSE RACING

Complete Guide to Thoroughbred Racing, by Tom Ainsley. Trident
Press, 1968.
This compares favorably with the statistical books put out
about baseball; it is full of statistical and factual data. It is aimed
primarily at the person doing horse handicapping but it answers all
the questions that can be answered statistically about the sport.

Horses and Courses, by David Hedges. Viking Press, 1972. (ISBN
0-670-37953-0)
This practical history of the "Sport of Kings" is filled with
pictures of famous horses, jockeys, owners, trainers and of race
tracks. There is a listing of the winners of the important stake
races through the years.

RADIO

The Radio Amateur's Handbook, ed. by The Headquarters Staff,
American Radio Relay League. Newington, Conn.: Radio Relay
League, annual since 1922.
Although intended to provide information on the proper hand-

ling and enjoyment of amateur radio, this handbook provides much more. It has a good brief history of the development of radio and an introduction to radio theory. Its main contribution is instruction in the making and use of radio transmitters, receivers, and antennas. It summarizes government regulations and license and insurance requirements. There is also a good glossary of radio terminology and the abbreviations used in the profession. This book has many diagrams and illustrations which make the construction of "ham" equipment much easier. This book is similar to but better than a book with the same title published by T. Y. Crowell.

The Radio Amateur's Handbook, ed. by Robert Hertzberg. 12th ed. T. Y. Crowell, 1970. (ISBN 0-690-66773-6)
Contains much the same information as book by the Radio League book but is less comprehensive in its coverage.

The Big Broadcast: 1920-1950. A New, Revised and Greatly Expanded Edition of "Radio's Golden Age"--the Complete Reference Work, by Frank Buxton. Viking Press, 1972. (ISBN 0-670-16240-X)
The subtitle "a complete reference work" is a little grandiose but the book is worth shelf space in any library. It is an alphabetical arrangement of the radio shows of the past and for each show gives the type of show that it was, the cast of characters, the announcers, the producers, date of first broadcast and final broadcasts and all the historical data available for each show. In addition there is a good bibliography of articles dealing with the golden age of radio and an index to all personal names mentioned in the historical articles.

North American Radio-TV Station Guide, ed. by Vane A. Jones. Howard W. Sams. Annual since 1963.
The information here is supplied by official FCC publications and lists by geographic location, by frequency, and by call letters all FM and AM radio stations in the United States, Canada, Cuba, Mexico and the West Indies. For each station listed there is given the radio frequency, the power of the station, its network affiliation and an indication whether it broadcasts stereo programs.

RAILROADS
see also
ENGINES - RAILROAD

Directory of World Electric Lines, ed. by Earl Clark. Cincinnati, Ohio: Earl Clark, 1971. Issued irregularly.
The title suggests a listing of electric power companies but actually it is a directory of the electrically operated railroads of the world. For each line listed (more abroad than in continental United States) the name, location, mileage, type of equipment used, gauge of track used and a short history of the line are given. The

lines are arranged geographically, first by continent, then country, and finally alphabetically by name. Of special interest are some of the subsidiary material included, such as lists of electric railroad museums, lists of lines no longer in existence, etc.

Official Guide of the Railroads and Steam Navigation Lines of the
    United States, Puerto Rico, Canada, Mexico. New York: Na-
    tional Railway Publication Co. Monthly since 1868.
        This has all the timetables of the U. S. Railways with maps showing the railway systems. It also contains schedules for inter-coastal shipping lines and a condensed airline schedule.

Rand McNally Handy Railroad Atlas of the United States. Rand
    McNally and Co., n. d. (ISBN 0-528-21102-1)
        This is an atlas of the railroad lines of the country. There is a map for the whole country and then individual state maps. Each map shows the railroad lines, the towns on the lines and the rail distances between the cities.

RECORDS
see
SUPERLATIVES

REFERENCE BOOKS
see also
ATLASES; DICTIONARIES; ENCYCLOPEDIAS

        Since this book is intended primarily for the working librar-ian, we will not annotate such obvious sources as Winchell, Cheney and others. Here are listed only those materials which evaluate more recent publications.

American Reference Books Annual, ed. by Bohdan S. Wynar. Little-
    ton, Colo.: Libraries Unlimited. Annual since 1969.
        This is a comprehensive annual reviewing service for refer-ence books published in the United States. It covers an amazing number of reference books and each review is signed by the re-viewer. The opinions are somewhat personal at times but one can normally trust the evaluations.

Reference and Subscription Book Reviews, ed. by Reference and Sub-
    scription Books Review Committee. American Library Associ-
    ation. Biennial.
        These are compilations of reviews of subscription and refer-ence books which appear in the American Library Association Book-list. The coverage is quite limited but the reviews are much more detailed than those in the Wynar book. The reviews give the history of the publication, the scope, the purpose, the authority, and the

usefulness to various types of libraries. Any excellent source of objective reviews, but of limited utility because of the length of time between publication of the book and the appearance of the reviews.

REPTILES
see
AMPHIBIANS AND REPTILES

RETIREMENT

Complete Guide to Retirement, by Thomas Collins. Prentice Hall, 1972. (ISBN 0-13-160382-5)
Each year sees many books on the subject of how to retire, what and what not to do, and most of them became dated almost as soon as they are printed. This one seems to have held up fairly well and the ideas expressed today are as good as when it was written. It gives the usual sort of information but adds at the end of each chapter a good bibliography of pamphlets, government documents and other books. The subjects covered include the financial problems involved in adjusting to a lessened income, the time problems created by the lack of a regular occupation, the health problems always present in older years, legal problems and many others.

Where to Retire on a Small Income, by Norman D. Ford. 18th ed. Harian Publications, 1973. (ISBN 0-448-06971-7)
This one is prone to the common faults mentioned above. The prices mentioned are necessarily out of date as soon as the book is written, so that one cannot depend upon the money quotations, but his suggested places for relatively cheap living are still valid even if the prices are not. It would be a better book if written without mention of prices.

RHYMES

For books dealing with Mother Goose or nursery rhymes see NURSERY RHYMES. For books dealing with verse in general see POETRY.
This section focuses on rhyming dictionaries. Most of those do about the same thing, i. e., give lists of words of one, two or three syllables which can be considered to rhyme. Most are arranged alphabetically by actual sound rather than by spelling and almost every one has a section devoted to the intricacies of the making of poetry. The following are arranged in order of preference.

Poet's Manual and Rhyming Dictionary, by Frances Stillman. T. Y.

Crowell, 1965. (ISBN 0-690-64572-4)
New Rhyming Dictionary and Poet's Handbook, by Burges Johnson.
    Rev. ed. Harper & Row, 1957. (ISBN 0-06-012205-6)
Complete Rhyming Dictionary, by Clement Wood. Doubleday, 1936.
    (ISBN 0-385-00046-4)

ROADS AND HIGHWAYS

Highway Statistics. U. S. Bureau of Public Roads. U. S. Govern-
    ment Printing Office. Annual since 1945. (TD 2.110:)
        This annual publication of the Bureau of Public Roads is
packed with statistics and analytical tables, including such things as
use of motor fuel and motor vehicles, the financing of state and
local highways, federal and state highway taxes and federal aid to
the building of highways.

Highway Progress. U. S. Bureau of Public Roads. U. S. Govern-
    ment Printing Office. Annual since 1904. (TD 2.101:)
        The title to this publication varies from year to year but it
is the annual report of the Bureau of Public Roads and describes the
work of the Bureau and the accomplishments of the Federal aid to
highways program for the past year. It also contains many statistical tables dealing with highways and highway construction.

Road Atlas: United States, Canada, Mexico. Rand McNally and Co.
    Annual since 1924.
        This is a supplement to the Rand McNally Commercial Atlas
and is published annually as a part of that service although it can be
purchased separately. It has excellent maps of all states and the
provinces of Canada as well as a general map of Mexico. There
are mileage charts and time zone charts. It will not take the place
of the maps distributed by the gasoline stations but it is a good
second choice.

ROCKETS
see
GUIDED MISSILES

ROCKS
see also
GEOLOGY; MINERALOGY

Field Book of Rocks and Minerals, by Frederick H. Pogue. 3rd ed.
    Houghton-Mifflin, 1960. (ISBN 0-395-08106-8)
        An excellent identification guide, with photographs of various

rocks and minerals and diagrams of the crystal formations of the
minerals described. For each rock, there is given the physical
properties, composition, a suggested test for identification, and other
distinguishing marks.

The Rockhound's Manual, by Gordon S. Fay. Harper & Row, 1972.
 (ISBN 0-06-011218-2)
 This handbook by a geological engineer serves as a clear and
precise guide to all aspects of rock collecting and identification. The
final section deals with the identification of the most commonly
sought stones and minerals of the United States. There are many
black and white illustrations and eight color plates to assist in identification.

RODEOS

Rodeo Reference Yearbook.   New York: Rodeo Information Foundation.   Annual since 1955.
 The Rodeo Information Foundation is the public relations
agency for the whole rodeo world and its annual reference yearbook
is the Bible for the sport. It lists the latest champions, the results of championships for the past year and the scheduled events
for the upcoming year.

 For a mere listing of Rodeo Championship Standings for the
past year or for a listing of the men who have won the All Around
Championship for the past fifteen years, see:

World Almanac and Book of Facts, ed. by George Delury.   Newspaper Enterprise Association.   Annual since 1868.
 In index under RODEOS.

ROYALTY
see
KINGS AND RULERS

SAINTS

Butler's Lives of the Saints, ed. by Bernard Kelly.   Westminister,
 Md.: Christian Classics, 1962.   5 vols.
 Originally published in 1756, this has long been an authority
on the lives of Catholic saints.   This latest edition has shortened
some of the biographies and increased the coverage of others, while
some minor saints have been omitted entirely.   It remains, however, one of the outstanding works in the field with a coverage of

almost 2500 saints.

Heavenly Friends, by Rosalie M. Levy. Boston, Mass.: Daughters
of St. Paul, 1958.
This is a chronological arrangement of the saints by saints'
days and, while nowhere near as complete a listing as either the
Butler or the Baring-Gould books, it is a loving depiction of the
many saints on the clerical calendar.

Lives of the Saints, by Sabine Baring-Gould. Finch Press (Reprint
of 1914 ed.). 16 vols.
The standard work on the lives of the saints, including the
English martyrs and Cornish, Scottish and Welsh saints, with a full
index for the whole work. The use of the index is important since
the lives of the saints are arranged chronologically by the day of
the year on which the saint's day is celebrated. This mammoth
work may be more than the average small library will need or use.

Saints and Their Emblems, by Maurice Drake. Burt Franklin, 1971
(Reprint of 1916 ed.). (ISBN 0-8337-0902-X)
This is a standard work on the symbolism of sacred art.
There is a dictionary of the saints giving brief coverage of the life
and then the symbols used to depict the saint in religious art. In
addition, there are appendices which list the patron saints of various arts, crafts, professions and trades as well as patron saints of
cities, countries, etc.

SAYINGS
see
QUOTATIONS

SCHOLARSHIPS
see
COLLEGE COSTS; FELLOWSHIPS AND GRANTS

SCULPTURE

Sculpture Index, ed. by Jane Clapp. Scarecrow Press, 1970. 2 vols.
Vol. 1: Sculpture of Europe and the Contemporary Middle East.
(ISBN 0-8108-0249-X)
Vol. 2: Sculpture of the Americas, the Orient, the Pacific
World and the Classical World. (ISBN 0-8108-0311-9)
This set is intended as a guide to pictures of sculpture which
have appeared in over 950 different publications ranging from art
histories to exhibit catalogs. Items are listed by the sculptor, the
title of the work, and by subjects.

New Dictionary of Modern Sculpture, ed. by Robert Mallard. Tudor
    Press, 1971. (ISBN 0-8148-0479-9)
    This is a translation from the French of a standard work on
modern sculpture and sculptors. It contains biographies of over 600
sculptors beginning with Rodin and has extensive illustrations of their
works. Although it is designated as a dictionary it does not discuss
the art other than as applied to the individual.

History of Sculpture, by George H. Chase. Greenwood Press, 1972
    (Reprint of 1925 ed.). (ISBN 0-8371-5681-5)
    This standard work has numerous illustrations and an excel-
lent bibliography as well as an index to the locations of various
works of sculpture. It is organized first by periods of history and
then by country but there is a good index.

SEX

        One is tempted to say that one should learn about sex other
than in a library and let the whole thing go at that, but you do get
questions.

Psychology of Sex, by Havelock Ellis. Emerson Press, 1960.
    (ISBN 0-87523-013-X)
    This is the best or certainly the most famous book dealing
with the psychology of sex and should be in every library.

Marriage Manual, by Hannah Stone. Rev. and enl. ed. Simon &
    Schuster, 1968. (ISBN 0-671-45101-4)
    A how-to-do-it manual for the wedding night and beyond. This
is possibly the most respected book of its type and answers many of
the questions which bother prospective mates or married couples
having sexual problems.

Sexual Behavior in the Human Female, ed. by Alfred Kinsey.
    Saunders, 1953. (ISBN 0-7216-5450-9)
Sexual Behavior in the Human Male, ed. by Alfred Kinsey. Saunders,
    1948. (ISBN 0-7216-5445-2)
    When these books appeared in the late forties and early fif-
ties, they caused quite a stir. Today the findings seem rather
mundane, but these remain among the best studies of the sexual behavior of humans.

SHAKESPEARE

Dictionary of the Characters and Proper Names in the Works of
    Shakespeare, by Francis G. Stokes. Somerset Press (Reprint
    of 1960 ed.).

This includes in one alphabetical arrangement all the names which appear in the works of Shakespeare, including historical, fictional and legendary characters as well as the names of places and titles of the plays. For each play, there is a summary of the plot and the source of the original work on which the play was based.

Shakespeare Commentary, by Arthur E. Baker. Ungar Press, 1957. 2 vols. (ISBN 0-8044-2018-1)
A commentary on the plays and poems of Shakespeare.

Shakespeare Companion, 1564-1964, by Frank E. Halliday. Rev. ed. Schocken Press, 1964. (ISBN 0-8052-3237-0)
This is a handbook covering every aspect of Shakespeare's life and works. It is an alphabetically arranged list of subjects and includes brief biographies of his chief associates, his publishers, players, critics and anyone else associated with him. There are summaries of all his plays and comments on his various poems. It is aided by an excellent bibliography and a picture section.

Shakespeare Concordance, ed. by John Bartlett. Gordon Press (Reprint of 1894 ed.).
The most complete concordance of Shakespeare's work available. Every key word in his plays and poetry is indexed, with reference to the Globe edition of his works published in 1891. Although keyed to a specific edition, it still is of great value with any legitimate edition of Shakespeare's works.

SHELLS

Field Guide to the Shells of Our Atlantic and Gulf Coasts, ed. by Roger T. Peterson. Revised edition. Houghton-Mifflin, 1951. (ISBN 0-395-08027-4)
Field Guide to the Shells of the Pacific Coast and Hawaii, ed. by Roger T. Peterson. Revised edition. Houghton-Mifflin, 1966. (ISBN 0-395-08029-0)
These two titles in the Roger Peterson Nature Guide Series together give an excellent coverage of the shells found on American seashores. For each type of shell, a simple description, often accompanied by pictures or color plates, make identification fairly easy. The arrangement is by family of shell but there is a good index. There is also a glossary which defines the unusual words used by shell collectors.

The Shell Book, by Julia E. Rogers. Rev. ed. Charles T. Branford, 1951. (ISBN 0-8231-2007-4)
Another easily used and understood guide to the seashells of America. The arrangement is by family and genera but a good index and illustrations make the identification of specific shells easy. There is a good glossary of shell terms.

Shell Collector's Handbook, by A. Hyatt Verrill. Putnam, 1950.
   (ISBN 0-399-10736-3)
   This is a part of the Putnam Nature Field Guide series and
is an excellent introduction to the art of collecting shells. It gives
an identification guide but its more important contribution is information about the way to hunt shells, the way to clean them, catalog
them and display them.

SHIPS

All About Ships and Shipping, by E. P. Harnack. Transatlantic
   Arts, 1964.
   This is a handbook type publication which gives diagrams,
plans, and photographs of the construction of all types of ships.
Particularly interesting are the color illustrations of the flags and
funnels, and decorations of various shipping companies and countries.
There are also illustrations of the international code flags and their
meanings.

Jane's Fighting Ships, ed. by Raymond V. B. Blackmon.   Franklin
   Watts.   Annual since 1897.
   This is the most important reference book dealing with fighting ships and is recognized by naval scholars as the most authentic
information available on the navies of the world. It is arranged by
country and covers not only the large countries but even countries
which have only one or two ships in their navies. For each ship,
there is full technical data with pictures, silhouettes, capacities,
firepower, and all needed information.

Jane's Surface Skimmers: Hovercrafts and Hydrofoils, ed. by Roy
   McLeavey.   Franklin Watts.   Annual since 1965.
   This is another in Jane's excellent series, this time devoted
to hydrofoils and hovercrafts.   It gives all technical data needed,
plus black and white photographs and diagrams.   The last word on
the subject.

Merchant Vessels of the United States.   U. S. Bureau of Customs.
   U. S. Government Printing Office.   Annual since 1869.
   This annual publication lists the names of all American
merchant vessels and yachts.   For each vessel, it gives the official
number, the radio call letters and frequency, name, classification,
capacity length, breadth and depth, year of building, place of home
port and type of business in which the vessel is engaged.

Ship Identification: Merchant Ships, by E. C. Talbot-Booth.   Naval
   Institute Press, 1970.   (ISBN 0-87021-875-1)
   This publication by the U. S. Naval Institute is an excellent
identification guide to the various merchant vessels of the world.
For each vessel described there is information about tonnage, pro-
pulsion and riggings.   Index to ship names and ship types.

SHORT STORIES

No attempt is made to list the many anthologies of short stories which are available, but the Houghton Mifflin annual publication is included as a continuing publication which is worth adding to any library.

Best American Short Stories, ed. by Martha Foley. Houghton Mifflin. Annual since 1915.
There are currently only the 1971-1972-1973 editions of this series in print but two other compilations are available which select from past editions. They are:

The Best of the Best, ed. by Martha Foley. Houghton Mifflin, 1952. (ISBN 0-395-07686-2)
Fifty Best American Short Stories: 1915-1965, ed. by Martha Foley. Houghton Mifflin, 1965. (ISBN 0-395-07687-0)

Short Story Index, compiled by Dorothy E. Cook. H. W. Wilson, 1953. (ISBN 0-8242-0384-4)
This volume indexes more than 60,000 short stories by author, title and subject. This index covers anthologies of short stories up through 1949. For each main entry which is the author entry, it gives the author's full name, his dates and the title of each of his stories and a citation where each story appears. Four supplements carry the coverage up to the year 1968:

Supplement 1950-54. (ISBN 0-8242-0385-2)
Supplement 1955-58. (ISBN 0-8242-0386-0)
Supplement 1959-63. (ISBN 0-8242-0387-9)
Supplement 1964-68. (ISBN 0-8242-0399-2)

SIGNALS

All About Ships and Shipping, by E. P. Harnack. Transatlantic Arts, 1964.
Although not primarily about signaling, this has an excellent section in full color giving the illustrations of the international code flags and their meanings.

Bluejacket's Manual. 18th ed. U. S. Naval Institute. (Order from Arco Press.) (ISBN 0-668-03048-8)
This handbook for the enlisted man in the Navy was originally published in 1902 and has served generations of Naval personnel as a source of practical information. Chapter 30, Visual Signals, is as good a summary of various signaling systems as it is possible to find. There is a diagrammed illustration of signaling by semaphore, explanation of signaling by lights, the use of code flags, and the meaning of each flag. In addition, since the international morse code can be used by radiotelegraph or by the navy

flashing light signals, there is a full listing of the international Morse code.   There is also a discussion of tug whistle signals and the hand signals used on river boats.

Scout Handbook, by Frederick L. Hines.   8th ed. Boy Scouts of
      America, 1972.   (ISBN 0-8395-6500-3)
        This includes a very good section on semaphore and the Morse code as well as hand signals.   It is not nearly so comprehensive as the Bluejacket's Manual but it is more likely to be found in the collection of the small library.

SIGNS AND SYMBOLS

American Symbols, A Pictorial History, ed. by Ernst Lehner.
      Tudor Press, 1957.   (ISBN 0-8148-0008-4)
        This is a pictorial representation of the signs and symbols which have played a part in the history of the United States, beginning with the flags planted by Columbus and continuing up to modern times.   There are advertising symbols, political symbols and sports emblems.   Each is clearly illustrated with black and white drawings.

Picture Book of Symbols, ed. by Ernst Lehner.   Tudor Press, 1956.
      (ISBN 0-8148-0250-8)
        A companion volume to American Symbols covering the use of symbols as a means of human communication, from the crude drawings on the walls of caves down to the modern day.   There are 29 sections, each dealing with a specific type of symbol or its applications.   These include magic symbols, religious symbols, patriotic symbols, good luck, etc.   Each section is illustrated by clearly drawn and easily copied reproductions of the various signs and symbols.

Symbols, Signs and Signets, ed. by Ernst Lehner.   Dover Press,
      1950.   (ISBN 0-486-22241-1)
        Much more complete than the other two books, this arranges several thousand signs and symbols in large subject categories. The important feature of the book is the reproductions of symbols; the text consisting only of brief histories as introductions to the twelve main sections.

SKIN DIVING

Complete Manual of Skin Diving, by A. P. Balder.   Macmillan, 1968.
      (ISBN 0-02-50641)
        This is a general handbook which can be used by both the beginner and the experienced diver.   It lists types of equipment and

various techniques for using that equipment.

Dive: Complete Book of Skin Diving, by Rick Carrier. Funk and
    Wagnalls, 1973. (ISBN 0-308-10056-5)
    An even more comprehensive handbook to skin diving tech-
niques and equipment.

SLANG

Dictionary of American Slang, ed. by Harold Wentworth. T. Y.
    Crowell, 1960. (ISBN 0-690-23602-6)
    This is the best of the dictionaries of American slang. It
has a full listing of many words which are not used in polite con-
versation, as well as more conventional words heard on the streets
and factories. For each term there is a good description of its
meaning and usage.

Dictionary of Slang and Unconventional English, ed. by Eric Par-
    tridge. Macmillan, 1970.
    This is an excellent work including terms used by members
of the underworld, colloquialisms and catch terms, as well as the
more conventional slang expressions. The dictionary is historical
in approach but omits any words not used after the year 1600.

Slang Today and Yesterday, by Eric Partridge. 4th ed. Barnes &
    Noble, 1970. (ISBN 0-389-03977-2)
    This is more a history of the use of slang in various parts
of the English speaking world than a dictionary of slang meanings,
although there is a section for this also. Either of the other titles
is more dependable for current definitions.

SNAKES
see also
AMPHIBIANS AND REPTILES

Field Book of Snakes of the United States and Canada, by Karl P.
    Schmidt. Putnam, 1941. (ISBN 0-399-10295-7)
    A handbook for the identification of almost every variety of
snake found on the North American continent. It has pictures as
well as descriptions of the snake, its habitat, its habits and its geographical distribution. This is a part of the excellent Putnam
series of Nature Field Books.

Snakes of the World, by Raymond L. Ditmars. Macmillan, 1966.
    (ISBN 0-02-53173)
    Originally published in 1933, this is written by the world's
greatest herpetologist and remains the standard work on snakes of the
world.

Snakes of the World, by John Stidworthy.   Grosset and Dunlap, 1971.
    (ISBN 0-448-00854-8)
    This is volume two of the Grosset and Dunlap All-Color
Guide Series, each volume of which deals with a specific type of
animal life and each of which is profusely illustrated with color
photographs.   This one, on the snakes of the world, is the very
best of the whole series.   It is quite comprehensive and for each
snake there is a color picture and an easily understood description
of the snake and its habits.   At the end of the book there is a listing of zoos and aquaria that have good collections of snakes.

SOCIAL SCIENCES

    There are two major encyclopedias in the social sciences and
both are still needed; neither can be considered as a substitute for
the other.

Encyclopedia of the Social Sciences, ed. by Edwin R. A. Seligman.
    Macmillan, 1937.   15 vols.
    This publication is now becoming quite dated in a rapidly
changing field but it remains an important reference work, particularly for historical perspectives and for movements which had their
beginnings in the earlier periods.

International Encyclopedia of the Social Sciences.   Collier-Macmillan,
    1968.   17 vols.
    This was originally projected to be a new edition of the En-
cyclopedia Of Social Sciences but it is actually an entirely new work.
It can be considered as a supplement to the earlier work but not a
replacement.   In both encyclopedias the articles are signed by experts, and both are reliable information sources.

DICTIONARIES

A Modern Dictionary of Sociology, by George A. Theodorson.   T. Y.
    Crowell, 1969.   (ISBN 0-690-55058-8)
    A good dictionary of contemporary sociological terms, es-
pecially those which occur in the popular press, newspapers, periodicals, books, etc.   The definitions are generally short but adequate.

BIBLIOGRAPHIES

A Reader's Guide to the Social Sciences, ed. by Bert F. Hoselitz.
    Free Press, 1970.
    Both more and less than a bibliography, this is a series of
essays by experts in specific fields describing the latest developments and listing the classical and contemporary writings in each
field.

Sources of Information in the Social Sciences, ed. by Carl M. White.

2nd ed. American Library Association, 1973. (ISBN 0-8389-0134-4)

An excellent source directory which identifies and evaluates many publications in the various disciplines.

INDEXES

Public Affairs Information Services Bulletin. Public Affairs Information Service. Weekly with annual cumulations since 1915.

A subject index to periodicals, pamphlet materials and government documents in all fields of public administration and related subjects. It is an excellent guide for the purchase of pamphlet materials.

Social Science Index. H. W. Wilson Company. Quarterly with annual cumulations since 1974.

A direct descendant of the International Index, which was published from 1907-1955. Its name was then changed to The Social Science and Humanities Index. Beginning in July 1974, the publication was divided into two separate indexes, The Social Science Index and the Humanities Index. It carries on the high tradition of Wilson indices and has coverage of 263 periodicals.

SOCIAL SECURITY

The best source of information concerning your social security benefits is the United States Government. For a good listing of publications dealing with social services in the United States see Price List # 78 of the Superintendent of Documents. (The complete list of price lists is available free of charge from the Government Printing Office.)

The following government publications will be helpful:

Estimating Your Social Security Retirement Check. July, 1972. (HE 3. 2:R31)
Planning For Later Years. 1967. (HE 3. 2: P69)
Social Security Benefits, How You Earn Them, How To Estimate The Amount. 1971. (HE 3. 52:47)

Social Security Handbook. (FS 3. 52:135)

This handbook is a distillation of the information needed to understand retirement insurance, survivor's insurance, disability insurance, health insurance or any questions concerning your Social Security benefits.

Medicare and Social Security Explained, ed. by CCH Editorial Staff. Chicago, Ill.: Commerce Clearing House, 1970.

This is a handy compilation of pertinent data on Federal Old Age benefits, covering not only Social Security but also medicare, survivor's and disability benefits, and related programs. It is

aided by a topical index.   This seems to be the best non-govern-
mental publication on the subject.

Social Security Programs in the United States.   U.S. Social Security
    Administration.   U.S. Government Printing Office, 1968.
Social Security Programs Throughout the World.   U.S. Social Se-
    curity Administration.   U.S. Government Printing Office, 1958.

SOCIOLOGY
see
SOCIAL SCIENCES

SOLAR ENERGY

Direct Use of the Sun's Energy, by Farrington Daniels.   Yale Uni-
    versity Press, 1965.   (ISBN 0-300-00399-4)
    With the recent development of the oil crisis and the result-
ing panic caused by the needs for energy, the possible use of energy
from the sun become more important.   In this book, one of the best
informed and easily understood experts outlines the problems, the
challenges and the possible benefits to be derived from solar research.   It is a fine summary of the state of the research at the
present time as well as a guide post for future developments.

Solar Energy Research, by Farrington Daniels.   University of Wis-
    consin Press, 1955.   (ISBN 0-299-01250-6)
    A listiong of persons and projects involved in solar energy
research and the type of projects that they are testing.   Rather
dated.

Coming Age of Solar Energy, by D. S. Halacy.   Rev. ed.   Harper &
    Row, 1973.   (ISBN 0-06-11714-1)
    Although written for a high school audience, this is an in-
formative book on the present state of solar energy research programs and the future of that research.   The writer may perhaps be
too optimistic in his rosy picture of future development.

SOLITAIRE
see also
CARD GAMES; GAMES

Complete Book of Solitaire and Patience Games, by Albert H. More-
    head.   Bantam Books, 1973.
    This is probably the most complete listing of one-man games
and their rules. Practically every solitaire game in existence is listed
here.

One Hundred and Fifty Solitaire Games, by Douglas Brown. Harper &
Row, n. d.   (ISBN 0-06-087033-8)
Rules and descriptions of 150 games for one person.

SONGS
see also
FOLK MUSIC

Song Index, ed. by Minnie L. Sears.   Shoe String Press, 1966 (Reprint of 1934 edition).   2 vols. in 1.   (ISBN 0-208-00548-X)
This reprint of the earlier H. W. Wilson index includes
author, title, composer and first line indexes to more than 19,000
songs.   It is useful for finding the words to songs, the complete
musical output of a composer, or poems which have been set to
music.

Popular Music: An Annotated Index of American Popular Songs.
Adrian Press, 1969.   5 vols.
An index to selected popular songs published between 1920-
1964, arranged by year then alphabetically by title.   Each entry includes the author, the composer, the publisher and, if the song was
recorded, the best selling or first recording (often both if they are
different).   There is also a list of music publishers in each volume.

SPEECHES

Documents of American History, ed. by Henry Steele Commager.
8th ed.   Appleton, 1968.   (ISBN 0-390-20369-6)
This is a collection of the important documents in American
history arranged chronologically and each with an introductory paragraph explaining its place in the history of the country.   Many of the
documents included are the texts of speeches delivered in Congress
or elsewhere.   There is a good subject index and author index.

Representative American Speeches, ed. by Waldo Braden.   H. W.
Wilson Company.   Annual since 1943.
This is an annual volume of the H. W. Wilson Reference
Shelf and each year presents the important speeches delivered in
the United States.   They may cover any subject and be delivered in
any forum.

Speech Index, ed. by Roberta Sutton.   4th ed.   Scarecrow Press,
1966.   (ISBN 0-8108-0138-8)
supplement 1966-70.   1972.   (ISBN 0-8108-0498-0)
Taken together, these two books index almost 300 collections
of world famous orations and speeches given on special occasions.
There is author, title and subject indexing in one alphabet.

Treasury of Great American Speeches, ed. by Charles Hurd. Rev.
  ed. Hawthorn Books, 1970.
  These speeches range from the time of John Winthrop in 1645
down through Nixon's first inaugural address in 1969. Each speech
is preceded by a brief introduction explaining the time and place as
well as the occasion for the speech and if necessary a summary of
the effect of the speech on the audience. The arrangement is
chronological but there is a good index to speaker and subject.

Vital Speeches of the Day. Pelham, N. Y.: City News Publishing
  Co. Bi-weekly since 1934.
  This periodical publication is indexed in Readers' Guide and
is simply a reprint of the texts of various speeches which the editor
feels have a vital effect on our nation or the world. The majority
of the speeches are by Americans but there are occasional foreign
speakers represented. Most of the speeches are printed in their
entirety, but if they are abstracted, this information is indicated.
This is a vital periodical for any library.

SPELLING

  The final authority concerning spelling remains the unabridged
dictionary and it should be consulted for any variants or secondary
acceptable spellings. There are other books, however, that are intended to help with the spelling of words and the listing of words
often misspelled.

Twenty Thousand Words, compiled by Louis A. Leslie. McGraw-
  Hill, 1972. (ISBN 0-07-037340-X)
Words Often Misspelled, by Ruth Gleeson and James Colvin. Pocket
  Books, Inc. 1963. (ISBN 0-671-77456-5)

SPIRITUALS
see also
FOLK MUSIC; SONGS

Afro-American Folksongs: A Study in Racial and National Music, by
  Henry E. Krehbiel. Ungar, 1962. (ISBN 0-8044-5571-6)
  A good history of the development not only of spirituals but
of all types of Negro folk music.

Black Music in Our Culture, by Dominique-Rene de Lerma. Kent
  State University Press, 1970. (ISBN 0-87338-110-6)
  This is a result of a seminar held on black music at the
University of Indiana and it covers all aspects of black music--jazz,
modern, spirituals, traditional, etc. Much of the seminar was de-
voted to the feelings of black composers and musicians about their

music and the black musical heritage. This book is particularly good for its bibliography of related material and its presentation of a proposed syllabus for the study of black music.

The Music of Black Americans, by Eileen Southern. Norton, 1971. (ISBN 0-393-02156-4)
    This is primarily a history of the persons who composed the music of Black America whether it was the slave in the cotton field or the modern composers of symphonic music. There is an excellent section on the history of Negro spirituals.

    Often your question will be for the words of a particular spiritual and the following are good collections of spirituals.

Book of American Negro Spirituals. Viking Press, 1940. (ISBN 0-670-18123-4)
Treasury of Negro Spirituals, by Henry A. Chambers. Emerson Press, 1963. (ISBN 0-87523-145-4)

SPORTS
see also
names of individual sports

Encyclopedia of Sports, by Frank G. Menke. 4th rev. ed. A. S. Barnes, 1969.
    This book presents a comprehensive history of nearly 80 sports, from pingpong to professional football. For each there is a brief history of the game and a listing of records and record holders and champions for the sport through the years. In addition to individual records in various sports, there is a compilation of Olympic records and champions since 1900.

Sports Rules Encyclopedia, ed. by Jess R. White. National Press, 1961. (ISBN -87484-063-5)
    This book is intended primarily for the physical education teacher or the playground director but it will be of help to anyone looking for the official rules under which various sports are played. For each sport is given the governing body for that sport and its address and then the official rules of the sport. At the end of each collection of sports rules, there is a good bibliography of books in print dealing with the sport.

STAMP COLLECTING

Stamp Collector's Handbook, by Fred Reinfeld. Doubleday, 1970. (ISBN 0-385-03183-1)
    An excellent introduction to the hobby, this book defines

philatelic terms, gives advice on type of specialization, albums and equipment as well as some information on the history of the postage stamp and stamp collecting.

Standard Handbook of Stamp Collecting, by Richard M. Cabeen. 2nd
    ed. T. Y. Crowell, 1965. (ISBN 0-690-76997-0)
    This is one of the very best introductions to the hobby of
stamp collecting. It has an excellent glossary to explain new terms
to the beginner as well as detailed tables of philatelic data and an
excellent index.

    The very heart of the hobby is the stamp catalog; without it
a collector is at a loss to evaluate his collection or the worth of
new acquisitions. There are two major catalogs available and either
is perfectly dependable. Actually, the preference will be determined
by the type of album that the collector uses to house his collection.
Each of the major catalogs is published by a philatelic supply house
that also supplies albums, and the catalog designations in one catalog will not coincide with the album designations of the other company.

Minkus New World Wide Stamp Catalog, ed. by Ben Blumenthal.
    Minkus Publications. Annual. 2 vols.
Scott Standard Postage Stamps of the World. Simon & Schuster,
    Annual. 3 vols.
    The Scott catalog is the older of the two catalogs and the
most often quoted. If only one catalog can be purchased, the writer
of this book would recommend Scott's even though he personally pre-
fers the Minkus for what seem to him to be clearer definitions and
identification.

STATE GOVERNMENT
see
GOVERNMENT - STATES

STATISTICS

    There are many sources of statistics and for statistics deal-
ing with specific fields of interest or of manufacturing, see the
appropriate subject heading in this book, i. e., for statistics concerning the production of COAL see that heading, for statistics concerning state governments, see GOVERNMENT - STATES.

Statistics Sources, ed. by Paul Wasserman. 3rd rev. ed. Gale
    Research Co., 1971.
    The sub-title to this book is "a subject guide to data on In-
dustrial, Business, Social, Educational, Financial and other topics
for the United States and selected foreign countries." This book

does not give statistical information but is possibly the best source
for locating source materials.   For each type of statistic sought one
finds not only the titles of suggested sources but also, wherever
possible, complete order information.

Handbook of Probability and Statistics with Tables, ed. by Richard
 S. Burington.   2nd ed.   McGraw-Hill, 1969.   (ISBN 0-07-
 009030-0)
 This is devoted to the presentation of the theories of probability and the application of those theories in scientific disciplines
such as physics, chemistry, biology, medicine and engineering.

Statistical Abstract of the United States.   U. S.   Bureau of the Census.   U. S. Government Printing Office.   Annual since 1878.
 (C 3. 134:)
 This is a one-volume distillation of the statistics of the social, political and economic organization of the United States as revealed by the decennial censuses.   It includes a comprehensive
selection of data from many important statistical sources both public
and private.   Good for locating statistics on any current problem or
activity in the United States.

Historical Statistics of the United States.   U. S.   Bureau of the Census.   U. S. Government Printing Office, 1960.   (C 3. 134. 2)
 This is an historical supplement to the Statistical Abstract of
the United States and as such summarizes the social and economical
development of the United States from colonial times through 1957.
It consists of 21 chapters and 51 sections and includes figures on
agriculture, armed forces, banks and banking, births and deaths,
climate, communications, construction and housing, crime, education, elections, foreign trade, government finance, immigration,
manufacturing, population and any other facet of American history
that can be portrayed statistically.   Particularly helpful is a separate chapter on Colonial statistics, which are hard to find elsewhere.

City and County Data Book.   U. S. Bureau of the Census.   U. S.
 Government Printing Office.   Every five years.   (C 3. 134.2:)
 This supplement to the Statistical Abstract of the United States
presents 144 items in tabular data format for each county, city,
state and region.   There are 113 items for each standard metropolitan area and 148 items for each city over 25, 000.

 In addition to these supplements, the Bureau of the Census
publishes individual census of agriculture, business, population, etc.

STEEL

Commodity Yearbook, ed. by Harry Jiler.   Commodity Research
 Bureau, Inc.   Annual since 1939.
 This publication gives the prices and production statistics for

each of the various commodities needed for our national welfare. Under IRON AND STEEL one finds statistics on steel production as well as salient statistics on iron ore production both here and abroad.

The Making, Shaping and Treating of Steel, ed. by Harold E. Mc-
     Gannon. 9th ed. U.S. Steel Corporation, 1971.
     This is the most complete one-volume quick reference work for authoritative information concerning the production and processing of steel. It covers everything from raw materials to finished product. Also an excellent source for information dealing with recent developments and future research projects now in the works.

STOCKS AND BONDS
see
INVESTMENTS

SUPERLATIVES

Guinness Book of World Records, ed. by Norris McWhirter. Rev.
     ed. Sterling Press, 1973. (ISBN 0-8069-0810-5)
     This is jam-packed with information on the lowest, the highest, the longest, the shortest of any type of activity, person or event. It was originally compiled by the Guinness Stout people for distribution to pub owners in England to settle arguments concerning superlative achievements, but became so popular that it has been enlarged and put on sale to the general public. It is a fascinating book of trivia which often answers questions not easily found elsewhere. There is a paperback edition available.

SUPERSTITIONS

Encyclopedia of Superstitions, ed. by Edwin Radford. Greenwood
     Press, 1949. (ISBN 0-8371-2115-9)
     A topical arrangement of over 23,000 superstitions with a definite British tint but including superstitions from all parts of the known world. Wherever possible there is a tracing of the origins of the superstition. There is a brief bibliography and a good index.

The Hand of Destiny, ed. by Charles John Samuel Thompson. De-
     troit, Mich.: Singing Tree Press, 1970 (Reprint of 1932 ed.).
     This is a listing of folklore and superstitions as they affect everyday life. Mr. Thompson defines folklore as a study to preserve popular beliefs and traditions and to trace them to their original sources. This book is a compilation of some of his findings of popular superstitions especially in the British Isles. Once again,

the arrangement is topical with a fairly good index.

Origins of Popular Superstitions and Customs, by Thomas S. Knowl-
son. Gale Press, 1968 (Reprint of 1910 ed.).
A good summary of the origins of various superstitious beliefs current today in America.

SUPREME COURT

The Justices of the United States Supreme Court, 1789-1969. Their
Lives and Major Opinions, ed. by Leon Friedman. R. R.
Bowker, 1969. 4 vols. (ISBN 0-8352-0217-8)
This is a compilation of biographical sketches and judicial
opinions of the 97 persons who have served as justices on the U.S.
Supreme Court.

SWIMMING

For records and winners of various swimming meets of the
recent past:

Information Please Almanac, ed. by Dan Golenpaul. Dan Golenpaul
Associates, Annual since 1946.
World Almanac and Book of Facts, ed. by George Delury. News-
paper Enterprise Association. Annual since 1868.

For rules of competitive swimming and official records:

Official NCAA Swimming Guide. National Collegiate Athletic Association. Triennial.
This gives the official rules by which NCAA sanctioned
events are judged and the official records of those events.

SYMBOLS
see
SIGNS AND SYMBOLS

SYNONYMS AND ANTONYMS

Any good unabridged dictionary gives a few synonyms and antonyms for the words defined in the dictionary but often persons
want a series of words illustrating various aspects of the same

meaning and this is not easily arrived at in a standard dictionary.
For these questions a good thesaurus is recommended. There are
many such books available but the following can be recommended
most highly.

New Roget's Thesaurus of the English Language in Dictionary Form,
ed. by Norman Lewis. Rev. and enl. ed. Putnam, 1965.
(ISBN 0-399-10579-4)
The name Roget is to the thesaurus what the name Frigidaire
is to the refrigerator. Roget's International Thesaurus was for
many years the only source of such information and it still remains
one of the very best. The original was arranged by broad subject
headings and one had to use the index to find the desired words, but
the one recommended here is alphabetically arranged and simpler to
use.

Webster's New Dictionary of Synonyms. Merriam Webster, 1968.
(ISBN 0-87779-041-8)
This is an alphabetical arrangement of synonyms and antonyms
and is probably the best and most easily used of all such dictionaries. It also contains a section on the history of English language
synonyms.

TAXES
see also
INCOME TAXES

For a quick summary of recent tax developments:

Congressional Quarterly Almanac. Washington, D. C.: Congressional
Quarterly, Inc. Weekly with annual cumulations since 1945.
This is an editorial research service intended to provide its
users with news and analysis of recent congressional actions. It
gives the latest actions of Congress, Congressional Committees, Executive Offices and Judicial actions. It is published weekly with
quarterly indices and annual cumulations. There is always a full
discussion of any new tax measures which may appear in Congress.

For texts of tax laws and discussion of applications:

Prentice Hall Federal Tax Handbook. Prentice Hall, 1974. (ISBN
0-013-312850-4)
The purpose of this handbook is to provide the taxpayer with
a full understanding of the federal tax law so that the taxpayer can
pay the least legitimate taxes possible. The handbook therefore discusses all new tax laws, legislation, court decisions and rulings as
they apply to either individual or corporate taxation.

State Tax Handbook. Commerce Clearing House. Annual.
This has up-to-date information on the general taxation laws

of each state in the United States along with forms, instructions and charts. This actually is a condensation and cumulation of the facts found in the various Commerce Clearing House publications which deal with the taxes of each state, for example, The Guide Book to New York Taxes, 1971. The Commerce Clearing House puts out one for each state and it might be wise to have the volume for your individual state in the library.

TELEVISION

Basic Television, by Paul B. Zbar. 2nd ed. McGraw-Hill, 1971. (ISBN 0-07-072751-1)
    This is basically a textbook which presents 33 experiments each designed to acquaint the student with a different aspect of television theory or practice. There are many diagrams and easy drawings which make the projected experiments easy to perform and understand.

The Emmy Awards: A Pictorial History. Crown Publishers, 1970.
    This is a year-by-year compilation of the winners of the Emmy Awards, which are the television equivalent of the Oscar Awards for motion pictures. It is well illustrated with black and white photographs of scenes from winning shows, and lists shows which were considered but did not win. Although not intended as a television history, it could serve very well in that capacity.

North American Radio Television Station Guide, ed. by Vane A. Jones. Howard W. Sams and Company. Annual since 1963.
    The information for this book is supplied by official FCC publications. It lists by geographic location, by frequency, and by call letters all the television stations in the United States, Canada, Cuba, Mexico and the West Indies. For each listing there is the channel, network affiliation and other technical information.

TENNIS

Official Encyclopedia of Tennis, by U. S. Lawn Tennis Association. Harper & Row, 1972. (ISBN 0-06-014479-3)
    This is an excellent work on tennis, comparing favorably with the best of the reference books on baseball. It covers every aspect of the game, its history, famous courts and players. There is a listing of the winners of every important tennis tournament held in America or around the world as well as biographical sketches of the important players. This is supplemented by a good glossary of terms and an adequate index.

    The section dealing with the hall of fame is complete with

photos of most persons selected and a brief biography.

Official Tennis Yearbook and Guide.   U. S. Lawn Tennis Association.
New York: H. O. Zimman, Inc.   Annual.
This is an official publication of the U. S. L. T. A. giving the
latest tennis rules and records as well as the current rankings of
Davis Cup and other ratings.

THEATER
see also
DRAMA

History of the Theater, by George Freedley.   3rd rev. ed. Crown
Publishers, 1968.
This is a good history of the world theater from earliest
time up to 1940, with supplements which bring it up to 1966.   It is
a chronological story of the history of the theater, showing its
gradual evolution from social and religious plays down to the the-
aters of today.   There are good bibliographies for each development
and the whole work is well illustrated.

Pictorial History of the American Theater, 1860-1970, ed. by John
Willis.   3rd ed.   Crown Publishers, 1970.
This is a pictorial history of the American theater which tells
in pictures the history of American buildings, actors and perform-
ances.   It concentrates primarily on the New York stage but does
include some provincial history.

Who's Who in Show Business: The International Directory of the Entertainment World, 1969-1971, ed. by Ken Hecht.   Who's Who
in Show Business, 1971.   (ISBN 0-913012-02-5)
Although the arrangement is difficult since it is arranged by
type of performer, i. e., dancers, comedians, musicians, etc., this
is still a good biographical directory of the people in show business.
It is particularly interesting in that it has a section called Who's
Who Off Stage in which outstanding choreographers, directors, composers, etc. are listed.   The good index makes the rather haphazard
arrangement usable.

Who's Who in the Theater, ed. by Robert Finley.   15th ed. Pitman,
1972.

TIDES
see also
NAVIGATION

Tidal Current Tables, Atlantic Coast of North America.   U. S. Coast and Geodetic Survey. U. S. Government Printing Office. Annual since 1923. (C 4. 22:)

Tidal Current Tables, Pacific Coast of North America. U. S. Coast and Geodetic Survey. U. S. Government Printing Office. Annual since 1923. (C 4. 23:)

These are annual publications giving advance information on the tidal currents for the Pacific and Atlantic Coasts of North America. Each one contains a list of publications dealing with tides and currents.

World Almanac and Book of Facts, ed. by George Delury. Newspaper Enterprise Association. Annual since 1868.

This has a good summary of the various tides and their causes and has a summary table of the average rise and fall for tides of various port cities.

TIME
see also
NAVIGATION

Rand McNally Commercial Atlas and Marketing Guide. Rand McNally Corporation. Annual since 1869.

This has a time-zone map of the world.

World Almanac and Book of Facts, ed. by George Delury. Newspaper Enterprise Association. Annual since 1868.

A good summary of world time zones and of the rising and setting of the sun and moon are listed.

TOYS

Toys of Other Days, by F. Nevill Jackson. Benjamin Blom, 1968.

A good illustrated history of the development of toys, especially in the British Isles.

The Wonderful World of Toys, Games and Dolls, ed. by Joseph J. Schroeder, Jr. Northfield, Ill.: Digest Books, 1971. (ISBN 0-695-80219-4)

This is a collection of advertisements for toys during the period 1860-1930, primarily from catalogs and manufacturers brochures. It lacks an index and therefore is limited in its reference applications but should be of interest to anyone looking for the historical development of toys.

TRACK AND FIELD

International Track and Field Coaching Encyclopedia, by Fred Wilt.
Prentice Hall, 1970. (ISBN 0-13-473645-1)
This is an international compilation from 12 different coun-
tries dealing with coaching and training techniques.

Official NCAA Track and Field Guide. National Collegiate Athletic
Association. Triennial.
This contains the official rules for various track and field
events participated in by the National Collegiate Athletic Association.
It also contains a list of official collegiate records, etc.

Official Track and Field Handbook. New York: Amateur Athletic
Union of the United States. Annual.
This is the competing association to the NCAA and is re-
sponsible for all but collegiate amateur sporting events in the United
States. This publication gives records for world, Olympic and U.S.
track events and field sports. It also lists the rules under which
AAU personnel participate.

TRADEMARKS AND TRADE NAMES

Famous American Trademarks, by Arnold B. Barach. Public
Affairs Press, 1971.
A collection of the histories of 100 of the most famous
American trademarks. For each one it gives the designer, the first
use of the trademark and other historical facts. These brief histories originally appeared in the Changing Times Magazine and are
therefore intended for popular use rather than research, but while
no documentation of facts is given, the book should prove useful in
answering trademark questions. Unfortunately, no index is furnished
and one must depend upon an inadequate table of contents.

General Information Concerning Trademarks. U.S. Patent Office.
U.S. Government Printing Office, 1956. (C 21.2:)
Index of Trademarks Issued from the United States Patent Office.
U.S. Patent Office. U.S. Government Printing Office. Annual
since 1928. (C 21.5/3:)
An annual index to trademarks and classifications of goods
which were granted during the past calendar year. For each trademark, there is a notation to whom it was granted, its registration
number and any decision concerning its use.

Thomas' Register of American Manufacturers and Thomas' Register
Catalog File. Thomas Publishing Company. Annual since 1910.
This is a reference guide to the manufacturers of any type of
equipment made in the United States. There are four sections to the
Register: section I, which takes up six volumes, is devoted to pro-

ducts and services listed alphabetically and then geographically by
state and city; section II (vol. 7) is a listing of company names
giving addresses, zip codes and telephone numbers listed alphabetically; section III (vol. 8) is an alphabetical American Trademark
Index listed by names under which various products are stamped,
labelled or advertised; section IV (vols. 9-11) consists of catalogs
of companies arranged alphabetically and cross referenced to the
first eight volumes.

Trademark Rules of Practice of the U. S. Patent Office.   U. S. Patent
     Office.   U. S. Government Printing Office.   Annual since 1947.
     (C 21. 15:)
          The official rules under which the Patent Office issues the
use of trademarks and brand name registrations.

TRAVEL

          The literature of the traveler and tourist is so varied and so
great that it would be impossible to list even a decent selection of
travel guides; however, there are several books which should be in
any collection.   The one set of books which carries the highest recommendation from all sources is:

The Michelin Green and Red Guides.   French and European Publica-
     tions.
          These two sets of books, originally published by the Michelin
Tire Company for the use of their customers, have over the years
become the authentic guide for travelers to all parts of Europe.   The
Red Guides are published about Easter of each year and present data
on various cities and towns of Europe, giving for each the population, principal attractions and most importantly a listing of the major hotels and restaurants which are graded by type of service and
official government rating.   The ratings given the hotels and restaurants are very accurate and highly prized by establishments listed
therein.   Hotel rates and restaurant prices are also given.   This is
a near must for anyone traveling by automobile in Europe.   The
following Red Guides are available.

France	Germany
Italy	Spain and Portugal
Benelux	Paris

The Red Guides for Benelux and Spain also carry sightseeing
information.
          The Green Guides are not revised annually and are intended
to point out places of interest and the most advantageous routes within each country within the time available.   For each town, the following information is given: a brief historical note, the main
tourist attractions (rated one, two or three stars depending upon importance) and a listing of other sights in the immediate area (also

rated one, two or three stars).   There are many maps to important
tourist areas and an estimate of how much time should be devoted
to each area.   There are nineteen Green Guides to various sections
of France and individual guides to the following countries:

Austria	New York City
Germany	Portugal
Italy	Switzerland

The Michelin Guides are in a class by themselves, but the
following sets can also be highly recommended.

Fodor Modern Guides, ed. by Eugene Fodor.   McKay.   Annual.
      This excellent set of travel guides is published annually.
Each travel guide gives not only an historical introduction to the
country but also information about the best ways to get there, the
probable costs of a day's hotel, meals and entertainment, as well
as a sectional description of the country giving excellent information
about each section and the principal cities in that section.   For each
city, there is a listing of hotels and restaurants with some indication of the price categories.   These price listings are not as reliable as those in the Michelin guides but overall, the Fodor Guides
are the second best set available.   There are guides for the following countries.

Austria	Holland	Peking
Belgium and Luxembourg	Hungary	Portugal
The Caribbean	India	Scandinavia
Czechoslovakia	Ireland	South America
Europe	Islamic Asia	Spain
France	Israel	Switzerland
Germany	Italy	Tunisia
Great Britain	Japan and	Turkey
Greece	the Far East	Yugoslavia
Hawaii	Mexico	
	Morocco	

No listing of travel information would be complete without
mentioning the books of Arthur Frommer who, a generation ago,
wrote the first Europe on Five Dollars a Day, and has remained
the guide to the budget traveler ever since.   Of course, he no longer
claims that you can travel on five dollars a day but his books provide a good economical introduction to world travel.   Often his hotel
recommendations do not live up to American standards but his travel
hints for saving money in other ways are quite valid.   The Frommer
books are revised annually and can be purchased from Simon and
Schuster.   The books available are:

England on Five and Ten Dollars a Day
Europe on Five and Ten Dollars a Day
Greece on Five Dollars a Day
Hawaii on Ten Dollars a Day
India on Five and Ten Dollars a Day

Ireland on Five Dollars a Day
Israel on Five and Ten Dollars a Day
Japan on Ten Dollars a Day
Mexico on Five and Ten Dollars a Day
New York on Ten Dollars a Day
Scandinavia on Ten Dollars a Day
South America on Five and Ten Dollars a Day
Spain on Five Dollars a Day
Turkey on Five Dollars a Day
Washington on Five and Ten Dollars a Day
Washington, D. C. on Ten Dollars a Day

Realistically speaking, no one can travel on the amounts mentioned in the titles but it may be possible for double the estimated amounts. A more realistic series edited by Frommer and also published by Simon and Schuster is the Dollar Wise Guides which follow the same format as the Five Dollars a Day but do not limit listings to that low a budget. Books in this series are available for the following countries:

England	Italy
France	Portugal
Germany	

TREATIES

Key Treaties for the Great Powers, 1814-1914, ed. by Michael
    Hurst. St. Martin's Press, 1972. 2 vols.
    This gives the precise text of the major treaties signed by the great powers from the time of Napoleon to the beginning of the first World War. This is an important collection since it obviates the need to search several places to find the desired information. There is no commentary concerning the treaty or its effect on the world; just the bare text. Treaties are arranged chronologically with an index by subject and by main words within the title of the treaty.

Major Peace Treaties of Modern History, 1648-1967, ed. by Fred
    L. Israel. McGraw-Hill, 1967. 4 vols. (ISBN 0-07-032085-3)
    This set of books is introduced by Arnold Toynbee and covers the important treaties of the world from 1648 to the present day. Each treaty, starting with the Treaty of Westphalia in 1648, considered to be the beginnings of modern diplomacy, is introduced by commentary in which the treaty is placed historically and an account given as to the effect the treaty had on its time and history. The full test of each treaty is given and treaties are arranged chronologically with a good index for the whole set.

Treaties in Force: a List of Treaties and Other International Agreements of the United States. U. S. Department of State. U. S.

Government Printing Office. (S 9. 14:)
This contains a list of treaties and other international agreements to which the United States has become a party. It includes all treaties which have not expired or which have not been revoked by the signing powers or superseded by later agreements.

Treaties and Other International Agreements of the United States of America, compiled by Charles I. Bevans. U. S. Department of State. U. S. Government Printing Office. Annual since 1950. (S 9. 12/2:)
This is an annual publication of the treaties which the United States became a party during the past calendar year.

TREES

Atlas of United States Trees: Vol. I, Conifers and Important Hardwoods, by Elbert L. Little, Jr. U. S. Department of Agriculture. U. S. Government Printing Office. 1971. (A 1. 38:1146.)
A collection of about 300 maps showing the natural distribution of the 200 native tree varieties in the continental United States and Alaska. All native soft woods are listed as well as 106 species of hardwood trees. In addition to the maps there are nine overlays which can be used to correlate the trees with such environmental features as growing season, rivers, rainfall and climate.

Checklist of Native and Naturalized Trees of the United States and Alaska. U. S. Forest Service. U. S. Government Printing Office. 1963. (A 1. 76:41)
This is the official listing of names for trees in the United States. It lists, by scientific name and the currently used common name, all the native and naturalized trees of the United States and Alaska and indicates the geographical distribution of each.

Know Your Woods, by 'bert J. Constantine, Jr. Scribner's, 1972. (ISBN 0-684-13078-.
This is possibly th. most comprehensive publication dealing with trees and the woods that they produce. The first part of the book deals with the trees themselves, their geographical distribution, how to recognize the varieties and how to determine the type of wood that you need for your individual needs. Part two is an alphabetical arrangement of the woods from all parts of the world, with a good general index for finding the wood or tree needed, either using the scientific or common names.

Knowing Your Trees. American Forestry Association, 1973.
This is an identification guide to the fifty-one most famous types of trees in the United States and gives methods of identifying each one by leaf, bark, flowers and fruits. In addition, each tree is pictured with both summer and winter photographs to help in identification.

Trees. Yearbook of Agriculture, 1949. U. S. Department of Agriculture. U. S. Government Printing Office, 1949. (A1. 10:949)

This was the second of the Yearbooks of Agriculture devoted to a specific subject and it is a book that can be used for reference purposes for a long time to come. There are several sections dealing with the history of trees, the use of trees, the cultivation of trees, insects and diseases of trees and a projection of the future use of forests and woods. In addition there are several good bibliographies on several related subjects and a key to the identification of woods and trees.

TROPICAL FISH

Complete Aquarist's Guide to Freshwater Tropical Fishes, by John Gilbert. Golden Press, 1970. (ISBN 0-307-49530-2)

Although this does not live up to the title "complete, " it remains an excellent guide to tropical fish and their enjoyment. Chapters, each by an expert on various aspects of home aquariums, present basic information on the establishment, management and filling your aquarium. There is information about many various types of fishes and the proper feeding and care of each variety mentioned. It is an excellent book and its full color illustrations make it a beautiful one as well.

Handbook of Tropical Aquarium Fishes, by Herbert R. Axelrod. Jersey City, N. J. : TFH Publications, 1971.

This is a much more complete handbook and gives intensive information about the care and maintenance of home aquariums and the proper food, care and selection of types of tropical fish. It has information on fish diseases and possible care. Probably the most complete current book on the subject.

Tropical Aquariums, Plants and Fishes, by Neil Wainwright. Warne, 1970. (ISBN 0-7232-1263-5)

This is a book about aquariums intended for the beginning hobbyist. It is a good guide to what to purchase, types of fish which are desirable and the ways to feed and keep them healthy. A good appendix lists tropical fish by both popular and scientific names. There is also a special chapter for the more advanced hobbyist about the breeding of tropical fishes.

Tropical Fish Identifier, by Braz Walker. Sterling Press, 1971. (ISBN 0-8069-3714-9)

This identifies over 120 different varieties of tropical fish suitable for home aquariums and for each one gives its proper scientific classification as well as its common name. It gives a physical description of each fish along with size, care needed, feeding habits, and a color photograph.

TYPOGRAPHY

Encyclopaedia of Type Faces, by W. Pincus Jaspert.   4th ed.
    Barnes and Noble, 1971.   (ISBN 0-06-492039-9)
    This is a comprehensive encyclopedia of almost 2000 different
type faces illustrated and arranged under three headings: Roman,
Lineales, and Scripts.   For each face presented there is given the
name of the type, the foundry making it, the designer and year of
the design, and a complete alphabet of each type face discussed.
There is also a good bibliography of materials dealing with typography and a listing of names and addresses of the makers of types
as well as an index to type designers.

UNIFORMS
see also
ARMED FORCES; DECORATIONS AND MEDALS

        Questions about uniforms are frequent and usually come from
little theater groups or from artists wanting to portray persons cor-
rectly either on stage or in portraits.   The very best source of information for uniforms of the Armed Services which have fought in
the continental United States is a periodical.   It should be in any
library having either a Military Arts collection, a theater collection
or a well defined art department.

The Military Collector and Historian. The Journal of the Company
    of Military Historians, ed. by Col. John R. Elting.   Washing-
    ton, D.C.: The Company of Military Historians.   Quarterly
    since 1949.
        The title of this publication is misleading; it is devoted al-
most entirely to information concerning uniforms and their accou-
terments, although occasionally there are articles about famous flags.
Especially important are the articles in each issue which describe
the uniforms of various regiments or troops and the accompanying
plates.   These plates, issued quarterly, are in full color and, together with the detailed descriptions in the quarterly itself, provide
the very best source of information on military uniforms of America,
primarily United States uniforms but occasionally featuring British
troops and others who fought on the American mainland.

        Although the Military Collector and Historian is the best
source, it is not normally available to the average library, so the
following books are recommended as giving authentic descriptions
and pictures of various types of military uniforms.

German Army Uniforms and Insignia, 1933-1945, by Brian L. Davis.
    Arco, 1973.   (ISBN 0-668-03359-2)
Military Uniforms, 1886-1918, by Rene North.   Grosset and Dunlap,
    1970.   (ISBN 0-448-00846-7)

Uniforms of the American, British, French and German Armies in the War of the American Revolution, 1775-1783, by Charles Lefferts. We, Inc. 1971 (Reprint of 1926 ed.). (ISBN 0-011964-20-7)
Uniforms of the Civil War, by Francis A. Lord. A. S. Barnes, 1969. (ISBN 0-498-06731-9)
Uniforms of the British Army, Navy, and Court, by T. H. Holding. Theater Arts, 1970.

UNITED NATIONS

There have been so many books dealing with the United Nations and its activities that the first place to look for information is in the card catalog of your library. If just a brief history of the formation and activities are desired, any good encyclopedia will suffice. For more detailed information the following are recommended.

Annual Review of United Nations Affairs, ed. by Barbara A. Kulzer. Oceana Publications. Annual since 1967.
This is an annual review of the activities of the United Nations and includes special documents or messages delivered in that body and a summary of the actions taken by that organization during the year. Unfortunately, the coverage usually runs about three to five years behind the date of publication.

Chronology and Factbook of the United Nations, 1941-1969, ed. by Waldo Chamberlain. 3rd rev. ed. Oceana Publications, 1970. (ISBN 0-379-00453-4)
Although only basically a chronology of the activities of the United Nations, this publication is excellent as a guide to determining exactly when actions were taken and as such can be used as a sort of index to the Yearbook of the United Nations. It does however have the full texts of such important documents as the Charter, a list of members, and other documents.

Yearbook of the United Nations. United Nations Headquarters. Annual since 1947.
Once again, the biggest difficulty with the publication is the time lag between coverage and publication. Despite this handicap, this is an indispensable reference book. It summarizes the events of the calendar year covered, has a complete listing of the membership, a breakdown of the budget and complete texts of all pertinent documents.

UNITED STATES

No attempt is made here to present a comprehensive listing of the many books dealing with American history. The books listed are those most helpful in answering quickly the general reference question.

ATLASES

Atlas of American History, ed. by James Truslow Adams. Scribner's, 1943. (Available on subscription only; not available through book trade.)
    This is probably the most usable of all the many atlases of American history. It was designed to accompany the Dictionary of American History but can be of equal use separately. It has 147 maps arranged chronologically, showing the territorial expansion of the United States, and an alphabetical index to places named on the maps.

Historical Atlas of the United States, ed. by Clifford L. Lord. Johnson Reprint, 1969 (Reprint of 1953 edition).
    This is a little more up-to-date and has considerably more maps (312) than the Adams Atlas, but it cannot really be considered a replacement for that work since the maps are not as detailed or as well indexed. It is however an excellent work.

BIBLIOGRAPHIES

Guide to the Study of the United States of America. U.S. Library of Congress. U.S. Government Printing Office, 1960.
    An excellent annotated bibliography of books dealing with the history of our country. It is divided both chronologically and geographically. There are some brief biographies of the authors whose works are annotated.

Harvard Guide to American History, ed. by Oscar Handlin. Harvard University Press, 1954. (ISBN 0-674-37550-5)
    Although now twenty years old, this still remains the most definitive bibliography on American history for the period it covers. It is arranged chronologically and topically to interpret all phases of American life.

BIOGRAPHY

Dictionary of American Biography. Scribner's, 1957-1964. 11 vols. (Available by subscription only; not available through book trade.)
    This is the standard work of American historical biography and covers all important American historical figures who died prior to 1941. Each article is signed and there is a bibliography of works by and about the biographee. This is a reprint of the original work and each volume contains two of the original volumes.

GENERAL HISTORIES

Dictionary of American History, ed. by James Truslow Adams.
    Scribner's, 1958-1961. 7 vols. (Available by subscription only;
    not available through book trade.)
        This is an excellent ready reference source for American
history questions. The articles, although quite brief, are all au-
thenticated and signed by experts and some have brief bibliographies.
Although arranged in dictionary order, there are many cross references which enable the user to move from one idea to another
easily.

Oxford Companion to American History, ed. by Thomas Herbert
    Johnson. Oxford University Press, 1969. (ISBN 0-19-500597-X)
        This is another alphabetically arranged dictionary of American
history in which short authentic articles are well written and documented. It is an excellent starting place for the location of the
time and the place of a certain event in American history.

Webster's Guide to American History, ed. by Charles Van Doren.
    Merriam, 1971. (ISBN 0-87779-081-7)
        This is a three-volume summary of American history ar-
ranged chronologically, with maps, statistical tables and biographical
sketches. There is an excellent index. A good starting point for
the preparation of historical papers.

INDEXES

America: History and Life; a Guide to Periodical Literature. Santa
    Barbara, California: Clio Press, American Bibliographical
    Center. Three times a year since 1964.
        This is an index to periodicals dealing with American history
and life, but it is an abstracting service as well. The materials
indexed all deal with the history of the United States and Canada but
can have been published in any part of the world. There is an annual index.

UNIVERSITIES
see
COLLEGES AND UNIVERSITIES

VALENTINES

A History of Valentines, by Ruth W. Lee. Lee Publications, 1962.
    (ISBN 0-910872-10-4)
        This is a good history of the development of Valentines and
the use of verse on the cards. Illustrated with pictures of many famous valentines, most in black and white but a few in full color.

In addition to this information, information on the celebration of St. Valentine's Day appears in the following books:

American Book of Days, by George W. Douglas. 2nd ed. H. W. Wilson, 1948. (ISBN 0-8242-0002-0)

Anniversaries and Holidays: A Calendar of Days and How to Observe Them, by Mary E. Hazeltine. 2nd ed. American Library Association, 1944. (ISBN 0-8389-0009-7)

Book of Days, A Miscellany of Popular Antiquities in Connection with the Calendar, Including Anecdote, Biography and History, ed. by Robert Chambers. Gale Publishing, 1967. 2 vols. (Reprint of 1862 ed.)

VEGETABLES
see
GARDENING

VENEREAL DISEASES

Venereal Disease Bibliography, 1966-1970, by Stephan H. Goode. Troy, N.Y.: Whitson, 1972. (ISBN 0-87875-023-1)
This is the first of a proposed series of bibliographies on the subject of venereal diseases to be published annually. The current issue covers a five-year period. There is both a subject listing and an alphabetical listing of the articles cited, plus an author index.

Current Literature on Venereal Disease: Abstracts and Bibliography. U.S. Public Health Service. U.S. Government Printing Office. Published quarterly since 1966. (HE 20.2311:)
This presents abstracts of the current materials in the field and is particularly good because it helps the individual to evaluate the possible value of the article before actually locating it. It is arranged topically, i.e., by diagnosis and treatment, research and evaluation and public health methods. There are both author and subject indexes.

VITAMINS
see
NUTRITION

VOCATIONS
see
CAREERS

VOTING QUALIFICATIONS

The best source of information concerning the voting qualifications for your particular state is in the Code of Laws for the state. These are usually published by the State Legislature.

There is another source which gives a summary of the voting laws for each state:

The Election Process - Voting Laws and Procedures, by A. Reitman. 2nd ed. Oceana Publications, 1972. (ISBN 0-379-11069-5)
This is another in the Oceana Legal Almanac series and gives in easily understood terms the main laws which control the voting in each of the various states of the United States.

In addition, the two almanacs will have brief summaries of voting eligibility requirements.

Information Please Almanac, by Dan Golenpaul. Dan Golenpaul Associates. Annual since 1946.
World Almanac and Book of Facts, ed. by George Delury. Newspaper Enterprise Association. Annual since 1868.

WEATHER
see
METEOROLOGY

WEDDINGS
see
ETIQUETTE; MARRIAGE--CUSTOMS

WEIGHTS AND MEASURES

For a simple listing of weights and measures and a comparison between the metric and the English systems, see the heading WEIGHTS AND MEASURES in:

Information Please Almanac, ed. by Dan Golenpaul. Dan Golenpaul Associates. Annual since 1946.
World Almanac and Book of Facts, ed. by George Delury. Newspaper Enterprise Association. Annual since 1868.

For a history of the use of weights and measures:

Measurements and How We Use Them, by Tillie S. Pine. McGraw-Hill, 1973. (ISBN 0-07-050084-3)

WILD FLOWERS
see also
FLOWERS

Although wild flowers in general are treated under the heading of FLOWERS in this book, there is one series dealing specifically with the wildflowers which should be mentioned separately.

Wildflowers of the United States, ed. by Harold William Rickett.
McGraw-Hill, 1967-74. 6 vols.
This is a comprehensive work dealing with the wildflowers of every part of the United States and identifying over 4,650 different species. It is illustrated with more than 2,400 illustrations in full color. The work is supervised by the staff of the New York Botanical Gardens and is the most important work of its kind ever undertaken for this or any other country. This is an expensive but incomparable work. The individual volumes of the series are as follows:

Vol. 1.	The Northeastern States		(ISBN 0-07-052614-1)
Vol. 2.	The Southeastern States		(ISBN 0-07-052630-3)
Vol. 3.	Texas		(ISBN 0-07-052633-8)
Vol. 4.	The Southwestern States		(ISBN 0-07-052636-2)
Vol. 5.	The Northwestern States		(ISBN 0-07-052640-0)
Vol. 6.	The Central Mountains and Plains		(ISBN 0-07-052643-5)

WILLS

Prefacing this section, as all sections dealing with legal matters, with the precaution that a librarian is not a lawyer and that legal interpretations can only be given by a lawyer, the following books are helpful to the individual wanting to construct his own will or to plan a will with the help of proper legal help.

How to Make a Will Simplified, by P. J. T. Callahan. 2nd ed.
Oceana Publications, 1952. (ISBN 0-379-11002-4)
This is another in the Legal Almanac Series and like the others is a very simple explanation of the processes by which a person prepares a will and assures its acceptance.

Will Laws of the United States. Gould Publications, 1974. (ISBN 0-87526-067-5)
This is a comprehensive book covering the laws relating to wills and decedents' estates throughout the United States. There are tabular listings of the laws, contrasting the various states and their requirements. There are also parts dealing with pre-death transfers of property by gifts and trust funds.

WOMEN

Womanhood Media: Current Resources about Women, ed. by Helen
    Wheeler. Scarecrow Press, 1972. (ISBN 0-8108-0549-9)
       Although the arrangement of this book leaves a lot to be de-
sired, it does quite a bit to answer the questions that come to a
library dealing with the problems of women and the feminist movement. The first part is devoted to 200 questions on various aspects
of the problems facing women working for equal rights, as well as
a section devoted to how to achieve equality. Probably the most
important section is a bibliography arranged by Dewey Classification
number. The items listed would be an excellent basic collection
on women for any library.

Women and Society, ed. by Donna Reische. H. W. Wilson Co.,
    1972. (ISBN 0-8242-0451-4)
       This is a volume in the excellent Reference Shelf Series,
which is intended to provide high school and college students with
information for research or debate on the current topics of the day.
This one deals with the role of women in the United States, the
feminist movement and the history and condition of women generally.
The book is arranged in four sections: The Quest for Options;
Women in the Marketplace; Some Perspectives--Social and Historical; and Biology and the Social Role.

Women's Rights Movement in the United States, 1848-1970, by
    Albert Krichmar. Scarecrow Press, 1972. (ISBN 0-8108-0528-6)
       This is a bibliography of the entire women's liberation move-
ment in the United States and lists over 5,000 works covering every
aspect of women's life in the United States but concentrating on the
movement for equal rights. There are several indexes.

WRESTLING

Official NCAA Wrestling Guide. National Collegiate Athletic Asso-
    ciation. Triennial.
       This is the official publication of the National Collegiate
Athletic Association dealing with the sport of wrestling as it is
practiced in colleges and high schools of the United States. It is
published every three years and gives the latest changes in amateur
rules as well as the records of the various colleges and high school
participating.

Wrestling. Amateur Athletic Union of the United States. Annual.
       This is the publication of the other Amateur Athletic Associ-
ation in the United States and the one which controls the participation
in the Olympic Games. This one gives the latest rules for Olympic
style wrestling and Greco-Roman wrestling as well as a listing of
Olympic record holders and state and regional champions.

WRITING

For information concerning individual writers consult either AUTHORS or LITERATURE in this book. This section is devoted to the problems of writing and getting published the things you write.

Literary Market Place; The Business Directory of American Book Publishing. R. R. Bowker Company. Annual since 1941.
This is not only a register of the personnel in the publishing fields but also a guide for persons either wanting to sell a particular type of writing or to locate a particular type of writing. It is arranged by Book Publishers, Author's Agents, Writer's Associations, Employment Agencies, and finally by periodicals and reference books. There is an excellent index.

Writer's and Artist's Yearbook. The Writer. Annual since 1907.
This is the standard directory of markets for writers and artists, for television, screen or books. The book is divided into four sections by the type of writing done. In addition to listing writers it gives a listing of the type of materials desired by various publishers and detailed information concerning the proper way to submit that material.

Writer's Handbook, ed. by A. S. Burack. Rev. ed. The Writer, 1973. (ISBN 0-87116-078-1)
This is an up-to-date manual for the writing of various types of commercial writing. It has over 75 sections devoted to various aspects of the author's problems and each section is written by a specialist. It also gives lists of markets for written materials.

Writer's Market, ed. by Lynne Ellinwood. Writer's Digest. Annual since 1930.
This is undoubtedly the best source of information on markets for written materials. It lists the various markets available and gives the addresses of the companies, the names of the editors for each type of material, information concerning the rates of pay, the time of reporting and any special requirements needed for each magazine or company. The arrangement is by type of publication and by type of material desired with a good index for finding the desired publication. This is a book that should be in any library which has questions from potential writers.

ZOOS

Animals Next Door: A Guide to Zoos and Aquariums of the Americas, by Harry Gersh. Fleet, 1971. (ISBN 0-8303-0088-0)
This lists in a very readable but informative way the important zoos and aquariums of the Western hemisphere.

<u>Mammals of the World</u>, by Michael Boorer.   Grosset and Dunlap,
    1971.   (ISBN 0-448-00860-2)
        Although primarily intended as a discussion of the mammals
of the world and their life styles and habits, this book also lists
the zoos of the world and tells where each type of animal can be
seen.